Farrell Dobbs emerged as a militant Teamster leader during the historic 1934 Minneapolis strikes. He was elected secretary-treasurer of Teamster Local 574 and then appointed as a general organizer on the union's national staff. A supporter of the class-struggle wing in the union, he led the first over-the-road campaign, which organized workers by the tens of thousands throughout an eleven-state area in the Midwest and laid the basis for the Teamsters' present power as a union.

Dobbs resigned from the Teamsters' national staff in 1940 to become labor secretary for the Socialist Workers Party. In 1941 he was prosecuted for his militant union and antiwar views. Dobbs and seventeen other leaders of the Socialist Workers Party and the Minneapolis Teamsters were then jailed as the first victims of the notorious Smith Act. He served twelve months in Sandstone federal prison.

From 1943 to 1948, Dobbs was the editor of the socialist newsweekly *The Militant*. From 1948 to 1960 he ran for president four times on the Socialist Workers ticket. During this period of witch-hunt and cold-war hysteria, he campaigned in support of the civil rights, antiwar, and union movements. He visited Cuba after the revolution and made opposition to U.S. aggression against Cuba one of the major issues of his 1960 presidential campaign.

Dobbs was the national secretary of the Socialist Workers Party from 1953 to 1972. He is currently working on a history of the Socialist Workers Party from the 1940s to the 1960s.

To All W. P. A. Workers and Relief Clients
Mass Meeting
Wednesday, July 12
7:30 P. M. SHARP
at the Parade Grounds

Action has been taken by the Minneapolis Building and Construction Trades Council that the strike be kept in force on all W.P.A. jobs until trade union wages and conditions have been re-established for all men involved and that we request support from the entire trade union movement and accept support from all labor organizations on the basis of our program and urge all W.P.A. workers to pull off from their jobs and join the strike and urge all relief clients not to accept employment on any W.P.A. jobs until this fight is won.

Keep all W.P.A. jobs closed down until the fight against wage cuts is won for all W.P.A. workers.

United we will win this fight against wage cuts which affect the wage standards of all workers

---

Chairman: PETER MURCK, President of the Minneapolis Building and Construction Trades Council, A. F. of L.

Speakers: ROY WEIR, Minneapolis Central Labor Union, A. F. of L.

WALTER FRANK, Chairman of W.P.A. Joint Committee of the Minneapolis Building and Construction Trades Council

MAX GELDMAN, Federal Workers' Section No. 544

B. EASTMAN, State President C. I. O.

ROBERT WISHART, Workers Alliance

LOUIS BOERBACH, Member of W. P. A. Joint Committee

Auspices of Minneapolis Building and Construction Trades Council and its W. P. A. Joint Committee, composed of Minneapolis Building and Construction Trades Council, and Workers Alliance and C. I. O. and Federal Workers Section No. 544.

Leaflet summoning Minneapolis workers to a mass rally during the 1939 WPA strike.

Teamster
Politics
Farrell Dobbs

MONAD PRESS, NEW YORK

First Edition, 1975
Second Printing, 1979

Published by Monad Press
for the Anchor Foundation, Inc.

Distributed by
Pathfinder Press
410 West Street
New York, N.Y. 10014

Library of Congress Catalog Card Number 75-17324
Manufactured in the United States of America
ISBN 0-913460-38-9 (cloth); 0-913460-39-7 (paper)

330866

To the members
of Local 544's union defense guard

Contents

List of Illustrations

Acknowledgments

Although the contents of this work are my responsibility alone, I wish to express gratitude to all who so generously responded to requests for assistance.

Marvel Scholl, my most intimate companion and collaborator throughout the years covered in this story, helped constantly in double-checking the facts and recalling unrecorded experiences that can be recovered only from memory. An extensive quotation has been taken, as well, from her writings in the *Northwest Organizer*. Sharon Lee Finer performed the laborious task of typing each chapter in quadruplicate, often doing so under circumstances in which it was difficult to put other matters aside long enough to do the job. Her competent performance made it easier for me in several important respects.

In preparing the section on the unemployed movement, I put a number of questions to Max Geldman about events during the 1930s. He answered them fully and unreservedly, so far as his memory would permit. In addition he taped considerable background information on the subject, much of which has been directly quoted in the text.

Jack Maloney and Louis Miller helped to draft the account of the federal trial at Sioux City, Iowa, in which they were among the defendants. They also supplied data used in writing brief sketches of their personal backgrounds. Ray Rainbolt and Harry DeBoer not only checked each chapter of the book for factual accuracy; they gave important aid in preparing the analysis of General Drivers Local 544's union defense guard and in describing how it functioned. Pauline (Swanson) DeBoer was equally cooperative in digging up information about the union defense guard and in handling correspondence on the subject from her end.

George Tselos furnished copies of official AFL correspondence obtained from public archives in the course of his researches into labor history. Helen Scheer and V. Raymond Dunne, Jr., aided in gathering information from the daily papers of the 1930s and searching out facts about key individuals. George Novack, who had urged and inspired me to undertake the writing project about the Teamsters, kept his promise to lend his editorial skill in the final polishing of the manuscript.

Some of the data appearing in this book came from files I accumulated while functioning as a Teamster organizer. Use has also been made of various publications. These include the Minneapolis Teamster paper, the *Northwest Organizer;* The Minneapolis *Labor Review,* official organ of the AFL Central Labor Union; *The Militant* and the *Socialist Appeal,* both reflecting the views of the Trotskyist movement; and capitalist dailies in Minneapolis and St. Paul, Minnesota.

Preface

In the closing passage of *Teamster Power*—the second volume in this series about a significant part of U.S. labor history—I indicated that the story would be completed with the present book. When it came to the actual writing, though, the subjects covered herein took more space than had been anticipated. For that reason another volume will be needed to finish the account.

The completion of several important developments remains to be described. These include the outcome of the fink suit against General Drivers Local 544 and the further evolution of the conflict inside the Minnesota Farmer-Labor Party, both subjects having been only partially treated in the present work.

The final volume will focus on the sequence of events in what became a life-and-death struggle over the issues of war and union democracy. It centered around yet another confrontation between Local 544 and Daniel J. Tobin, president of the International Brotherhood of Teamsters. In that climactic battle Tobin was openly backed by President Franklin D. Roosevelt, who launched a witch-hunt attack against the Trotskyist-led union and the Socialist Workers Party. Need for ample room to cover that whole episode adequately is the primary reason why a fourth book is being added.

THE POLITICS OF THE
TRADE-UNION MOVEMENT

Defendants in the 1939 Sioux City frame-up of Teamster organizers. From the left: Howard Fouts, Ralph Johnson, Jack Maloney, Francis Quinn, Louis Miller, and Walter K. Stultz. A seventh victim, Earl Carpenter, had not yet been released on bond when the picture was taken.

1. Antilabor Role of the FBI

The provocative interference of the Federal Bureau of Investigation in the legitimate affairs of the people in this country, including disruption of their political and trade-union organizations, was given large-scale exposure after the Watergate scandals. But the antidemocratic and antilabor activities of federal and other police agencies were already in operation during the 1930s.

That role was evidenced in the 1939 governmental attacks on the International Brotherhood of Teamsters, which occurred at a time when I was a general organizer assigned to the union's over-the-road campaign in the Midwest. In connection with the organizing drive—an action that helped lift the IBT into its present powerful status—several officials of Teamster locals were framed up and hauled into the courts on various charges.

Help in their defense was sought from Daniel J. Tobin, then general president of the IBT. He responded according to his political lights. But the effort fell short of what could and should have been done, as a review of the events will show.

On March 3, 1939, a truck operated by the Nielson-Peterson Company of Grand Island, Nebraska, was damaged in an explosion of some kind at Sioux Falls, South Dakota. As though following a prearranged script, the Sioux Falls authorities moved quickly against the strongest Teamster unit in the immediate area, Local 383 of Sioux City, Iowa. Indictments were issued against three officials of Local 383: Howard Fouts, Ralph Johnson, and Jack Maloney. They were charged with "malicious destruction of property with explosives."

Since the indicted unionists lived in Iowa, extradition proceedings were formally required to put them on trial in Sioux Falls. To

avoid that difficulty a geographical peculiarity was used to nab
Fouts and Johnson. Sioux City lies on the east bank of the Big
Sioux River, which marks the boundary between Iowa and South
Dakota. The airport serving the city was then located on the west
side of the river. It was in the vicinity of the airport—Dakota
territory—that the two men were arrested. Apparently they had
been tailed there by agents of the Federal Bureau of Investigation, who were cooperating in police attacks on the Teamsters
with local authorities throughout the region.

To avoid falling into the same trap, Maloney quit traveling by
air. Upon advice of counsel he also made bond before a Sioux
City magistrate so that he couldn't be charged as a "fugitive from
justice." This proved to be a wise move. About four o'clock one
morning, FBI agents banged on the door of his room in the
Milner Hotel with a "fugitive" warrant. When shown the
magistrate's bond, however, they backed off. Efforts made
thereafter to extradite Maloney were blocked, so he escaped
prosecution in the Sioux Falls case. But the FBI already had
something else in mind for him, as will be seen later.

An experience Johnson had after his arrest showed the
contrived nature of the case against the Local 383 officials. The
police had put him in a brightly lighted show-up line, along with
a few other men, for purposes of identification by an alleged
witness against him. Starting at one end of the line, the cop in
charge asked each man in turn simply to give his name. But
when he got to Johnson the cop stated: "You are Ralph Johnson,
aren't you, and you're connected with the truck drivers union as
an organizer." A woman back in the shadows then said: "That's
the man."

Upon being arraigned in a Sioux Falls court, Fouts and
Johnson pleaded not guilty and were released after posting $5,000
bail each.

Teamster locals throughout the area quickly came to their
defense. Money was contributed for bail, lawyer's fees, and court
costs. In addition, the antiunion implications of the case were
brought to Tobin's attention with a request for his support. In
response, he authorized an appeal within the IBT for defense
funds. He also made an effort to swing some political influence
inside South Dakota on behalf of the defendants, but it proved
unsuccessful.

As part of the defense effort, Jack Maloney prepared a full

account of the case. One passage in the report gave a rather graphic description of the atmosphere surrounding the trial of the victimized trade unionists.

"A few years ago in Sioux Falls," Jack wrote, "some gangsters had a dispute over the division of the swag. They shot a woman of the band full of holes and her husband was placed in a dynamite warehouse in a nearby stone quarry. The dynamite shack was then touched off, the man being blown to bits. The explosion blew practically all of the windows in Sioux Falls into the streets. Another incident occurred around April 1, 1939, when a preacher became envious of another preacher's personal belongings. In this dispute, over the ownership of an automobile, the first preacher blew up with dynamite the second preacher's automobile. He was tried, convicted, and sentenced to six years on this charge, just before Fouts and Johnson are to stand trial on the charges against them. These two incidents tend to make the citizens of South Dakota very hostile when the word dynamite is mentioned."

Such were the circumstances under which the two Local 383 officials were hauled into court on June 6, 1939, before Judge Wall. On top of that the prosecutor, Ed Baron, was careful to see that not a single trade unionist got on the jury. It was made up entirely of merchants and farmers.

Testimony introduced by the state alleged that the defendants were seen near the truck on the day it was damaged. In rebuttal, several defense witnesses testified that Fouts was in Sioux City at the time and that Johnson was in the Omaha-Council Bluffs area.

The trucking employer from Grand Island was allowed to tell about labor trouble he had experienced in Nebraska in 1937. Objecting vigorously, the defense contended that a labor dispute in another state two years earlier had absolutely no bearing on the case at hand. Although such irrelevant testimony could only be intended to prejudice the jurors against the defendants, the judge overruled the objection.

Both men were found guilty and given sentences of four years in the state penitentiary. Since the verdict was appealed, they were able to remain free on bond. Finally, in September 1940, the South Dakota Supreme Court reversed the convictions on the grounds that the "evidence" against Fouts and Johnson was insufficient.

By then, however, the two were in a federal prison at Terre Haute, Indiana. They had been put there as a result of another frame-up, one that had been openly engineered by the FBI. It stemmed from an earlier incident during a strike in which Local 383 was involved.

In July 1938 the Teamsters and Bakers unions had jointly tied up the wholesale bakeries in Sioux City. The strike was solid. Not a single worker sought to return to the job. Since this left the police with no pretext to attack the picket lines, there were no instances of violence in the city during the walkout.

The incident later seized upon to fabricate a case against the Teamsters was of an isolated and questionable nature. One of the struck firms, Metz Baking Company, operated extensively in the region of Sioux City. A Metz truck was allegedly burned during the strike near the Iowa-Minnesota line. The company blamed the Teamsters, and the charge became a one-day sensation in the papers.

Local 383 disclaimed any knowledge of the matter, observing that there would have been no point in the strikers taking such action in the hinterlands. The outcome of the struggle had to be determined in Sioux City, where the union forces were strong and in full control of the situation.

Maybe the company had burned its own truck to win public sympathy, the Teamster leaders suggested. Or there might be another explanation. The scab driver, who was working long hours, might have fallen asleep and gone off the road. Perhaps he then set fire to the truck, claiming pickets had attacked him, to cover up what really happened.

In any event, the conflict was actually fought out in Sioux City, and after a walkout of about a month the strikers won. A year later union contracts with the bakeries were renewed on improved terms, without need for strike action. By that time the false allegations against the Teamsters concerning the Metz truck were thought to have sunk back into limbo.

Not so. The FBI had long been working quietly on the case. This had led to secret indictments against several Teamster officials by a federal grand jury, which had been convened in Cedar Rapids, Iowa, at the opposite end of the state. They were alleged to have participated in the burning of the truck during the 1938 strike.

There were five counts against them: violation of the Dyer Act (transporting a stolen vehicle across state lines); interference with interstate commerce; conspiracy to do both of the above; conspiracy to steal bakery goods; and possession of stolen bakery goods.

The first three of these counts were the most vital, since they were used to assume federal jurisdiction over the case. Such action conformed with the line that President Franklin D. Roosevelt had laid down by then. His aim was clearly to provide a basis for federal police actions designed to weaken strong trade unions.

None of this was known to the IBT until September 23, 1939. At four o'clock that morning FBI agents descended upon the homes of the unsuspecting victims. The dragnet caught up Teamster officials in three cities: Louis Miller and Walter K. Stultz in Omaha, Nebraska; Francis Quinn in Des Moines, Iowa; Howard Fouts and Ralph Johnson in Sioux City. (Jack Maloney was also on the list, but he was attending a union conference in Chicago at the time. Upon his return to Sioux City he surrendered himself through a lawyer.)

After the arrests, obstacles were put in the way of the defendants making bail. Fellow union officials, who sought help from bonding agencies to get them out of jail, were shadowed by FBI agents. Pressure was then brought against the bondsmen to scare them off. Despite such harassment, release of the six was finally obtained by posting $5,000 bail for each one.

A seventh victim was Earl Carpenter. He had been an officer of the Omaha IBT local until late 1938 when he moved to Oakland, California, and took a job as a bus driver. He, too, was picked up by the FBI and held in an Oakland jail pending later transport to Iowa for his trial.

Ominously enough, the attack had not been limited to Sioux City Local 383, the only IBT unit involved in the 1938 bakery strike. Omaha Local 554 and Des Moines Local 90 had also become targets of the FBI. All three locals were among the key links in the eleven-state formation through which the Teamsters were organizing over-the-road drivers across the entire upper Mississippi valley. Thus it was plainly evident that the Metz incident was being used as a cover for a union-busting attack of major proportions, and strong countermeasures were needed to ward off the danger.

As a general organizer assigned by the IBT to its over-the-road campaign, it was my responsibility to take initiative in preparing the defense of the victimized union leaders. After first helping to get them out on bail, I had a discussion with Tobin about the problem as a whole. He agreed that it was a dangerous situation for the organization. Then he stressed that he could use his connections in the Democratic Party to arrange for me to have a talk with Attorney General Frank Murphy about the case. Seeking to influence the chief federal prosecutor seemed a feeble way to fight back against the frame-up. But the IBT head wanted to take such a step. Since there was nothing to lose by the attempt, I went through with it.

Tobin's son, Fred, the Teamsters' legislative representative in Washington, D.C., went with me to see the Attorney General. He greeted us at the door of his plush office with extended hand. Everything about him reflected the essence of affability except his eyes. They were as cold as a banker's when asked to make a loan without collateral.

Murphy listened courteously to my protest against the attack on the union. Then he gave us a lot of double-talk that boiled down to the following: the Justice Department was sworn to uphold the law without fear or favor, and we could feel assured that in doing so it would guarantee the IBT defendants a fair trial. What had already happened showed that such assertions were patently false. It followed that the Attorney General remained determined to go through with the frame-up. Tobin's assumed political influence had failed to touch him.

Meanwhile, counsel had been secured for the indicted men. They were represented by five prominent lawyers in the region: David Weinberg and Louis Carnazzo of Nebraska; John Connelly and C.I. McNutt of Iowa; and Henry Mundt of South Dakota. From the outset the government sought to make their task doubly difficult at every juncture.

Early in October all those indicted, except Carpenter, were arraigned in Sioux City, at which time they pled not guilty. Two of them, Miller and Stultz, had posted bond in Omaha where they lived. When they got to Sioux City, however, they were held in jail eight days on the nit-picking pretext of a minor technical error in the Omaha bonds. That created a serious obstacle to consultation with their lawyers, who practiced in Omaha. When the two were finally released, only a few days remained to prepare their defense before going to trial.

Carpenter was brought east by train in the custody of U.S. marshals. FBI agents, led by Eugene Combs, were on hand to meet him at the Sioux City station. There they put on a show calculated to give a public impression that Earl was a dangerous criminal and hauled him off to jail. He had arrived in town only thirty-three hours before the trial was to begin. Thus he had virtually no time to consult the lawyers and prepare to defend himself against the frame-up.

The trial opened October 30, 1939, in the federal district court at Sioux City, with Judge Scott presiding. A jury was picked from a panel stacked against labor. Among its members were a couple of bankers, a public utility official, a lumber yard manager, and two loan sharks.

A major clash quickly developed over the issue of federal jurisdiction in the case. On that point the government presented FBI testimony about the site of the 1938 truck incident, in which the Metz driver had been traveling south from Minnesota into Iowa on U.S. highway 75. Right at the boundary between the two states the road makes a 90-degree turn and goes east a short distance. Then it makes another 90-degree turn to the south into Iowa. The section of highway at the boundary had been elaborately surveyed by FBI agents. Their object was to present claims that the Minnesota-Iowa line ran along the center of the piece of road going east; that the defendants had stopped the truck on the Minnesota side of the highway and moved it a few feet across the narrow pavement to the Iowa side; and that the case was therefore interstate in character.

Their argument was as crooked as the road. Nevertheless, the judge overruled defense objections and let the FBI testimony stand. In equally outrageous fashion the prosecution then set out to link the defendants to the alleged crime. It was charged that seven officials from IBT locals in three different cities had combined to stop one truck. Seven union leaders were said to have undertaken the action without involving a single rank-and-file member from any of the three locals. On the face of it the charge was preposterous. In fact, it was doubly so, because over two-hundred union members were on strike in Sioux City and available for picket duty at the time of the Metz incident.

To introduce "evidence" against the victims, a trick was used. It centered on a written chart specifying where each defendant was to sit in the court room. The chart was apparently shown to government witnesses, no doubt by the FBI agents who had lined them up. Such a ploy was indicated by the manner in which these witnesses conducted themselves in making "identifications."

Concerning one count in the indictment, however, U.S. District Attorney Dunn, the prosecutor, tended to back off. It involved the alleged "possession of stolen bakery goods." Even the most devious legal mind could not explain how the bakery goods could be both burned and possessed. So Dunn failed to push that particular charge.

When the case went to the jury all the defendants were found guilty on the other four counts of the indictment. They received sentences of two years on each count, the prison terms to run concurrently. Notice of appeal was then filed by defense counsel, along with a request that the bonds posted before the trial remain valid. The request was granted for only five of those involved.

Jack Maloney and Earl Carpenter were required to post new bail of $5,300 each. As a pretext for this discriminatory order, the judge cited Earl's residency in California and the "transient" nature of Jack's sojourn in Sioux City. (He had gone there two years before from Minneapolis, Minnesota, as an organizer for the North Central District Drivers Council, a formation initiated in Minnesota and thereafter extended into the contiguous states.) Defense counsel was then notified that the two men would be held in the local jail for five days, and if new bail was not posted for them within that period, they would be sent to the penitentiary.

During the course of these events, I prepared a memorandum for circulation among the over-the-road unions in the eleven-state area. One passage in it indicated the lethargic response of the IBT general officers to the needs of the victimized Teamster leaders.

"Immediately upon receipt of the news of the conviction of the defendants in the Sioux City federal court case," my memorandum stated, "I telephoned Acting President John M. Gillespie to explain the situation and request assistance in obtaining the appeal bond. I was informed by Brother Gillespie that it was not possible for direct aid to be given by the International Union without the approval of the International Executive Board. He suggested that I contact those Local Unions which I thought might be in a position to advance some funds for this purpose, and authorized me to inform them that if the International Executive Board, at its next meeting, granted the request for financial aid, that these donations from the Local Unions would then be refunded. He emphasized that this might be possible but was not guaranteed."

Gillespie, with whom I held the conversation, served as Tobin's chief of staff. He routinely used the title "acting president" when the IBT head was away from the national headquarters.

Having no alternative, we followed his suggestion and asked for financial help from over-the-road locals throughout the area. We planned to use funds thus raised to pay the premiums involved in arranging bail through a bonding agency. That course was decided on because it would be a tall order to raise $10,600 in cash to spring Maloney and Carpenter, especially in the short time we had. But matters didn't work out as planned. A four-day quest showed that none of the Sioux City agencies would do business with us. It seemed the case was "too hot" for them.

Our next step, taken with the help of Minneapolis Local 544, was to have a Minnesota bondsman rushed in to handle the matter. He arrived in Sioux City early in the morning on the deadline day. After getting a rundown on the situation, he set out to arrange the desired bonds, confidently assuring us that with his connections he would be able to do so before noon. In a couple of hours, however, he returned empty-handed and crestfallen, unable to understand why he had run up against a stone wall. It was something entirely outside the realm of his experience.

Bonding agencies do business in considerable part with underworld figures. Such clients are usually allowed to ply their "trades" with minimal police interference, provided their offenses are against people and not against capitalist private property. If an underworld figure gets arrested now and then, some capitalist politician can usually be found who will pull strings to help ease the legal situation. Experienced bondsmen consider such practices more or less routine. But in the present case none of the usual norms applied. The federal government, acting as the executive body of the employers generally, was attacking a trade union. A clash of opposing class forces was going on in which the political influence of bonding agencies was nil.

By the time the Minneapolis bondsman reported his failure, only a few hours remained before Maloney and Carpenter would be taken to the penitentiary. If that was to be prevented, cash bail would have to be raised in a hurry. So I began telephoning an emergency appeal to the biggest IBT locals. My first call was to

T.T. Neal, the head of Kansas City Local 41. Unlike Gillespie, who had hemmed and hawed when I contacted him earlier, Neal was ready to go all the way.

"How much do you need all told?" he asked.

"$10,600," I replied, "and right now."

"We have about $14,000 in Local 41's treasury," he then responded. "There isn't time to consult the executive board about it, so I'll telegraph you $11,000 of that on my own responsibility. As soon as other locals send contributions, please rush some of it back, so I can plug the hole I'm making in our treasury."

My calls to other IBT units also got a swift response. A total of $8,500 was sent from Chicago Local 710, Detroit Local 299, Milwaukee Local 200, Minneapolis Local 544, St. Louis Local 600, and South Bend Local 364. That made it possible to quickly return $6,500 to Neal and still have funds available to meet other expenses involved in the appeal.

Meantime, the lump sum telegraphed by Neal had arrived about three hours before the deadline. Cash bail was then put up for Maloney and Carpenter, who were released from jail. It had been a near thing.

By this time, feelings of intense anger over the government's brutal attack had been generated among rank-and-file Teamsters. The membership of Sioux City Local 383, for example, unanimously adopted a resolution stating: "We are especially convinced that the FBI did everything possible to make the charges severe beyond all rules of decency in an effort to publicly brand these union officials as criminals."

The authorities not only turned a deaf ear to such protests from trade unionists, but they launched still another frame-up against Local 383. This time a complaint from the Gibson Trucking Company of Havelock, Iowa, was used for the purpose. Gibson, who had refused to sign the IBT's area contract for over-the-road operations, was paying his drivers scab wages. In March 1940 three drivers on Havelock-Sioux City runs came voluntarily to Local 383's hall. Two of them were members of the local, and all three wanted aid in getting the union scale. They asked that their employer be notified that he could no longer operate in Sioux City until the area contract was signed. Howard Fouts then telephoned Gibson at Havelock and served notice on him to that effect.

Within a short time two Sioux City police came to the union hall and asked if the Gibson drivers were present. They were, but they didn't identify themselves. The cops then went away.

A few days later three officials of Local 383 were arrested: Howard Fouts, Ralph Johnson, and Charles Cunningham; also a job steward, Jack Webster. The four were charged with kidnapping the Gibson drivers and holding them for ransom. Newspaper headlines screamed that they were being denied bail because the charge could involve the death penalty. They lay in jail for seventeen days until they were indicted by the county grand jury on the kidnapping charge. After that the four were released on bond of $15,000.

At this juncture a strong delegation representing over-the-road locals in the eleven-state area had a session with Tobin. He was asked to give more effective support to the union leaders who had become frame-up victims. Tobin then sent Joseph L. Padway, general counsel for the IBT, to check into the situation. Padway visited Omaha, Grand Island, Sioux Falls, and Sioux City. In each place he issued press statements denouncing the legal assault on Teamster leaders. He also consulted with counsel for the defendants in the various cases. After that, Padway departed from the region and did not return, even though his visit left things about where they stood before he came.

Fouts, who had been the one to telephone Gibson about signing a union contract, was brought to trial first in the "kidnapping" case. The drivers who had asked union help were scared off from testifying in his defense. He was convicted, sentenced to six months in the county jail, and fined $600. It was such a crude frame-up, however, that the conviction was reversed on appeal. After that the charges against the other three were dropped.

While the "kidnapping" conviction was being appealed, there was a new development in the case of the seven who had been sentenced for allegedly burning the Metz truck. In May 1940 the U.S. Circuit Court of Appeals heard arguments in this case. A few weeks later their appeal was denied and they were ordered imprisoned at the beginning of August 1940 to serve two-year terms.

Earl Carpenter, Jack Maloney, Francis Quinn, and Walter K. Stultz were put in the federal prison at Sandstone, Minnesota. Howard Fouts and Ralph Johnson were sent to Terre Haute, Indiana. Louis Miller was locked up at Leavenworth, Kansas. Before entering prison Miller sent me a letter expressing his feelings about the situation.

"As you know," Lou wrote, "a decision has been made which

seems to be final and under these circumstances there is nothing left for me to do but take the consequence. I want you to know that in spite of the verdict which has declared me guilty, I shall serve time as a free man, in thought.

"I have at all times tried to play the game as a true unionist, fighting for those principles which every true union man has in his heart. I do not intend that this letter should in any sense be an obituary, rather I want to arouse the union consciousness of every working man and woman.

"Let the injustice which has befallen me serve as a warning to every ardent unionist to guard against the pitfalls and dangers which may be in his fight for economic freedom. I should then feel that the price which I have been called upon to pay will not have been paid in vain.

"Remember me as one making a plea for continued organization, continued courageous leadership and a continued fight for justice in the Fraternity of Labor."

2. Roosevelt's Aims

Basically, the legal assault on the IBT was intended to curb militancy in its ranks, for by 1939 organizers of the over-the-road campaign were in the forefront of the union's general advance. Hence the federal government made them primary targets, as shown by the frame-up in Sioux City. Before assessing more fully the Roosevelt administration's motives for that outrageous act, however, a closer look should be taken at the worker militants who were under attack. This can be done through background sketches of Jack Maloney and Louis Miller, two of the frame-up victims. In a broad sense their stories reflect the evolution of the many outstanding fighters who were in the process of transforming the Teamster movement.

Shaun McGillin (Jack) Maloney, the third child of Irish immigrant parents, was born September 10, 1911, in Minneapolis, Minnesota. He never saw his father, Thomas. His mother, Katherine McGillin, later remarried. Her second husband, Ole Severson, was a second generation Norwegian-American whose surname Jack used until he was in his twenties.

At an early age Jack began to acquire radical sentiments from both his mother and his stepfather. Katherine sang songs and told stories to her children about the Irish struggle for independence from Britain. From this they developed an instinct to rebel against any form of regimentation. Ole's radicalism, in turn, helped the process along. At various times he had worked in the harvest fields and logging camps where he involved himself in struggles waged by the Industrial Workers of the World (IWW). In addition he was a supporter of Eugene V. Debs, the great socialist and trade-union leader. Like Debs, he was opposed to U.S. involvement in imperialist war. Such views, strongly held by Ole, tended to rub off on the children, along with the spirit of militancy they gained from their mother.

During the latter part of his school years, Jack worked with his

27

stepfather whenever circumstances permitted. Ole, a staunch
union man, had been blacklisted in the Minneapolis teaming
industry after an IBT strike was broken in 1916. Later he got
enough money together to buy his own team of horses. That
enabled him to find employment on construction jobs—scooping
out basements, hauling sand, etc.—and in general teaming. It
was on such jobs that Ole was able to use Jack as a helper,
mainly to drive the team while Ole did the heavier labor involved.

Then, after quitting high school while in the ninth grade, Jack
got an official work permit at the age of fourteen. By that time he
had learned enough about driving trucks to get employment on
his own in that line, which was rapidly replacing the teaming
trade. His first job of the kind was in the shipping room and
delivery service of a big department store. From there he shifted
to truck driving on construction work. After that, with hard times
brought on by an economic slump in 1926, he went to the harvest
fields for several seasons.

Upon returning to Minneapolis, Jack worked as a driver in
various kinds of retail delivery and transfer service and in the
construction industry. For a time he also drove trucks for
carnivals, circuses, and athletic shows on the road. Then, in the
summers of 1930 and 1931, he worked as a deck hand on the ore
boats plying the Great Lakes. Following that, he again based
himself in his home town where he drove for trucking firms
engaged in local and long distance hauling of freight and
household goods.

By that time, however, the depression that followed the 1929
market crash was reaching severe depths. Steady employment for
drivers had become increasingly hard to find. They had to put in
a lot of time waiting on company premises without pay, hoping to
get work for a few hours or, if lucky, a few days; and they had to
take whatever jobs came along, at whatever rates the bosses
decided to pay. Those who "made trouble" about being gouged in
this manner by the trucking firms were blacklisted, left stranded
with no way to fight in defense of their interests. As a result,
thousands of workers in the Minneapolis trucking industry were
ready for battle; and they responded heartily when the General
Drivers Union launched an organization campaign in 1934
designed to lead them into action against the bosses.

In May of that year the drivers, helpers, and inside workers
struck most of the city's trucking industry. The bosses responded

by using the police department, backed up by special deputies, for an all-out attack on the union forces. Meeting the assault club against club, the strikers fought successfully to defend their picket lines. During the combat, in which he came forward as a picket captain, Jack learned rich lessons about the class struggle, as did his fellow workers. As a body they picketed so effectively that the trucking companies had to make a settlement on terms favorable to the union.

Not yet ready to concede defeat, the bosses soon repudiated the May agreement, and the union was forced to resume the walkout. In the renewed conflict, Jack served as a member of the democratically elected Committee of 100 that led the strike.

This time the cops used riot guns against the workers, killing two and wounding many. At that critical juncture Jack served as one of the field commanders responsible for leading large picket detachments in confrontations with the scab-herding police that followed the massacre. Before long the governor declared martial law, seized the strike headquarters, ordered the arrest of the central strike leaders, and asked that a rank-and-file committee meet with him to negotiate a settlement of the controversy. Jack was a member of a committee of three that went to see the governor. They refused to negotiate, demanding instead that he return the strike headquarters and release the arrested leaders. Their stand was strongly backed by those central leaders still at large—who were organizing effective picketing in defiance of the military—and the governor was forced to back down. Finally, in August 1934, the union won a definitive settlement with the bosses that firmly established it in the trucking industry.

For the next period Jack served on the union's organization staff whenever its finances permitted; during the intervals he took truck-driving jobs. As time went by the growing Teamster forces in Minneapolis were able to initiate the North Central District Drivers Council as the vehicle for a regional unionization campaign. As part of that project the NCDDC assigned Jack, in the fall of 1937, to help a newly chartered IBT local in Sioux Falls, South Dakota. There he played a large role in a hard-fought strike against some freight outfits. Thanks to previous experience, he knew how to take the lead in resisting police attacks on the picket lines. The workers won, and the union gained a foothold in the local trucking industry. Soon afterward the regional organizing committee shifted him to Sioux City,

Iowa, where the help of an experienced organizer and strike leader was also needed.

While making the shift in assignments, Jack was sent on a side trip to establish contact with IBT units in Omaha and Des Moines. On the way he spotted a truck from Omaha parked at a roadside diner in Missouri Valley, Iowa. He went in, took a seat next to the driver, and introduced himself. The Omaha driver was Louis Miller, whose story will account for his enthusiastic response to Jack's explanation of the broad organization campaign that had been set into motion.

Louis Miller's father, Anton Mileroviz, was a Pole born in Germany. As a young man, Anton went over-the-hill from the Kaiser's conscript army and fled to Poland. After that he found work as a coal miner in the Krakow region. There he married Hattie Czaplewski and the couple later migrated to the United States. They settled down in St. Joseph, Missouri, where Anton became a packinghouse worker and the family name was changed from Mileroviz to Miller. Their son, Louis, was born in St. Joseph on June 15, 1901.

Lou's formal education ended after one year in high school. The family, which was devoutly Catholic, had been pressing him to train for the priesthood, but he was dead set against it. So when he was about seventeen, he took off, heading first for the harvest fields, where he joined the IWW. By then the U.S. had entered World War I and the organization was being subjected to vigilante attacks and legal frame-ups. It was in such circumstances that Lou began to get his feet wet in the class struggle. After that he got employment on road work, traveling across a stretch from the Dakotas to Texas. Then he went west, finding whatever work he could as a boomer along the Pacific coast between Los Angeles and Seattle. From there he made his way back toward home by way of the Rocky Mountain states.

Upon returning to St. Joseph, he began to haul bootleg whiskey. Although this was popularly viewed as socially necessary labor during the prohibition era, the authorities treated it as an illegal occupation. One thing led to another and Lou wound up doing considerable time. While in prison he read whatever he could get his hands on and took such study courses as were available, in an effort to further his education.

After regaining his freedom he got a job at the St. Joseph terminal of the Watson Brothers Transportation Company. At first he

worked on the docks and as an apprentice driver learning to handle over-the-road equipment. Then he was transferred to the company's main operational base in Omaha, where he was assigned
to a run between that terminal and Kansas City.

Drivers' wages in Omaha then averaged about 25¢ an hour. An
eighty-hour work week was not unusual, and job conditions were
generally very bad. Under these circumstances the workers were
more than ready to fight for an improvement in their situation,
but they had no ready means of getting themselves organized.
Although IBT Local 554 already existed in Omaha, it was little
more than a paper setup. The officials in charge of the local had
failed to show the necessary leadership qualities, with the result
that the workers had no confidence in them.

In the spring of 1937 a way was found to overcome the bind.
Lou and a half-dozen other drivers took the initiative in launching a spontaneous walkout at various terminals of the Watson
system. Having thus made sure that there would be a fight, the
workers involved joined Local 554 in a body. By mid-June they
were able to win contracts with several Omaha trucking firms
providing union recognition, wage hikes, and other concessions.
That same year new local union officers were elected from the
ranks, Lou becoming vice-president.

Later on Watson shifted Lou to an Omaha-Sioux City run. Toward the end of 1937 he was making such a trip when he met
Jack Maloney in the Missouri Valley diner. Jack went on from
there to Omaha to talk with other Local 554 officers about the
NCDDC's regional campaign. Lou joined in the discussion as
soon as he got back from his run, pressing strongly for Omaha's
participation in the project. The upshot was that a Local 554
delegation attended a broad Teamster conference held at St. Paul,
Minnesota, in January 1938.

Lou was among those present and, while he was there, Jack
took him on a tour of the Teamster movement next door in
Minneapolis. As Lou later described the experience: "I liked what
I saw and found out what it meant to have a strong union." Soon
thereafter he went on the Local 554 organization staff full time,
ready to help carry out what he now understood had to be done.

An obstacle to the campaign projected by the NCDDC arose
when Tobin issued an order to its St. Paul conference that the
regional formation had to be dissolved. This angered the delegates, who sent a committee to meet with the IBT head and de-

mand the latitude needed for their unionization drive. Under this pressure he backed off some, offering a compromise proposal that the action be confined to over-the-road drivers. Since that in itself represented a major advance, his proposal was accepted and the organization activity went forward with renewed vigor. In a few months an eleven-state area structure was created. It extended from Michigan and Ohio in the east to the Dakotas and Nebraska in the west. This formation recruited tens of thousands of new members into the IBT. In August 1938 it won the first uniform area contract, providing higher wages and better working conditions for over-the-road drivers.

Trucking companies in the Missouri valley region tried to hold out against signing the area-wide agreement. This led to a series of struggles. Walkouts of a relatively short duration forced the Des Moines and Sioux Falls employers into line, but in Omaha, other Nebraska towns, and Sioux City, the bosses fought viciously. A strike lasting from September 1938 to February 1939 was needed to make them sign the area contract.

Having finally emerged victorious from the battle with the long distance trucking firms, the IBT locals became the spearhead for all organized labor in Iowa, Nebraska, and South Dakota. Wages were low and job conditions bad for workers generally in those states. Now that they had seen proof that concessions could be wrested from the bosses through strike actions, thousands began to join the unions of their trades. In the struggles that followed they looked to the Teamsters for help, and they got it. A new day was dawning for militant trade unionism in that benighted territory.

This caused deep concern among the bosses in those open-shop states. So they set out to reverse the trend, picking the Teamster locals as their main target. Agencies of capitalist rule at the city, county, and state levels were activated in frame-up attacks on IBT officials. They sought help from the federal government against the union militants, and their request got a ready response from the Roosevelt administration, which was then making a rightward turn away from its earlier policies.

When Roosevelt first took office in 1933, the nation's economy was almost paralyzed. Conditions of life for the workers had become so intolerable that rebellious moods were rapidly spreading among them. Fears of a revolutionary uprising gripped the capitalists, so they allowed the incoming president wide latitude in acting to stem the threat to their rule.

After proclaiming a "New Deal" for the country, Roosevelt quickly pushed several new measures through Congress. Among these was legislation to restrict competition between capitalist enterprises within the various industrial sectors, which opened the way for price hikes and increased profit taking. Although the policy served mainly to promote the growth of corporate monopolies, it was demagogically presented as the only way to get the economy going again. On the same premise, federal spending was channeled wherever possible into the coffers of the fat cats. Everybody would gain from this in the end, it was slyly argued, as benefits "trickled down" from the top of the economic pyramid.

Parallel with the foregoing measures, Roosevelt purported to assure labor the right to organize trade unions and to bargain collectively with the bosses. But it was a hollow promise. In practice he continued to use the federal government as a strikebreaking agency, simply resorting to subtler methods than those previously utilized for such purposes.

As the carrot accompanying the club, a few social concessions of a secondary character were made to the workers. These centered on "social security" legislation and were designed to raise labor's hopes of meaningful progress through gradual reforms within the capitalist system.

Reformist illusions of this kind were also propagated by trade-union bureaucrats and other misleaders within the radical movement who supported the New Deal policies. With their help, Roosevelt was able to prevent the workers from taking an anticapitalist political course, and the labor upsurge was contained at the trade-union level.

Even so, the capitalists were not yet out of the woods. During 1937-38 another industrial slump set in, and it was again a deep one. As this development showed, the New Deal measures could not, in themselves, overcome the economic crisis. Additional steps were needed, and by that time Roosevelt had new means at hand to tackle the problem. He had already taken the lead in ruling-class preparations to plunge the country into the imperialist conflict that was soon to erupt on a world scale. He now intensified that course of action, using increased outlays for armament both to artificially stimulate the economy and to prepare for military combat. The New Deal was becoming a War Deal.

In an imperialist war the exploited masses not only do the fighting and dying, but heavy material sacrifices are forced upon them as well. Meanwhile, new contingents of millionaires and billionaires spring up, as the capitalists rake in blood profits from the holocaust. Protests against these inequalities are bound to develop, so Roosevelt made advance preparations to stifle them. A series of legislative acts and presidential decrees was shaped, step by step, to restrict civil liberties. The FBI openly began to assume the role of political police. Together with other federal agencies, it moved to clamp down on the more aggressive sections of organized labor; and the Teamsters were not the only target.

A direct clash with the national administration had developed in still another sphere during 1939. It involved a nationwide strike on federally operated "made work" projects, where the workers were fighting against wage cuts and layoffs. Brutal repressive action—which will be described later in some detail—was taken by the government. That, in turn, was followed by another form of attack on the AFL building-trades unions, whose members had taken part in the strike on the federal projects.

The U.S. Department of Justice obtained a series of indictments against AFL building-trades officials. They were charged with "criminal conspiracy in restraint of trade" within the private sector of the building industry. In this case the aim was not so much to secure convictions as it was to throw a scare into the labor bureaucrats. They were being shown how the governmental power could be used against them if they obstructed policy changes set into motion by the ruling class as it prepared for war.

Since the message was really addressed to the labor movement as a whole, it was plainly the duty of all top union officials to launch a broad movement in defense of those under government attack. Moreover, the defense should have taken the form of a direct, militant confrontation with the primary instigator of the legal assaults on trade unionists, Franklin D. Roosevelt. As it was, though, none of the top labor bureaucrats had the outlook needed for such a fight. All of them defaulted on their responsibilities to the union ranks, including Tobin.

When cracking down on a rank-and-filer or a local union, the Teamster president was tougher than boarding house meat; but when it was a matter of going up against the bosses and their government, he became as timid as a rabbit.

Jack Maloney described the situation this way: "When we stressed to Tobin that the federal government was persecuting us, he showed no class outlook regarding the problem. He seemed to feel that we were too rough in our organizing work, that we didn't do enough politicking with the powers that be. As for him, he had no thought of using the IBT's strength in a clash with the government. His idea was to pull strings for off-the-record favors, like a ward heeler. He kept saying that he couldn't compromise the union, apparently thinking that we were giving it a bad image. Well, if he wants an image the bosses' government will approve, you can make book that the membership will pay through the nose for it."

The accuracy of Jack's appraisal can be verified through a more complete account of official Teamster policies, especially as these were revealed in earlier clashes the IBT chief had with the Minneapolis General Drivers Union.

3. Mentality of a Union Bureaucrat

Since 1907 Daniel J. Tobin sat astride the Teamster organization as its general president. During those years he became wholly committed to the concepts of business unionism. As the term implies, that outlook is designed to assure the capitalists of organized labor's cooperation, both within industry and at the governmental level. In return, it is fatuously assumed, grateful employers will make a few significant concessions to the workers. On that premise the ruling hierarchy in the trade unions—today as yesterday—displays "statesmanlike" sensitivity to ruling-class needs, thereby stripping itself of any capacity to lead struggles in defense of the workers' interests.

Organizationally, business unionism first took shape through the establishment of the American Federation of Labor along narrow craft lines. (The structural base widened later on, however, when the Congress of Industrial Organizations became extensively bureaucratized.) From the beginning, the AFL concentrated on recruitment of skilled and semiskilled workers. In the case of its IBT affiliate, efforts along that line focused primarily on select categories of drivers, helpers, and platform workers. Being somewhat better paid than the average laborer, they could more readily be drawn into contractual relations with the employers on class-collaborationist terms, especially when the arrangement also provided little job trusts for them.

In seeking contracts with trucking firms on this basis, Tobin put emphasis on *gradual* improvements for the workers. He insisted that union demands be "within reason." If a working agreement could not be obtained through direct negotiations with a given company, the Teamster president called for an effort to secure arbitration of the dispute. Only when an employer rejected that proposal as well was a strike to be considered, and even then strict procedures were laid down for taking a vote on the question in an IBT local. It was done in a way intended to "cool off hotheads" and give full play to any expressions of hesitation that might emanate from the ranks. When a strike was voted despite these obstacles, the decision was not yet final. Formal approval of the action was still required from the IBT's general executive board.

Strict control over strikes was only one aspect of the Teamster head's bureaucratic arbitrariness. The union's constitution contained a set of "laws" designed to serve his objectives at the expense of rank-and-file democracy. "Official policy" was laid down by him through freewheeling interpretation of resolutions adopted by IBT conventions, which were held at five-year intervals. He kept a staff of watchdogs on the alert for signs of dissidence within the organization, and anyone who got out of line could expect harsh discipline.

Tobin's scheme of things had no place at all for workers whose occupations fell outside the elitist categories of craft unionism. To him they were "rubbish." He said as much in the official IBT magazine, adding that the union didn't want such members, "if they are going on strike tomorrow." His reference was, of course, to the underprivileged masses who were radicalizing under the impact of the post-1929 depression. For their part, these workers were ready to fight in defense of their interests, if a way could be found for them to get organized with the help of competent leaders. But to do that in the trucking industry some basic alterations had to be made within the Teamster movement.

Steps toward the necessary changes were initiated in 1933 by revolutionary socialists who worked in the coal yards in Minneapolis. They belonged to the Communist League of America, the organizational form then taken by the Trotskyist movement. Plans for their course of action in the IBT had been carefully thought out in advance. As the Trotskyists saw the situation, the key to success in a clash with Tobin over union policy lay in his failure to adjust to the new times. A program of militant struggle to advance the workers' cause was required, as against his line of cozying up to the employers. To carry out that course, all workers in and around the trucking industry had to be organized. The democratic rights of the rank and file had to be counterposed to the IBT head's dictatorial methods inside the union. Given the accomplishment of those aims, new content could be infused into the old Teamster structure, making it an instrument for progress.

Tactically, it would have been unwise to begin with a head-on challenge to Tobin's rule, attempting forthwith to displace his apparatus in the leadership of the Minneapolis Teamsters. That would simply have played into his hands. A hue and cry could have been raised about "reds" trying to take over the organization. Conservative and uninformed members alike could have been mobilized against the challengers, and the fight would have been over almost before it got started.

Instead, the Trotskyists used flanking tactics. Demands upon the trucking companies were drawn up through a process of democratic consultation among the workers involved. With the assurance of general rank-and-file support of the demands, a fight to win them was set into motion. Tobin and his bureaucratic underlings were thus put in the middle. They could lend effective aid in the battle against the bosses and gain increased leadership authority, or they could fail to play a constructive role and wind up losing standing within the movement.

A further advantage resulted from this procedure. Officials in the lower echelons of the IBT hierarchy, being closer to the ranks than Tobin, were more susceptible than he was to the pressures of rising worker militancy. Among them were some who saw that changes in perspective were needed if the union was to prosper. They found merit in the trade-union program and combat ability of the Trotskyists and were favorably influenced by association with energetic young militants who arose from the union ranks to play leading roles in the conflicts that developed. As a consequence, such officials tended to oppose the Teamster president, in varying degrees, on some important issues.

Matters of tempo also had to be considered in shaping the plan of battle. As the struggle against the employers gained headway, a clash with the IBT chief was bound to develop. Yet it was important not to stumble into a premature showdown with him over secondary matters. At the start, all tactical steps had to be shaped in conformity with the basic strategy of an all-out fight against the enemy class. In that way a degree of mass momentum could be developed that Tobin would be unable to control, and despite obstructive actions on his part, the workers would be able to make gains.

Proceeding as outlined above, the Trotskyists began their campaign among Minneapolis workers engaged in the delivery of

coal. General Drivers Union Local 574 had the AFL jurisdiction
in that sphere, but the Tobinite majority of its executive board
was opposed to organizing those workers on an industry-wide
basis. So the first task was to help them fight their way into the
union.

Toward that end a voluntary organizing committee was formed
in the coal yards. The committee proceeded to develop mass
pressure on the petty bureaucrats in Local 574 for a change in
recruitment policy, receiving support from a minority of the
executive board. A breakthrough was soon accomplished, and the
coal workers began to pour into the local. When contract
demands were presented to the employers, however, they refused
even to negotiate with the union. At that point Tobin was
notified, simply for the record, of the workers' intention to go on
strike. John M. Gillespie replied for him, recommending that the
local seek, instead, to arrange government mediation of the
dispute.

Ignoring such advice as meaningless, the workers struck the
entire coal industry in February 1934. In the conflict that
followed, the voluntary committee led the picketing so effectively
that the bosses had to make a settlement with Local 574. They
were forced to yield wage concessions and, most importantly, to
grant union recognition.

While the settlement was being negotiated, word came from
Gillespie that approval of a strike was denied. By that time,
however, the battle had been fought and won. Sanction of the
action by the top IBT bureaucrats was no longer a relevant
question, since they had been effectively bypassed. On top of
that, it had now become possible to cross Tobin's craft-union
boundaries.

The victorious coal strike provided the stimulus needed for a
broad unionization campaign throughout the city's trucking
industry. In moving forward accordingly, the voluntary committee took advantage of the "general" jurisdictional designation in
Local 574's IBT charter. Recruitment was not confined to those
employed on trucks and loading docks, as Tobin had decreed, but
was expanded to include inside workers whose jobs were in any
way related to trucking. A few thousand new members were soon
enlisted on that basis, and the local began to assume a semi-
industrial organizational form.

Parallel with this growth a situation of dual leadership authority was taking shape within the changing union. The split within the executive board was hardening. On one side stood the Tobinite majority, which continued to follow an obstructionist course. On the other was the dissident minority, acting in concert with the voluntary organizing committee. The latter alliance was gaining ascendancy within the organization, since its policies coincided with the needs and aspirations of the ranks. In sum, formal authority remained with the executive board, but the voluntary committee now wielded sufficient power to overcome resistance to its preparations for a showdown fight with the trucking employers generally.

In May 1934 another walkout took place (the broad action cited before in describing Jack Maloney's background). While the strikers were battling the cops and deputies in that conflict, Tobin undertook a highhanded intervention. He sent a telegram instructing Local 574 to propose arbitration of the dispute with the trucking companies. But his order was ignored. The workers fought on and compelled the bosses to come to an agreement with the union.

Before long the employers undertook to repudiate the May settlement, making it clear that Local 574 was about to be forced into what would be the toughest fight of all. In preparing for the anticipated struggle the local solicited aid from its potential allies, and the response was magnificent. Heavy backing came from the city's AFL movement, the unemployed, farmers in the vicinity, students, and sections of the urban middle class. A massive coalition had come into being, ready to support the embattled Teamsters in what all understood would be a labor showdown with the entire Minneapolis ruling class.

At precisely that point Tobin committed a treacherous act. Through editorials in the IBT magazine he launched a red-baiting attack on the Trotskyists within Local 574, demanding that they be purged from the union. His diatribe was gleefully picked up by the employers and reprinted in the local newspapers. But the union members reacted angrily. They voted unanimously to begin the new walkout that the ruling class had forced upon them, including some harsh words to the IBT president in the strike call.

"If you can't act like a Union man, and help us, instead of

helping the bosses," he was told, "then at least have the decency to stand aside and let us fight our battle alone."

After that, neither Tobin nor his handraisers within Local 574 could influence the shaping of the local's policies. Thus it was possible to create a new leadership mechanism to conduct the struggle that followed during July and August. A broad strike committee was elected by the rank and file, and it was voted full executive authority for the duration of the conflict. To force compliance with the decision on the part of the official executive board, that body was both incorporated into the broad committee and made subordinate to it. Although such an arrangement conflicted with IBT "law," it was made to stick.

Toward the end of August 1934 the workers emerged victorious from the long fight against the trucking bosses. Their union had become consolidated within the trucking industry, and in the process it had developed into a powerful force within the Minnesota labor movement.

To assure the preservation of its internal dynamism, Local 574 held new elections after the strike was won. Only those who had acquitted themselves well in battle were returned to their posts. All the Tobinites were defeated in the voting. They were replaced in office by Trotskyists who had earned the support of the membership through their role on the voluntary organizing committee. These results brought the executive board fully into step with the militant rank and file. There were no longer any class collaborationists holding key official positions. A solid basis had been laid for the organization to follow a firm class-struggle course.

This favorable situation was further enhanced by changes occurring on a wider scale. The Minneapolis working class generally—including both members of existing unions and workers aspiring to become organized—had been stirred by the truck drivers' victory. As a result, new forces moved into action, and they developed increased momentum as one strike followed another. Then, in the midst of this process, Tobin decided to throw a monkey wrench into the trade-union machinery. In April 1935 he revoked Local 574's charter, callously disrupting the labor solidarity that had been generated during 1934.

He proceeded to set up a paper organization, "Local 500," with the expectation that it could displace Local 574. A decree was handed down that the leaders of the 1934 strikes were to be excluded from IBT membership, as were all inside workers, and that "Local 500's" policies were to be decided by a Tobin appointee. In short, everything was to revert to the pre-1934 state of affairs. To achieve that reactionary objective, the Teamster bureaucrat arrogantly demanded that the entire AFL help him destroy the splendid union that he purported to "outlaw."

Local 574 responded by campaigning for reinstatement into the IBT, with full democratic rights and with its organizational structure intact. While doing so, it beat off membership raids by "Local 500" and continued its efforts to complete the unionization of the city's trucking industry. At the same time, support was extended to AFL struggles in industrial spheres where help from the truck drivers was needed and valued. As a result, a big majority within the AFL continued to accept the proscribed union as an entirely legitimate organization.

Tobin had failed in his attempt to use the city's labor movement to crush Local 574. So he turned to AFL President William Green for help. Green dispatched one of his henchmen to Minneapolis with orders to force the unions there into compliance with "official" Teamster policy, but that didn't work either. Having grown desperate by that time, the IBT tyrant next resorted to naked force. A strong-arm gang was sent in from Chicago to break up Local 574 through methods of intimidation and terror. Quite a hassle followed. In the end, that attempt was also defeated and, with that setback, Tobin's string had about run out. In August 1936 he changed his line and agreed to take the "outlaws" back into the IBT.

The reinstatement was made through the issuance of a new charter bearing the designation Local 544. All the officers and members of former Local 574, including the 1934 strike leaders and the inside workers, were accepted into the new unit. By mutual agreement a new executive board was selected, composed of representatives from both former Local 574 and former "Local 500." In basic terms, Local 574 had been reinstated intact under a new charter number. Both its class-struggle policy and its organizational structure continued to prevail in the new setup. Even the difficulties involved in the formal leadership change were soon ironed out. Before long the Trotskyist trade-union program became as generally accepted in the executive board of Local 544 as it had previously been in 574.

Now that the infighting was over, the expansion drive that

Tobin had disrupted could at last be fully set into motion. It didn't take long for the united Teamster forces to assert their power everywhere in the Minneapolis trucking industry. Through the medium of the North Central District Drivers Council, the unionization campaign was extended all across Minnesota and into the adjoining states. Then the IBT president butted in again, dictatorially ordering that regional collaboration between local unions be discontinued. Once more, however, he found himself utterly out of touch with changing rank-and-file moods. As recounted in the previous chapter, he was forced to back down. The campaign went ahead, culminating in the consolidation of an area structure for over-the-road drivers on an eleven-state basis.

The latter accomplishment signified growing acceptance within expanded Teamster circles of policy changes first instituted in Minneapolis. In fact, even the IBT chief veered somewhat toward the new course for a time. He did so, for example, in backing the 1938–39 strike against the long-distance trucking outfits in Omaha and Sioux City. In part this was due to pressure from the ranks, but there was another motive that also came into play. Under the impetus of the over-the-road campaign, union recruitment was expanding throughout the trucking industry. That, in turn, swelled the payment of per capita taxes into the International treasury. In their combination these developments intrigued the Teamster president, as shown by the way he began to strut around in the pose of a "big time" labor official, and he was ready to go a certain distance in promoting organizational growth.

Tobin's posturing was, of course, merely a subjective byproduct of the basic transformation occurring within the IBT. Its rigid craft structure of yesteryear had been cracked wide open. Broader, more combative layers of workers were being drawn into the organization. They were ready for militant confrontations with the employers in support of progressive union aims. Young secondary officials were arising from their ranks, prepared to challenge the top bureaucrats on policy issues.

In short, the quantitative rise in the union's strength was producing a qualitative change in its internal features. The IBT had not only grown by 1939 to near 500,000 members, it was also becoming a dynamic movement capable of wielding great power in the class struggle.

This aggressive force naturally became a prime target in the government's drive to weaken the trade unions. For that reason Tobin, as general president, had the central responsibility for action in support of the seven Teamster officials framed up in the Sioux City case. In fact, prompt steps were required to mobilize the broadest possible movement to defend all victims of the government's legal assault—Teamster leaders, building trades officials, militants on federal "made work" projects, everyone under attack. A general fund was needed for bail, lawyers, and court costs, as well as to finance appeals to the higher courts, so as to carry the legal fight through to the bitter end.

Parallel with those activities the defense campaign should have been raised to a political plane. It was necessary, for example, to organize protest demonstrations and strikes aimed at forcing the government to back off from its attack. Educational measures were in order to explain the link between Roosevelt's efforts to undermine the labor movement and his preparations to take the country into World War II. Once that interconnection was understood, recognition had to follow that opposition to the war-makers was basic to defense of the workers' rights.

Action of the foregoing nature would inevitably have brought a direct political confrontation between the trade unions and the capitalist government. In such a clash, valuable lessons in class-struggle realities could have been driven home to the workers. Many would have perceived the need to turn away from the swamp of capitalist politics and begin a new advance along the road of independent working-class political action.

An effective struggle could have been waged under the objective conditions then existing. But the IBT lacked the top leadership needed to carry it through. Tobin, the business unionist, was incapable of fighting in that manner. As he saw things, the union had to restrict itself to the courtroom; and each case had to be handled separate and apart from all the others. With respect to political pressure, he would do no more than authorize public statements complaining about what was going on. Any idea of launching protest demonstrations and political strikes was alien to him. Instead of pointing to the relationship between the war preparations and the attacks on trade unions, he supported the foreign policy of U.S. imperialism. He was so deeply immersed in capitalist politics that he had headed the National Labor Committee of the Democratic Party during the campaign to reelect Roosevelt in 1936.

Because of those class-collaborationist views and practices,

Tobin defaulted on his responsibilities to the victimized IBT members. They went to prison for doing nothing more than attempting to provide the kind of leadership the workers needed. On top of that, the whole organization was dealt a setback. The vicious blow struck by the government in the Sioux City frame-up threw a scare into Teamster officials generally. They became cautious about laying themselves open to FBI-engineered attacks, fearing that they, too, might wind up in a federal jail. As a result the union began to lose the struggle momentum that it had developed.

There is much food for thought in this episode. Study of its meaning can be especially rewarding to worker militants who mistakenly believe they can best serve labor's cause by sticking entirely to trade-union matters and leaving politics to others. As the Sioux City case showed, unionism and politics cannot be separated. These two seemingly distinct spheres are in reality closely intertwined, one conditioning the other. If political action is left to the capitalists and their servitors within the labor movement, power generated at the trade-union level can be blunted, and even shattered, through blows from a government under ruling-class control.

Conversely, if the workers enter the political arena as an independent class force, with their own party, they have the strength to wrest state power from the hands of the capitalists. That step could put an end to governmental assaults on trade unions, like the one that struck the Teamsters. A labor government could qualitatively increase the workers' power, elevating it to a high plane on which all their basic problems as a class could be solved through the necessary transformations in the nation's social structure.

The complexities involved in guiding labor toward that independent political course can be scrutinized more closely by outlining the Trotskyist approach to the task, as it was developed when the depression of the 1930s began to radicalize the working class.

4. Dynamics of the Labor Upsurge

Under the present system, workers are conditioned from childhood to accept capitalist exploitation as something decreed by natural law. Indoctrination of this kind begins within the family, where the young are influenced by their brainwashed elders. From there the process is taken over by the propaganda media—schools, churches, television, radio, newspapers, and other sources of misinformation and manipulation.

As young workers enter the labor force they are subjected to refinements in ruling class doctrine. Without capitalist employers, they are told, there would be no jobs; so those benefactors deserve unswerving loyalty from their employees in order to promote the "common good." It is also stressed that the bosses got where they are by practicing rugged individualism. That preachment is intended to encourage the workers to do likewise if they hope to get ahead. The norm for personal conduct thus becomes: don't think about others, just take care of yourself.

As another means of dividing labor's ranks, use is made of factors serving to demarcate one group of workers from another. Skin color, ethnic background, sex, religion—anything that will help to sow dissension between groupings—is turned to capitalist advantage. Whites, for instance, are given an edge over people with black, brown, red, or yellow skins. Further differentiation then takes place along ethnic lines among whites themselves. Most favored historically are white, Anglo-Saxon protestants—Wasps; next come other categories of whites having European forebears; and, despite gradations in the degree of social acceptance that they enjoy, all in those categories are given advantage over people with different colored skins.

Numerous ironies result. A case in point is the situation of the

47

Indians, this country's true natives; they are way down in the pecking order.

Similarly, men take precedence over women in the work force. That discriminatory policy applies to women generally, even to the Wasps among them. It follows that for those in less-privileged categories a compound problem exists. Their status is determined not only by sex, but also by racial and ethnic factors. Women caught in that bind thereby become doubly victimized.

Such differentiations play a role in employment practices generally. Individuals in the more favored groupings are likely to get the better paying, skilled jobs. Those in the less favored categories, more or less in descending order, are next in line for the unskilled work and, after that, the menial tasks. For people at the bottom of this preferential sequence, the situation can be summed up in the phrase: last to be hired, first to be fired. Through such patterns of discrimination the bosses are able to pit one category of workers against another—skilled versus un-skilled, to cite a single example.

Relative economic privilege thus takes its place alongside race and sex bias as a device for splitting the working class so as to minimize organized resistance to capitalist exploitation.

Life on the job being what it is, however, other factors intrude to cause difficulties for the ruling class. Motivated by what is delicately called "the profit incentive," capitalists develop insatiable greed. Lust for private gain makes them strive to hold down wages, extend the hours of labor, disregard health and safety hazards, and impose poor job conditions. As a result, workers are constantly reminded through daily experience that they have problems in common as a class, and that collective action is needed to obtain redress of their grievances against the bosses.

This clash of class interests is what gave rise to trade unions on a world scale; because of the elementary level of class consciousness involved, these formations, as a rule, originated and developed as a movement for economic and social reform under capitalism.

Due to that reformist outlook, the business unionists in this country have been able to maintain control over the movement. The imposition of their policy obstructs further progress of the class consciousness first shown when workers organize on the job. When union members seek to use and improve labor's fighting capacity—acting under the pressures of harsh treatment at the hands of exploiters—they meet stubborn resistance from the top hierarchy. An official course of a diametrically opposed nature is followed. It consists of attempts to wheedle gratuities from the capitalist rulers by collaborating with them in both industry and government. From the labor bureaucrats' viewpoint that seems an ideal arrangement, whereby they, personally, can drift comfortably down the stream of life.

It happens, though, that snags are encountered along the way. Capitalists are notoriously loath to do anything that cuts significantly into their profits. Concessions may be coaxed from them on minor points, but it takes a fight to force their compliance with serious demands. As a result, strikes occur because of pressure from the workers, who don't have it as easy as the bureaucrats.

Still another vicious side of capitalist policy comes to the fore when a walkout takes place. Efforts are made to continue operating the struck facility with scabs. Whatever employees can be sucked in—due to the uneven development of class consciousness—are used as scabs, along with imported strike-breakers and hired thugs. These private actions are backed up by the repressive arms of government—police, courts, military— while at the same time the strikers are being subjected to the trickery of government mediators.

All this deceit and pressure is accompanied by a barrage of lying propaganda laid down by the capitalist news media. Inconveniences caused by the stoppage, real or imaginary, are given a big play. An attempt is made to strip workers not directly involved in the conflict of their class identity and make them part of a catchall "public" over which the propagandists shed crocodile tears. The employer's refusal to give fair consideration to the strikers' demands is glossed over. It is made to appear that the union is to blame for what is happening.

In this manner all sections of the ruling class gang up on the embattled workers. Their primary aim is to crush the strike. Failing that, they concentrate on forcing a settlement favorable to the specific employers involved. Under such circumstances the union ranks, stuck with class collaborationist leaders, usually come out holding the short end of the stick.

Strikebreaking represents only one form of capitalist attack on the workers' movement. Through executive orders and legislative acts various legal fetters are fastened upon labor organizations. When alleged violations of these governmental decrees occur, the courts are quick to issue injunctions, levy fines, and impose jail sentences against trade unionists. Here again the repressive actions are accompanied by a smear campaign against the victims.

On a broader scale, ruling-class strategists also busy themselves in cooking up "national crises," when necessary, on one or another fake premise. Scare propaganda is then used to trick workers into subordinating their own class interests to supposedly "larger needs." In that way they are cheated out of hard-earned gains and at the same time the capitalists are able to put over new swindles. Despite the obvious chicanery, the union bureaucrats invariably go along with such boss schemes, even though they may whine a little for the record.

In this overall situation the workers find themselves frustrated by multiple obstacles—employer resistance, governmental opposition, and misleadership in their own organizations. Not knowing how to cope with such a complex of problems, many simply decide to let matters take their course, hoping for a break here and there. Their attention thus begins to center more and more exclusively on making the most of personal life under existing conditions. This, in turn, creates the superficial impression that virtually the entire working class has voluntarily become immersed in peaceful collaboration with the employers, and that what the capitalists call "normalcy" has been made a permanent condition within industry.

At given intervals, however, an entirely different situation arises. The change results from contradictions inherent in a system devised to enrich a small capitalist minority at the expense of a big worker majority. Due to these contradictions, economic dislocations accumulate. Problems related to housing, education, health care, and other social needs grow worse. Conditions in general become less and less tolerable, until a stage is finally reached when all the ingredients for a major explosion come together.

Mounting discontent leads the workers into a search for some way to defend themselves effectively as a class. Divisive walls—built of self-centeredness, prejudice, special interest, class collaboration, and lying capitalist propaganda—begin to crumble. New potential develops for strengthening labor solidarity, elevating class consciousness, and raising the anticapitalist struggle to a higher plane.

A dramatic change of that nature took place in the aftermath of the 1929 stock market crash, which heralded the onset of severe economic depression. As the slump deepened, millions lost their jobs. Earnings were slashed for those who still had employment. Working conditions went from bad to worse, as did living standards in general.

At first the workers accepted these blows in a more or less passive manner. They had been stunned by the economic debacle and it took time to recover from the shock effect. Then, when they did begin a quest for ways to defend themselves, only scant means were at hand. Less than three million were organized into the AFL, mainly workers in skilled trades. The great bulk of the working class, especially in basic industry, was not unionized at all. On top of that, the AFL bureaucrats showed no real concern about the plight of the unorganized, whether employed or unemployed. In short, labor was caught in a crisis of organization and leadership.

But limited patterns of struggle gradually began to emerge, characterized by ups and downs in scope and tempo. In the initial stage the actions centered mainly on protest demonstrations by the unemployed. Then, during 1933, strikes broke out here and there in industry, the biggest one being conducted by textile workers. These walkouts resulted from the interaction of two basic factors: the workers' determination to regain ground they had lost in the depression and their rising confidence—stimulated by partial economic recovery under the New Deal—that their objective could be attained.

Developments of this kind were viewed by the AFL business unionists as a threat to their class-collaborationist line rather than as an opportunity to strengthen organized labor. So those worthies helped government mediators snooker rebellious workers into formal agreements with the bosses that brought precious few gains to the union rank and file.

But sellouts engineered in that way could not be made to stick very long. Combative moods among the workers continued to grow in intensity, and within the unions radicals were able to increase their leadership authority. As a result, miniature civil wars were fought in 1934 by Minneapolis truck drivers, San

Francisco longshoremen, and Toledo auto workers. In each case, labor emerged victorious. Inspired by proof that strikes conducted militantly could be won, the main detachments of the working class in basic industry began to move toward action against the monopoly corporations.

Before the end of 1934 struggles erupted in auto, rubber, and steel. In every instance these were sabotaged by AFL bureaucrats, who pushed through acceptance of special government boards to "study" the situation and recommend improvements. The crime was compounded through an organizational hoax. Workers in that sphere were first taken into the AFL on a plant-wide basis; the bureaucrats then proceeded to chop off craft units from the main body, undermining the industrial union form so vital to effective action in basic industry. On every count the newly recruited AFL members had been double-crossed, and they reacted angrily.

This created a new problem for the labor bureaucrats. If these workers were not allowed to organize on an industrial basis, and if they were not given more effective leadership, radicals would soon gain considerable influence among them. Everything would then be up for grabs, including the future of the bureaucrats themselves.

Foremost among the more alert business unionists who sought to do something about this danger to their kind—and also take advantage of the opportunity to advance their organizations—was John L. Lewis, head of the United Mine Workers Union. He led a fight for inclusion of industrial union forms, alongside existing craft setups, within the general AFL structure. When the effort failed, he headed up a bloc of unions that split from the AFL in 1936 to form what became the Congress of Industrial Organizations.

With the appearance of the CIO as an independent force, workers throughout basic industry flocked into its ranks and, during 1936 and 1937, a series of bitter struggles followed. These included massive sit-down strikes involving the occupation of plants in total disregard of the alleged "sanctity" of capitalist private property. Action at the scene of battle was guided by broad strike committees. Following the initial contract settlements, committees were elected in the plants to enforce the terms; during the first period of the CIO's existence these committees were quick to call work stoppages whenever needed to obtain adjustment of grievances.

All in all, trade-union practices were undergoing significant modification. But the changes were of a limited nature in the following respects: they lasted only until rank-and-file democracy was later strangled in the CIO; and the use of class-struggle methods was restricted entirely to the industrial sphere.

Frightened by the breadth and intensity of the developing conflict, the top CIO officials looked from the outset for a way to bring the situation back within class-collaborationist bounds. As a means toward that end they seized upon the 1936 presidential campaign. Steps were taken to center union attention on support of Roosevelt's candidacy for reelection. That backing, it was hoped, would induce him to use governmental influence to get the CIO a few concessions from the giant monopolies in basic industry, thereby helping to restore more peaceful class relations.

Roosevelt, who knew a good class-collaborationist scheme when he saw one, welcomed the development as something that would serve his own ends. As a capitalist leader, he too hoped to steer the workers away from militant struggle and divert them toward concentration on reformist political action. Being a slick demagogue he could help to do so by making campaign promises intended to generate confidence that his reelection would result in significant gains for labor. Then, upon being returned to office, he could forget all that. His actions could focus, as usual, on protection of ruling-class interests, and no matter what he did, the labor movement would be stuck with him for another four years.

The workers themselves had illusions about the demagogue in the White House. Many were unable to perceive that the few positive steps he had taken, seemingly on their behalf, were actually due to political repercussions from the struggles they were conducting. Influenced by his glib talk, they considered him an enemy of big capital and a friend of labor. For example, many workers credited him with the formal recognition of labor's right to organize, even though, in practice, he had helped to obstruct their efforts to exercise that right. In addition, he was widely considered a lesser evil compared to the presidential candidate of the openly reactionary Republican Party, Alfred M. Landon. On the whole, Roosevelt was the recipient of a great deal of unearned gratitude and misplaced trust.

While using the workers' illusions about the "squire from Hyde Park" as the primary means to entrap them politically, John L. Lewis also took advantage of another factor operating in his favor. His leading role in founding the CIO had caused the rank and file to place great hope and confidence in him. As a result, he was in a good position to spearhead a general labor mobilization in support of the Democratic Party ticket.

In January 1936 Lewis started the ball rolling by putting a resolution through the United Mine Workers convention endorsing Roosevelt for reelection. Other CIO unions followed suit, as did numerous AFL organizations. Toward spring the CIO set up a formation called Labor's Non-Partisan League (LNPL), whose main objective was to mobilize support for the Democrats. Although the AFL did not create any similar apparatus at the time—remaining neutral as a federation in the campaign—most of its affiliates backed Roosevelt and, as mentioned previously, Daniel J. Tobin headed up the National Labor Committee of the Democratic Party.

Creation of the LNPL gave rise to a contradictory situation. On the one hand it was a political machine, seeking to organize labor voters as a bloc. That factor, taken alone, represented a new and progressive step within the trade-union movement. On the other hand, this positive feature was negated when the LNPL crossed class lines to support Democratic Party candidates.

In carrying out their policy the union bureaucrats got help from misleaders within the radical movement. Social-democratic reformists, who constituted the right wing of the Socialist Party, supported Roosevelt more or less openly. A similar course was followed by the Stalinist breed of opportunists, except that they acted in a sneaky manner. To present an outward semblance of independent politics, they nominated Earl Browder as the Communist Party's presidential candidate. Browder then campaigned indirectly for the Democrats by urging defeat of the Republican ticket "at all costs."

While this gang of class collaborationists busily peddled their pro-Democrat line, something else began to develop. Sentiment arose for the formation of a national labor party. A proposal of the kind was put forward, for example, by the 1936 convention of the United Auto Workers Union. There was a progressive aspect to the proposal, in the sense that it would constitute an organizational break with the capitalist two-party system. In that respect it would represent an advance beyond the LNPL, which had only a pseudo-independent character. But in terms of political line, such a formation would have started out as a reformist movement. That would be the normal orientation of a mass party launched through the trade unions. By their very nature the unions are conditioned to view such a step as merely an extension into politics of their fight for reforms within industry.

Due to this political connotation, revolutionists did not call for the building of a labor party during that period. As matters then stood it was not at all certain that the workers would have to go through a reformist stage in the course of a breakaway from capitalist politics. The social crisis was impelling them in one swift leap from a generally atomized state toward union organization in advanced industrial form. And that dynamic was still operative. It was thus possible that in the struggles to come the workers could make another big jump, this time to revolutionary politics.

In such an eventuality, moreover, the class collaborationists would probably act on their own to set up a reformist labor party in order to slow down the leftward political trend. There was no reason to give them a boost in that direction.

As revolutionists saw the situation, massive labor support to Roosevelt in 1936 did not, in itself, remove the prospects for extensive political radicalization. On the strike front the main CIO battles were yet to be fought, especially in auto and steel. In those clashes—which came in 1937—the workers would be directly up against major components of the ruling class. This would occur at a time when the capitalists were beginning to prepare for World War II and could, therefore, be expected to put up unusually stiff resistance to the CIO drive.

A potential class showdown was thus in the making, during which the government would become more fully exposed as an agency of the bosses. As a result, more and more workers might be able to see through Roosevelt, clear to his patrician bones.

Developments might also be affected by the labor radicalization then unfolding in Western Europe. Intense class struggles had erupted there, ranging from massive strikes in France to civil war in Spain. If a big advance toward a social overturn were to occur in any of the countries involved, profound repercussions could be expected in the United States. To an increasing degree, workers here would become ready for revolutionary action. A sweeping social conflict might then ensue, leading toward a confrontation over the issue of state power. In that case the way would be open to abolish outlived capitalism, put an end to the injustices it inflicts upon humanity, and proceed to the constuction of an enlightened socialist society.

As of 1936, such possibilities definitely existed under the objective conditions then prevailing. Only the further passage of time and events, however, would show whether the implied opportunities could be converted into political reality.

Meanwhile, there was vital need to concentrate on assembling revolutionary cadres, since it takes a party comprised of conscious revolutionists to lead the workers to complete victory. Building such a movement is an exceedingly difficult task, since it encompasses all aspects of the class struggle. Before all else a correct program has to be hammered out. A system of strategic and tactical perspectives must also be developed as a guide to action. Party members need to be fully educated in all the basic concepts involved, so that they may fulfill the key role that objective necessity requires of them in class conflict. And in keeping with its perspectives and tasks, the party must constitute itself as a disciplined formation capable of acting effectively in the fight for a socialist future.

Once the capacity to meet the above requisites is attained, the foremost tasks become the numerical strengthening of the organization and the sinking of its roots in the mass movement. From its inception—after the Trotskyists were expelled from the Stalinist Communist Party in 1928—the Communist League of America had devoted itself to such efforts. At first the CLA concentrated on trying to salvage as many revolutionists as it could out of the Stalinist wreckage. Wherever a chance arose, the Trotskyists also participated in workers' struggles, managing in the process to recruit new members by ones and twos. (In my own case, for instance, it was these party activities that brought me into the CLA in March 1934 as an individual recruit.) At the same time a lookout was kept for the spontaneous rise of new formations showing a tendency to move leftward. Such developments were of prime importance, since they presented an exceptional opportunity to expand the revolutionary forces, through either a fusion with any formation of the kind or an entry into it.

The first important break of this nature came toward the end of 1934. Earlier that year members of the American Workers Party had led the Toledo auto strike, mentioned above. This was one indication of significant motion within the AWP toward revolutionary positions. Therefore, the CLA approached it in a friendly way and a fusion of the two organizations resulted, the newly united body indentifying itself as the Workers Party of the United States.

About a year later another opportunity for substantial expansion of the revolutionary cadres arose. By then young militants were joining the Socialist Party in increasing numbers. After doing so they began to grope toward the formulation of a revolutionary program, but right-wingers in the SP sought to block the trend. That led to the organization of a left wing within the party. At that point the Workers Party negotiated acceptable terms for entry into the SP as a body. The step was taken in mid-1936. Our object, of course, was to help the left wing evolve toward full revolutionary positions.

In more immediate terms, the move also gave us a means of intervention in the 1936 election campaign. Despite right-wing reluctance, the Socialist Party was running Norman Thomas for president in opposition to both Roosevelt and Landon. As a socialist candidate, Thomas left much to be desired. Yet, by presenting our own material in his support, it was possible to circulate some effective propaganda against reformists of all stripes. That activity helped us reach open-minded militants who were receptive to revolutionary ideas.

Proceeding along the lines described, the Trotskyist forces nationally opposed both the Roosevelt supporters and the labor party advocates. In Minnesota, however, there was an extraordinary complication. A reformist labor party of significant dimensions already existed there. As a result some unusual problems confronted us.

POLITICAL CONFLICT
IN MINNESOTA

Memorial Day Massacre at Republic Steel plant in South Chicago (1937). CIO leaders' failure to respond to vicious government attacks led to defeat of Little Steel strike and loss of class-struggle momentum nationally.

5. Reformism in Action

In the summer of 1918 the AFL State Federation of Labor issued a call for the formation of a new political movement in Minnesota. The proposal met with a favorable response from the Non-Partisan League, a large organization based on working farmers. An agreement resulted whereby the two forces cooperated in forming the Farmer-Labor Party, which ran a slate of candidates in the state elections that year. Although defeated in this first effort the party remained viable, and it proceeded to consolidate its ranks for the long pull ahead.

While appearing on the electoral arena as the Farmer-Labor Party, the new movement designated itself the Farmer-Labor Federation in its character as an organization with an enrolled membership. (In 1924 the latter name was changed to Farmer-Labor Association.) Trade unions, which were accepted into affiliation as a body, became a major component of the formation. Group participation was also allowed in the case of farmers' organizations, cooperative movements, workers' benefit associations, cultural societies, etc. Ward clubs in the cities took in members as individuals, as did township clubs in rural communities.

Socially, the basic forces organized in this way represented an alliance of workers and farmers. The movement also received a degree of support within the urban middle class.

The founders of the Farmer-Labor Party viewed it as a means of defense against harsh exploitation and acts of repression by the capitalist rulers during World War I. After the war ended in November 1918 that sense of need did not disappear. Conditions in Minnesota gave continued impetus to the party's development. In the cities, open-shop practices held sway, enabling the bosses to gouge the workers to the point that not much of the "prosperity" of the 1920s rubbed off on them. Things were no better for the working farmers. A depression hit agriculture in 1921 and persisted for years, causing many tillers of the soil to fall on hard times. Meanwhile, both workers and farmers watched the rich get richer.

Under these circumstances the FLP was able, bit by bit, to gain clout at the polls. By 1922 it had won a seat in the U.S. Senate and two in the House of Representatives. Within the state, FLP candidates were elected to represent some districts in the legislature. Others were voted into posts here and there in county, city, and township governments.

After the 1929 stock market crash, the Farmer-Labor Party gained new momentum. In 1930 Floyd B. Olson, a lawyer running on the FLP ticket, was elected governor of the state. The party also increased its representation in the legislature, but not enough to wrest majority control of either house from the overtly capitalist politicians. Despite that flaw in its victory, this independent political movement of workers and farmers had achieved a major breakthrough. It had won the state's chief executive post, a seat of power that had been held continuously by the Republican Party for the previous sixteen years. In effect, the FLP was displacing the Democratic Party in Minnesota politics as the main opponent of the Republicans, a trend that was further affirmed when Olson was reelected governor in 1932.

Even though the Farmer-Labor Party ran candidates against both the Republicans and Democrats, its line was not anticapitalist. The party's program centered simply on reforming the existing system. That outlook, moreover, became counterposed to the objective need for the workers and their allies to abolish capitalism and reconstruct society on a socialist basis. Instead of adopting this political course, as the situation required, the FLP confined its policies and methods to what was possible within the prevailing social framework.

It thus became a de facto contributor to preservation of the capitalist ruling structure, thereby impeding a working-class advance toward a revolutionary orientation.

This opportunist course was accentuated in practice by FLP candidates for public office, who moved arbitrarily to assume control over the party. Their main aim was to get elected and then reelected. Toward that end they were prone to make freewheeling deals with liberal capitalist politicians.

A key factor leading toward blocs of this kind was a mutual desire to substitute maneuvers on the parliamentary arena for mass action by the workers and farmers. As an additional means of cementing the alliance, FLP candidates strove to water down the reforms called for in their election platforms, giving the timidity of liberal politicians precedence over the desires and demands of the party rank and file.

Foremost among the blocks of that nature was a setup called "All-Party Committees for Olson," initiated during the 1930 election campaign. Its aim was to mobilize support among dissident liberals within the Democratic and Republican ranks. Liberals ready to make the shift in political allegiance, at least temporarily, were motivated in part by grievances against their own party machines. More important, though, they sensed a new groundswell of voter backing for the FLP; in keeping with their mentality as timeservers, they were ready to climb on the bandwagon in order to advance their own careers.

After being elected governor, Olson gave a further demonstration of the importance he attached to the alliance with liberal capitalist politicians. In staffing his administration he accorded considerable patronage to people in the "All-Party Committees." His action was apparently intended as advance preparation for the 1932 campaign to get reelected. In that sense it represented an earnest of the rewards to be granted for political support.

But there was another side to the coin. Having liberals as part of the administration contributed to Olson's default on his obligations to the workers and farmers who had voted him into office.

In still another respect the FLP officialdom steered the movement into the swamp of capitalist politics. Under Olson's leadership a course was set in 1932 toward support of Franklin D. Roosevelt in the national elections, accompanied by collaboration with his administration after he assumed the presidency.

That caused the shaping of governmental policy at the state level to become intertwined with measures emanating from the White House. Roosevelt's line of granting only the most grudging concessions to the needy masses thus had a restraining effect on initiatives for change by FLP office holders. The result was further impairment of the party's capacity to carry out even the most limited reforms within Minnesota.

Such rightward trends in its top circles represented only one of the contradictory factors to be considered by revolutionists in shaping their policy toward the FLP. Despite the unprincipled maneuvers with liberals, the movement had broken organizationally with the capitalist two-party system. That was especially significant because it had a mass base among workers and farmers, who aspired to carry out genuinely independent political action without capitalist politicians having any voice whatever in party affairs.

Yet these FLP supporters remained handicapped by the illusion that their problems could be solved through improvement of the existing system. Accordingly, they backed the reformist politicians at the polls, counting on them to take effective action in public office.

It is not in the nature of capitalism, however, to allow mass needs preference over corporate profits. Demands for serious changes in social conditions were vigorously opposed by the ruling class. The capitalist-designed electoral system was used to corrupt FLP representatives in seats of power. As a consequence, time passed without any sign of significant progress on the governmental front. This caused increasing dissatisfaction among the exploited masses, thereby opening the way for intensified action in the economic sphere.

Confronted with these unique circumstances, the Communist League of America shaped a special policy for political work in Minnesota, deciding that FLP candidates for public office could be accorded critical support. That meant they could be backed in election campaigns, as against their capitalist opponents; but such support at the polls would be accompanied by criticism of the FLP's reformist program and of the policies followed by its elected representatives. This course, which was taken flexibly, did not exclude revolutionary opposition to the reformists in the electoral arena. Whether the Trotskyist party would run its own candidates against both the capitalists and reformists, for the purpose of emphasizing programmatic issues, was left open for determination according to specific conditions in each election period.

Through such a procedure encouragement could be given to the trend toward independent political action in opposition to the capitalist parties. That aim could be accomplished without giving a mistaken impression that revolutionists saw some virtue in reformist concepts. And at the same time well-intentioned FLP supporters could be induced to give open-minded consideration to revolutionary ideas.

Application of this policy did not signify that Trotskyist activity was to focus primarily on the FLP. Just the opposite. The central issue, it was stressed, boiled down to the class struggle for workers' power and a socialist future. Attempts to substitute reformist politics for mass action were resisted by counterposing a synthesis of revolutionary politics and mass confrontations with the ruling class. In this way political consciousness could be raised within the ranks of the workers and their allies and the most advanced could be recruited into the revolutionary party.

In Minneapolis we were able to shape the desired class-struggle course principally through General Drivers Union, Local 574. To attain our objective, however, obstacles in addition to those put in our way by reformist politicians would have to be overcome. We could, for example, expect difficulties with the AFL bureaucrats. They were blood kin to the political reformists in their desire to substitute class-collaborationist maneuvers for a class-struggle line. In any dispute we had with Governor Olson they could be expected to side with him, if not openly, at least covertly. Moreover, they had little stomach for the kind of fight that would have to be waged against the boss class, and they could be expected to run for cover when the going got rough.

There could be no doubt that a serious unionization campaign would lead to a major battle. A ruling-class organization known as the Citizens Alliance exercised unofficial, but none the less real, governmental control over the city. For years it had moved viciously against any significant attempt at a trade-union advance, breaking strike after strike. It was bound to react violently when, in the spring of 1934, Local 574 mobilized the trucking workers for a showdown with the bosses.

In such a harsh conflict, Olson was certain to create problems for us. Due to his contradictory political situation, he could be expected at first to pose as an arbiter between the opposing classes. As the battle sharpened, the bosses would bring pressure on him to use the powers of his office against Local 574. He would be reluctant to do so openly, since that would cost him much of labor's political support. But the need would still remain, in his view, to show that he was acting "responsibly" as a public official. For that reason he would most likely undertake maneuvers that could put the union in danger. Hence the Olson problem had to be included among the major factors to be taken into account in preparing for the fight within the trucking industry.

We decided to seek advantage from a positive aspect of the governor's contradictory stance. He had to show sympathy toward the struggles of workers who backed him at the polls. That enabled us to force him into expressing support for Local 574's objectives prior to the opening of the conflict with the ruling class. A similar declaration was also obtained from the city's AFL bureaucrats, most of whom aligned themselves with Olson politically.

It did not follow that these assurances brought the workers reliable allies. Neither the governor nor the union bureaucrats were about to make a change in line because of such a commitment. But it did mean that a double-cross from either quarter would be harder to put over.

While taking such precautionary measures, we centered our main attention on mobilizing thousands of workers in the trucking industry for action. That step opened the way to winning support for Local 574's struggle among other workers in the city. Parallel with that, backing could also be obtained among farmers in the vicinity and to a certain extent within the urban middle class. Through a mass mobilization of this kind, developed step by step as the fight unfolded, the Citizens Alliance could be defeated. To achieve that outcome, however, the struggle had to be waged power against power. It followed that the instrument of mass pressure would also be valuable in preventing the political reformists and union bureaucrats from diverting the action into the dead-end of class collaboration.

As our preparations for battle neared completion, Local 574's demands were served upon the trucking bosses. They refused even to negotiate. A strike was called and the workers, who responded in great numbers, quickly swept all scab trucks off the streets. A fierce conflict developed, putting every tendency within the labor movement to the acid test.

With trucking tied up generally, the Citizens Alliance took command of ruling-class strategy, aiming to smash the strike and crush the union. Olson was plainly considered unreliable for such an operation, so the Alliance tried to achieve its goal through the use of the city government's repressive mechanisms. The regular police were heavily reinforced by special deputies. These forces assaulted the union's picket lines, but without success. After two days of bloody combat, the strikers emerged victorious and were now in a position to exercise the rudiments of dual power, if only momentarily and on a strictly city scale.

Using the AFL bureaucrats to run interference for him, Olson then stepped in to arrange a truce in the fighting. Under the terms of the truce the bosses promised not to undertake any truck movements and the union agreed to limit its picketing to making sure that they kept their word. But something else had happened. The governor had mobilized the National Guard, an act having ominous implications for the strikers. Local 574 responded by initiating a mass protest against the threat, and the pressure had the desired effect. Olson backed away from any notion of intervening militarily in the strike and confined his actions to mediation between the bosses and the union. A negotiated settlement of the dispute resulted.

As matters turned out, though, the governor had been deceptive in his role as a go-between during the negotiations. He had assured the strikers that all were included in the clause granting employer recognition of the union. The bosses, on the other hand, claimed that they had extended recognition to Local 574 for only limited categories of its membership. The union naturally refused to be decimated in that manner, so despite Olson's assurances, nothing had really been settled. Moreover, when he was pressed to publicly reassert what he had told the strikers' representatives during the negotiations, he equivocated.

In those circumstances it was clear to the workers involved that the governor they had helped to elect had been of no help to them. That left them with no recourse but to resume their strike action.

During the ensuing walkout the Citizens Alliance became even more ruthless. Riot guns were issued to the cops, who used them against the pickets with murderous results. But the assault failed to break the union's morale. In fact the strike gained in vigor, as revulsion against police brutality stimulated a new, big wave of mass support. Plainly enough, Local 574 held the upper hand, and the bosses were now under strong pressure to come to terms with their embattled employees.

From labor's viewpoint there was no cause for the governor to intervene in the situation, except to bring added pressure on the trucking firms to capitulate. But for Olson, a different consideration was paramount. In the fall of the year he would be coming

up for reelection. Meanwhile, the ruling class was castigating
him for allowing Local 574's leaders to thrust "communism"
upon the city. His political image was being impaired in liberal
capitalist circles, and he wanted desperately to avoid further
damage to his personal career. Hence he became determined to
put an end to the strike in one way or another, using his powers
as commander-in-chief of the National Guard for the purpose.

Although the interests of Olson's worker constituents would be
harmed in the process, he hoped to minimize the political cost in
labor circles by clever machinations. What resulted was a scheme
devised in collusion with two federal mediators sent in by the
Roosevelt administration, which was designed to give the
planned military intervention a surface appearance of impartial-
ity.

Proposed terms for a "fair" settlement of the dispute were
arbitrarily promulgated by the mediators. The governor then set
a deadline for voluntary acceptance of their recommendations by
the union and the bosses. If either side rejected the terms, he
threatened, martial law would be declared to impose a settlement
on the basis dictated by Roosevelt's agents.

If Local 574 rejected the ultimatum, a military assault on its
picket lines would surely follow. That would put the strike in
great jeopardy because of the confusion Olson's tactics had
created within the labor movement. For that reason the union
leadership recommended that the mediator's terms be accepted,
even though they fell considerably short of the strikers' demands.
After thorough discussion of the matter the membership
concurred and the governor was notified of the union's decision.
Meantime, the bosses had been waiting until the last moment to
give their reply. They obviously hoped that the strikers would
provide Olson with the pretext he sought to move against the
union. When that failed to happen, the trucking employers simply
defied the governor, refusing to comply with his ultimatum.

Martial law was then proclaimed. Under the military regime
that followed, picketing was outlawed and, supposedly, only
firms accepting the mediators' settlement terms would be allowed
to operate their trucks. Before long, however, military permits
were granted for various kinds of scab trucking. As a result, the
strike was being broken piecemeal. Protests to Olson against this
outrage were unavailing, so Local 574 mobilized to resume full-

scale picketing. That got action—but against the union, not the scab trucking operations.

Using the flimsy pretext of an alleged violation of military regulations concerning Local 574's mobilization rally, the governor launched a direct attack on the organization. The National Guard seized its headquarters and began a roundup of top strike leaders. Parallel with that, Olson probed into the workers' ranks, seeking a pliable committee through which he might "negotiate" a strike settlement on whatever terms the trucking bosses would concede.

Within a matter of hours, however, the whole move began to backfire on him. He had underestimated both the depth of the union's secondary leadership structure and the caliber of its ranks. The strikers fought back courageously, going after the scab trucks in defiance of the military. While that was going on, protests began to pour in on the governor from angry members of trade unions and Farmer-Labor clubs. By the day's end he had been forced to call off the military occupation of union facilities and release the arrested strike leaders. He also had to make a pretense of doing something about the scab trucks.

In the course of the clash with Olson, it was discovered that several AFL officials were conniving with him. When the battle was over the offending bureaucrats were asked to appear before Local 574's strike committee and explain their conduct. A few showed up, but their alibis didn't wash. They were warned to refrain from undertaking any future maneuvers that might affect the strike without first consulting the democratically elected committee that was leading the action.

After that the union-employer confrontation settled into an endurance contest. The bosses figured that, with the passage of time, the strikers could be starved into submission. Their hopes of ultimate success were further buoyed by the role of the military. National Guard officers continued to issue permits for scab trucking on the slightest pretext and persisted in harassing the union forces in all conceivable ways, short of precipitating another major battle. But Local 574 managed to hang tough, and the strike remained effective.

Finally, toward the end of August 1934, the governor felt compelled to change his tactics. He sought White House aid in a new attempt to push through a negotiated settlement of the dispute. Roosevelt, who had to offer something in return for the Farmer-Labor support he received in the 1932 elections, responded by sending a new federal mediator to Minneapolis.

What happened next indicated that this latest envoy from Washington came equipped to do some arm twisting within the local ruling class. Before long he submitted new settlement terms to the union, accompanied by his written assurance that the trucking bosses were ready to sign a contract on the basis he had outlined. The union membership voted to accept the new proposal and the strike ended. After a long bitter struggle, Local 574 had emerged with a solid victory.

Olson was now able to concentrate on the campaign for reelection as the Farmer-Labor Party's candidate for governor. His 1934 platform marked a change in approach from that taken in his 1930 and 1932 programs. There was less squeamish adaptation to the timidities of liberal capitalist politicians. Instead, the latest document sought to express, in guarded form, the radical moods reflected in the mass actions of the recent period. But experience would show that it was all talk, designed to catch votes. There was to be no essential change in the class-collaborationist outlook of the reformist politicians who ran the FLP.

We Trotskyists did not intervene to any great extent in the preelection activities. At that time our Communist League was concentrating on preparation of its fusion with the American Workers Party to form the Workers Party of the United States. Those of us within Local 574 who belonged to the Communist League were also preoccupied with numerous problems confronting the union in the aftermath of the wearing battle it had fought. In the given circumstances, we could do little more than explain our views about reformist politicians to whatever workers we could conveniently reach.

Politically, our main efforts centered on counterposing revolutionary politics to the reformist outlook. We were helped by the way in which strike experiences had opened the minds of various workers to our views. Those experiences in the class struggle also enabled some among them to grasp the need for a vanguard party capable of leading a fight to abolish the whole rotten capitalist system. As a result, we were able to recruit a number of individuals into the Trotskyist ranks.

The workers generally had mixed attitudes toward Olson. He

was certainly no prize candidate in the eyes of most Local 574 members. Some simply stayed away from the polls, feeling no one deserved support. Many others voted for the incumbent governor as a lesser evil than the Republican. The latter view was prevalent to a considerable extent elsewhere in the trade unions, along with a significant amount of unqualified support for Olson. Taking the voting patterns as a whole, it was the working class that reelected him in 1934.

Those workers who gave Olson unqualified support had in many cases been taken in by the devious manner in which he carried out his maneuvers against the striking truck drivers. In just a few months, however, they were to see a much cruder performance, in yet another governmental quarter, that would reveal more clearly the essentially treacherous nature of reformist politics.

6. A Farmer-Laborite in City Hall

For a considerable time the Republicans had governed in Minneapolis. As matters now stood, however, they were in deep political trouble. Recent events had openly branded A.G. Bainbridge, the incumbent mayor, a pliant tool of the Citizens Alliance. During the Teamster strikes he had obediently sought to carry out orders handed down by the ruling-class gang, no matter how inhumane, how brutal their dictates proved to be.

Widespread criticism of that course was aimed not only at the mayor but at the Republican Party. Olson had, in fact, profited from that trend in the 1934 gubernatorial race.

Since municipal elections were coming up in June 1935, this added a new complication to the problems facing the capitalist overlords. They were already concerned enough over the emergence of Local 574 as a strong, militant force within the city's labor movement. On top of that, the Teamsters' victory had inspired workers in other sectors of local industry to launch unionization drives of their own. These developments had made the bosses more determined than ever to maintain tight control over the executive arm of city government, so as to continue its use for naked union-busting purposes. But how could they swing it with their political minions slipping so badly?

After weighing the matter, the Citizens Alliance decided to go all-out in pushing for the reelection of Bainbridge. A big slush fund for this purpose was raised among the fat cats. The propaganda mills were then set into motion, grinding out praise of the Republican hopeful and smears against the labor movement. The bosses contested the 1935 elections with the same arrogant contempt for the masses that they had shown during the 1934 strikes.

The main opposition to Bainbridge came from the Farmer-

Labor Party. Its candidate for mayor, Thomas E. Latimer, did not personally carry any significant political weight. But he was strongly backed by aroused AFL members throughout the city, who were determined to oust the Republican strikebreaker from office.

Key issues were thus at stake, and class lines were quite sharply drawn in the hard-fought campaign. It was also apparent that a relatively narrow majority would determine the outcome of the contest. In those circumstances the Workers Party decided to extend critical support to the FLP ticket. A statement was issued accordingly by the Minneapolis branch of the party and published in *The Militant* of May 19, 1935. The essence of the Trotskyist view was summed up in the following passages:

"While the Workers Party urges the defeat of Bainbridge by the election of Farmer-Labor candidates, it declares that the Farmer-Labor officials will not and cannot give the working class any real lasting benefits—these will have to be won by the workers themselves through their fighting organizations: the unions, unemployed organizations and revolutionary workers party.

"Workers of Minneapolis: Elect the Farmer-Laborites to office *but watch their every move, do not trust them.* They will serve the workers' movement only if the workers' organizations force them to." (Emphasis in original.)

Earlier in the year Local 574 had been expelled from the International Brotherhood of Teamsters. In resisting Daniel J. Tobin's attempt to read it ·out of the labor movement, the union was fighting to win AFL support locally. For that tactical reason, its paper, the *Northwest Organizer,* presented criticism of the Farmer-Laborite performance in public office somewhat obliquely. Main stress was placed on support to the FLP ticket in the fight against Bainbridge and the other open political tools of the Citizens Alliance. At the same time, the workers were urged to vote *especially* for William S. Brown, the president of Local 574. Brown, a Trotskyist sympathizer, was running as the FLP candidate for alderman from the city's third ward, where he resided. Although he had no chance of winning in that ward, his action helped to emphasize a vital point.

Bill Brown, the *Northwest Organizer* stated editorially, "has been tested in the fire of great working class battles—tested and found good."

When the votes were counted, Latimer was shown to have

unseated Bainbridge as mayor. The news was greeted with great elation among the workers. They felt they now had a representative in City Hall who would help fight the bosses instead of using his powers against labor. But it was soon to be discovered that the assumption was mistaken.

Latimer had scarcely taken office when a strike was called by ornamental iron workers, and a second walkout developed at a hosiery mill. In both instances he launched vicious police assaults on the embattled trade unionists. As a cover for these strikebreaking attempts, an Employer-Employee Board was rigged up. It was pictured as an instrument to maintain "industrial peace" by passing judgment on issues in dispute between labor and capital.

Comparable tactics were used against the unemployed. Demonstrators fighting for improved public relief measures were subjected to the same violent treatment by the cops that strikers within industry were receiving.

Essentially, the new mayor's policies were akin to those customarily followed by reformists in seats of power. Unlike Olson, however, Latimer had quickly knuckled under entirely to the Citizens Alliance, not even making any significant pretext of defying its dictates. Several factors contributed to this particular development.

To begin with, some of the reactionaries appointed by Bainbridge were kept on in important official positions under the new regime, flagrantly violating a specific campaign pledge Latimer had made. Besides that, he abetted FLP members of the city council in forming a coalition with their liberal counterparts. A further means was thereby provided for the capitalists to maintain direct influence over the shaping of FLP policies in municipal government. To make a bad matter worse, the more conservative AFL officials backed Latimer's rightward course. They were especially quick to provide a "labor" cover for his Employer-Employee Board, volunteering to serve as members of the phony setup as well as publicly touting it as a desirable substitute for strikes.

Workers victimized by Latimer's policies took an altogether different view of the situation. They reacted angrily to the betrayal of their hopes and expectations. That made it possible for Local 574 to initiate a broad left opposition within the labor movement, centered around three issues of immediate urgency:

rejection of all forms of class collaboration with the bosses; working-class solidarity and reciprocal aid in labor struggles; and full trade-union support to the unemployed.

This militant course was quickly put into practice through help to the ornamental iron and hosiery workers in fighting off the would-be strikebreakers. In addition, those comprising the left wing were ready to struggle for Local 574's reinstatement into the IBT, so as to reestablish the labor unity that Tobin had disrupted.

Toward the end of September 1935 a conference of fifteen left-wing unions was convened. All the organizations participating were affiliated with the AFL, except Local 574. The gathering issued a general warning about the dangers arising from collaboration by a right-wing bloc in the labor movement with the city administration, which had prostituted itself to the Citizens Alliance. Specific demands for corrective action were also put forward: dissolution of the Employer-Employee Board; reaffirmation of the workers' right to strike; and expulsion of Latimer from the FLP for strikebreaking.

Not long after this conference, the Minneapolis branch of the Workers Party issued a statement drawing a balance sheet on the Latimer regime. In describing reformism in general, this statement quoted from the national WP's declaration of principles.

"In the period of capitalist decline, so-called reformist parties cannot pretend to the progressive role they have played decades ago. Political and economic concessions can now be wrested from the capitalist class only by means of the most resolute and militant class struggle. Besides, any party which purports to represent two or more classes on an equal footing, or to direct its appeals 'to all classes' is essentially a middle class party doomed to irresolution and surrender to the big capitalists in every decisive test. . . .

"The revolutionary party will show by theory and historical example, and above all by its own activities that the actual consequences of the policies of reform movements, here as in all other countries, are directly opposed to their avowed aims, that they act to preserve capitalism, and hence are inimical to the interests of the workers."

Concerning the Minneapolis situation in particular, the branch statement itemized actions by the FLP mayor that confirmed the above evaluation of reformism. A real workers' party, the WP then pointed out, would have ousted all reactionaries from appointive office. It would have increased relief allowances for the jobless. Governmental power would have been used to shut down struck plants until the bosses conceded the union demands.

The workers were asked to join the Trotskyist movement and help to build such a truly fighting party. If they were not yet convinced of the need for this, the statement added, "we say, stay in the Farmer-Labor Party and try to make it function for the workers. The Workers Party will aid you in every possible way, but history mocks the idea of a reformist party winning permanent gains for the workers."

By that time the left-wing forces were steadily gaining headway in their offensive against Latimer and the conservative AFL hacks. In Local 574's case, it carried far more weight in the trade-union ranks than did the Tobinites who strove to isolate the local. This caused the IBT head to solicit help from AFL President William Green. Between them a plan was devised to send a special agent to Minneapolis to impose bureaucratic discipline over the AFL membership. One of Green's organizers, Meyer L. Lewis, got the assignment.

Shortly after he arrived in town, toward the end of October 1935, Lewis sent a preliminary report to Green.

"I have been in conference on three different occasions with the Mayor of the City of Minneapolis, Thomas Latimer. In the presence of Organizer Bradley, he pledged to me one hundred per cent cooperation on the part of the city. [Local] 574 has put Mayor Latimer on the spot and the only way that he can clear himself with the Labor movement and with the City of Minneapolis is to act definitely and without reservation. . . .

"He spoke to me today and he felt that it was important that the Labor Movement begin to wage its campaign to indicate that it was in cooperation with the City in an effort to bring about a drive against the Communistic leadership as evidenced by 574. . . .

"The newspapers of the Twin Cities have been strongly publicizing your Convention statements with regard to cooperation with the American Legion. They have given a great deal of space in a favorable light to the possible campaign of the Federation against the 'reds.' I am in a position to advise you that I have the finest connections with the newspapers in the Twin Cities dating back to a period of time which I spent here some years ago, and I can get the fullest cooperation from them when and if we need it."

Meyer Lewis not only had a cocky attitude, as his report to Green shows, but he was also crude and dictatorial in his methods. As a result, his intervention served to broaden and deepen the rebel trends inside the AFL. That, in turn, precipitated a panic within local bureaucratic circles. A flurry of protests against the Lewis approach followed, sent mostly to national labor figures other than Green and Tobin, asking that they intervene in the situation.

One such protest came from R.D. Cramer, editor of the AFL organ in Minneapolis, the *Labor Review*. On November 12, 1935, he fired a telegram to Henrik Shipstead, a Farmer-Laborite from Minnesota sitting in the U.S. Senate. The key sentences in the message follow:

"Red drive of representatives American Federation of Labor against Local 574 threatens to split labor movement here. . . . Split in labor movement will mean split in political movement and disaster all along the line."

Cramer seemed to think that Shipstead could induce Tobin to ease his campaign of pressure on the AFL for backing in his drive against Local 574; but he didn't know the Teamster president. Politically, the IBT head was a Roosevelt Democrat. His attitude toward the Farmer-Labor Party was conditioned accordingly. Since Roosevelt had a loose alliance with the FLP, Tobin raised no objections when IBT affiliates in Minnesota supported its candidates over those of the Democrats. But he wasn't about to let FLP problems take priority over his bureaucratic interests within the Teamsters.

Not only was Meyer Lewis allowed to continue the course he had been following within the trade-union movement, but his disruptive tactics were soon extended into the Farmer-Labor Party. In a March 1936 "progress report" to Green, he gloated: "I am enclosing a clipping which further explains some of the effect our work is having here on the Communist group, the dual organizations, and those organizations which have caused us so much trouble."

The lead paragraphs of the news story Lewis sent to Green read: "Communist influences in the Farmer-Labor party became a major disturbing factor within the party Saturday as various moves were under way to 'purge' the party.

"The Thirteenth Ward Farmer-Labor Club, in a strongly worded resolution, demanded that membership in the party of Truck Drivers union No. 574 and two other organizations be barred until further investigated, and proposed that delegates from the union be refused seats in the state convention because of apparent Communist leadership."

(It happened that Latimer himself lived in the thirteenth ward, one of the city's silk stocking districts.)

As was apparent to most FLP members, the attempt to exclude Local 574 from the organization was part of an effort to stem mounting demands for Latimer's expulsion from the party. At a March 8, 1936, party convention in Hennepin County (of which Minneapolis is the seat), a strong attempt had been set into motion to strip the mayor of his FLP membership forthwith. But the right wing succeeded in warding off the attack by having the proposed action referred to the central committee of the county body.

Even so, the rebels were not entirely blocked. They forced through a resolution demanding that all elected candidates submit to party discipline, and that those who broke such discipline be publicly expelled.

Shortly thereafter the effort to bar Local 574 from FLP gatherings was renewed at a session of the state central committee. Quite an argument resulted. The dispute wound up with the matter being referred to the Hennepin County central committee for further consideration. That maneuver served to keep the issue alive until the upcoming state convention, but there was also a deeper meaning involved. As the *Northwest Organizer* stressed, the state committee had countenanced an antidemocratic policy toward the union. To emphasize the point, the Teamster paper added that Local 574 undoubtedly had a larger membership than did the whole Hennepin county section of the FLP to which the proposal to exclude it had been referred.

When the Farmer-Labor Party state convention met on March 28, 1936, the left and right wings came to a standoff. Efforts to have Latimer expelled failed, as did attempts to bar the "outlaw" Teamster local. The credentials committee voted thirteen to two in favor of seating the delegates from Local 574. Upon hearing the committee's decision, the convention floor responded with a roar of applause.

Generally speaking, the ranks of the FLP, like those of the

AFL, had warm feelings toward the rebel union that had licked the Citizens Alliance. Our fight was with the bureaucrats who sat at the top of both movements.

Also important at the state convention were the nominations of FLP candidates for the fall 1936 general elections. Floyd Olson, who had large ambitions, was designated to run for a seat in the U.S. Senate. Elmer A. Benson, a small-town banker, was chosen to campaign for the governorship, soon to be vacated by Olson. Before the main electioneering got under way, however, several things happened that were to have significant political effects upon the Minnesota labor movement.

By midsummer Tobin had been forced to reinstate Local 574 into the International Brotherhood of Teamsters, with its charter designation changed to Local 544. A new, broad labor upsurge quickly followed. That, in turn, served to intensify working-class pressures on the reformists holding public office.

At the same time reformist politicians and union bureaucrats alike were stripped of a diversionary tactic they had been quick to use against the Trotskyists. We could no longer be falsely branded as disrupters who had recklessly led the Teamster ranks into an "officially" proclaimed state of "outlawry." In opposing our class-struggle views, the right-wingers would now have to face up more directly to the political issues involved.

Parallel with those developments, the Workers Party was in the process of carrying through its 1936 entry into the Socialist Party. In Minnesota the immediate effects on the SP were exceptionally pronounced for several reasons.

Back in 1919 the great bulk of the SP membership in the state had pulled out to help found the Communist Party. Since then the Socialist Party had failed to prosper. Individuals with a social-democratic bent had tended to join the Farmer-Labor Party instead of the SP; in the early 1930s the Trotskyists had displaced the SP on the left as the main rival of the Communist Party within the Minnesota radical movement.

Those who did belong to the Socialist Party became influenced in their thinking by the class war that erupted in Minneapolis during 1934. Many of them developed into political sympathizers of the Trotskyist movement, which had led the epic Teamster struggle. As a result, the Socialist Party was transformed virtually overnight when we entered it. To all intents and purposes, the Minnesota SP became a Trotskyist section of the national party. Important reinforcements had thus been secured in the fight for class-struggle policies on both the trade-union and political fronts.

Concrete evidence of that accomplishment was contained in a newly adopted SP resolution on the Farmer-Labor Party question. It denounced the strikebreaking by Olson and Latimer. The reformists were also criticized for their blocs with capitalist politicians, for the support they gave to the most reactionary sections of the trade-union movement, and for their stifling of democracy within the FLP.

Then, on August 22, 1936, Governor Olson died. This precipitated several major problems for the surviving rulers of the Farmer-Labor Party. Olson had long played a key role in drafting the party's election platforms and shaping its general policies. He had also been the one who settled quarrels within the top echelons, maintaining the organization's internal equilibrium. Now that he was gone, a gap existed in its leadership structure that would be hard for the right-wingers to fill. No one was on hand who came anywhere near being Olson's equal in keeping the reformist ship afloat in the stormy political waters of the time.

What took place in the immediate aftermath of the governor's death was more or less automatic. Lieutenant Governor Hjalmar Petersen, also a Farmer-Laborite, stepped in to serve the remaining few months of Olson's unexpired third term. A campaign was then opened in support of Elmer Benson's candidacy for the governorship, as had been decided earlier at the state convention. He was backed by a seemingly united party. (It was not until after the fall elections that the developing crisis within the FLP came out into the open.)

The Trotskyists entered the 1936 election campaign with a partial slate of candidates, working now through the Socialist Party. Nationally, we backed Norman Thomas, the party's nominee for president. At the state level we centered our efforts on running V.R. (Ray) Dunne, an outstanding Trotskyist and a Teamster leader, as the SP candidate for Minnesota secretary of state. Where the SP was not running its own candidates, including the contest for governor, the workers were urged to support the Farmer-Labor Party aspirants.

Ray Dunne conducted his campaign around key questions of program. In doing so he explained that the SP would accept no

responsibility for anyone elected on the FLP ticket, not even in
the case of posts for which the SP had not run. Further
experience with the reformists, he stressed, would teach that only
a revolutionary party can champion the needs of the workers.

When the election returns came in, Benson had outpolled his
Republican rival for the governorship. His success had resulted in
part from FLP backing of Roosevelt, who swept the presidential
elections. Against Roosevelt, Norman Thomas got 2,500 votes in
Minnesota. Ray Dunne came out a bit ahead of Thomas,
receiving 4,000 votes, three-fifths of them from Minneapolis.

An extensive postelection editorial appeared in the *Northwest
Organizer,* which had been made the official organ of the
Minneapolis Teamsters Joint Council when Local 574 was
reinstated into the IBT. It issued a fresh warning to the workers
about the slippery role of reformists in public office, again calling
attention to their repeated violations of campaign pledges. The
editorial sharply reminded the victorious Farmer-Labor candidates that the party rested chiefly on support from the trade-
union movement. But it did not follow, the editorial noted, that
labor should rely primarily on the FLP. The workers were
advised, instead, to build strong, militant unions; to keep abreast
of the times through a fighting policy; to promote a better
understanding of parties they could call their own; and not to
take for granted the good conduct of the reformists who had just
won at the polls.

In yet another quarter some postelection thinking was going
on. The Citizens Alliance was beginning to recognize that old-
time strikebreaking, union-busting, and openly reactionary
politicking no longer got results. Under Trotskyist leadership the
workers had whipped the Alliance in the trucking industry. Then
Tobin's attempt to cripple Local 574 had been beaten off, thereby
frustrating the employers' hopes to take early revenge on the
local. A new, expanding wave of trade-union activity had
followed, and the Republican Party was taking one beating after
another in the electoral arena.

So, as the *Northwest Organizer* aptly put it, the leopard
changed its spots. In January 1937 the Citizens Alliance was
dissolved into a new ruling-class setup called Associated
Industries. A change in tactics accompanied the move. Guile
began to replace attempts to put down worker uprisings through
brute force. Politically, a more subtle, more deceptive posture was

substituted for the former crudely reactionary stance. Greater attention was paid to rifts within the labor movement that could be exploited to the advantage of the bosses. Whatever the capitalists could think of was tried as they sought to regain ground they had lost to the insurgent proletariat.

Unfortunately for the workers, a new situation was arising within the labor movement that would make it easier for the bosses to alter the relationship of class forces in their favor. This adverse development stemmed from a 180 degree turn in line that the Communist Party was in the process of carrying out.

7. Stalinist Flip-Flops

The Trotskyist attitude toward the Farmer-Labor Party was not new; it continued and extended the policy that had been worked out in the early years of the Communist movement in the United States and elsewhere.

Before the Communist Party became infected with the Stalinist virus, it undertook a revolutionary intervention into the reformist political movement. The aim was to help create an elementary instrument for promotion of a massive labor breakaway from entrapment in the capitalist two-party swindle. This measure was viewed as a first step toward the political radicalization of the working class; and in the given objective situation the projected tactic was valid, despite the fact that mistakes in implementation cut short its development.

At the outset the CP gave conditional support to promotion on a national scale of an independent party based on the trade unions. In those days—before corporate farming had attained its present dominant position—the assumption naturally followed that a formation of this kind could attract small farmers in numbers that would give them quite substantial weight inside the movement. The CP urged mass support at the polls for the candidates of a party evaluated in that dual sense, as against the candidates of the Democrats and Republicans. At the same time the CP stressed that the problems of the toilers could not be solved through a reformist program and that only a revolutionary political course would meet their needs.

This general line had the approval of the Third International, then led by V. I. Lenin and Leon Trotsky, and it was designed for application under the specific political conditions existing in the United States after World War I.

The war had scarcely ended when a major strike wave developed. Under the impact of the class battles fought during the upsurge, sentiment arose for the building of a national labor party. This led to a conference in Chicago late in 1919 at which steps were taken to launch a political movement based on the trade unions, into which farmers were invited. The move was made through expansion of the Farmer-Labor Party. But even though that formation had thus been extended beyond Minnesota, from which an initial impulse had come, it was still confined primarily to midwestern states.

In a further effort to broaden FLP influence, candidates were named for the 1920 national elections. The nominee for president of the U.S. was Parley P. Christensen. According to the official returns, he received 265,411 votes, a significant mark of progress for the new movement.

It was in the light of these developments that the Communist Party undertook its intervention into the reformist movement, beginning in 1922. Prospects seemed good for a bloc with trade unionists who supported the FLP, a step that would help to expand CP influence and recruitment within the labor movement. To serve that end, collaboration was developed with key figures in the Chicago Federation of Labor, AFL. But the interventionist tactics were then carried to extremes which caused the whole thing to backfire.

By the time of the 1923 Farmer-Labor convention, held in Chicago, the CP found itself in a position to control the gathering. This strength was used to ram through a decision to restructure the movement as a "Federated Farmer-Labor Party" in which the CP forces would have decisive weight. The action was taken despite opposition from trade unionists, even though their support was needed to maintain a viable national formation, and a major blow-up resulted.

Many trade unionists, including those most influential in the Chicago Federation of Labor, simply walked away from the whole setup. They turned, instead, to support of Robert M. La Follette, a Wisconsin Republican who was getting ready to campaign as a "Progressive" candidate for the U.S. presidency in 1924.

With this loss of trade-union support, the expanded Farmer-

Labor movement came apart at the seams. Only the Minnesota wing survived the debacle; to differentiate itself from the "Federation" devised by the CP, the Minnesota party changed its organizational designation from Farmer-Labor Federation to Farmer-Labor Association.

Hoping to salvage something out of the mess, a section of the CP leadership proposed to link the now-isolated "Federated Farmer-Labor Party" to the La Follette movement. The Third International pointed out to them that it would be wrong to become involved in what amounted to a third capitalist party. So the CP wound up with its own presidential ticket, headed by William Z. Foster, who conducted a nominal campaign. The attempt to intervene in the Farmer-Labor movement had come to an ignominious end.

While these events were unfolding, Lenin died in January 1924: developments that followed in the Soviet Union and the Third International were to have profound repercussions for the labor movement in the U.S.

The Bolshevik Party had earned great respect among the world working class because it had led the Russian workers to victory in the October Revolution of 1917. But unfavorable objective conditions were to bring about a reversal of this revolutionary role. Lenin's death was one of the factors, but there were others.

The young workers' state had inherited a low level of culture and technology from czarist society, which made it very hard for the masses to overcome the conditions of poverty that plagued them. Meanwhile, none of the post-1917 revolutions in other countries had succeeded. After years of civil war and imperialist intervention, during which great losses were suffered—both in lives and in further devastation of the country's resources—the Soviet Union found itself isolated in a hostile capitalist world.

In this situation of increasing exhaustion and demoralization, the Stalinists began to seize control of the Bolshevik Party and impose their bureaucratic rule over the Soviet masses. Taking cynical advantage of the Bolsheviks' prestige, the Stalinists at the same time assumed dictatorial authority over the Third International. It was transformed into an instrument for promoting the narrow national interests of the ruling Soviet bureaucracy. Thereafter, the Third International was used to put the world Communist movement through a series of flip-flops in basic policy.

Whatever the convulsions involved, one factor remained constant throughout the ensuing years. Every Communist Party was required to jump quickly into conformity with the latest change in line, which each party had to carry out regardless of national conditions at the time. This dictate served to emphasize the narrow, Russian-nationalist character of Stalinist policy. Communist parties everywhere were used as mere pawns of Kremlin diplomacy. The aim was to promote friendly capitalist relations with the Soviet Union. Until 1928 collaboration was ordered with liberal and reformist politicians, as well as trade-union bureaucrats, who might help to secure capitalist recognition of the workers' state created in Russia. Moreover, all class-struggle issues were subordinated to that objective.

Then, at the Sixth Congress of the Third International in 1928, the Stalinists executed a complete turnabout, and the "third period" line was decreed. Among the central features of this new policy was the prediction of an early outbreak of spontaneous labor uprisings in capitalist countries. To give the masses "revolutionary" leadership in the anticipated conflicts, a frenzied course was laid down for quick action. Existing labor organizations that could not be captured intact were to be split. That was supposed to clear the way for their replacement by new formations developed under CP control.

As could be expected, this sectarian, ultraleft policy was accompanied by blind factionalism. Opponents of the new line were branded "social fascists." The Stalinists in this country hurled the epithet not only at their hated critics, the Trotskyists; they also used it indiscriminately against all opponents in the labor movement, from the AFL hierarchy to the social democrats and, in Minnesota, the Farmer-Labor Party.

It followed, of course, that no cooperation could be extended to "social fascists" in actions directed against the capitalist class. Hence, the Stalinists played a disruptive role during the 1934 Teamster struggle in Minneapolis. Throughout the long conflict their main fire was centered on the Trotskyists in the union leadership, denouncing them as "agents of the bosses." The same tactic was repeated later on when Local 574's charter was high-handedly revoked by Tobin. Twisting the facts around, the CP blamed the local's officers for that development, thereby serving to cover up for the IBT bureaucrat.

Special note should be taken of yet another application of the "third period" line, which will become all the more striking in the light of subsequent events. The matter was pinpointed through a June 1934 statement in the *Daily Worker,* a CP paper. It was made by William F. Dunne, a one-time revolutionary militant who had capitulated to the Stalinists. Part of his statement was devoted to blasting the Trotskyists for recommending that the workers accept a compromise settlement with the trucking bosses. In doing so, however, he also took a swipe at the Farmer-Labor Party. According to him, "The exposure and defeat of [Governor] Olson should have been the central political objective of the Minneapolis struggle."

As late as the mayoralty campaign in Minneapolis during the spring of 1935, the Stalinists continued to attack the Farmer-Labor Party. In the course of that campaign a public debate took place between Ray Dunne, a Trotskyist leader, and Harry Mayville, who spoke for the CP. Dunne advocated critical support to the FLP candidates in the political showdown then going on with the Citizens Alliance, while Mayville urged that no support whatever be extended to the reformist party's slate.

Perhaps Mayville didn't know it, but at that very time—when Communist Party members were still dutifully carrying out the 1928 directives—the Kremlin acrobats were preparing another political somersault. As a result, the CP hacks would soon be talking out of the other side of their mouths concerning the FLP.

The new line had been developed in the aftermath of a great tragedy that struck the German working class in 1933—Hitler's seizure of power without serious opposition. His easy victory was made possible by a deep rift in the labor movement, for which "third period" misleadership was in large part responsible. Not only were the German workers, including Communist Party members, betrayed into the brutal hands of the fascists; the Soviet Union itself was placed in grave danger of attack from the military machine that the Nazis quickly began to build up.

Thrust into a panic by this threat to their bureaucratic privileges, the Kremlin gang began a quest for military allies elsewhere in the capitalist world. Feelers were put out for "collective security" liaisons with imperialist countries whose interests might conflict with those of the German ruling class. The search brought a treaty with France, which was signed in the late spring of 1935.

A heavy price was to be paid for this diplomatic arrangement—

at the expense of the French workers. The line now put forward by the Stalinists amounted to defense of the capitalist system.

Parliamentary maneuvers were assigned the central role in working-class politics. A "people's front" was called for, as the instrument to establish a "people's government." Membership in the new setup was to be open to "all antifascist elements."

This policy represented a complete reversal of Lenin's concept of a united front. Under Lenin's guidance, such a formation served as a means of fighting the capitalists with the strongest possible forces that could be mobilized around specific class-struggle issues. Its adherents were confined to the workers and their allies, and there was no crossing of class lines into the ruling-class camp.

Under the Stalinist people's front concept, on the other hand, the aim was to lead the workers into a political coalition with direct agents of the boss class. In addition, capitalist politicians were accorded freedom of action within the "front"; but the workers were subjected to restrictions, as determined by the limited program to which the capitalist "allies" might agree.

To justify this line it was argued that the only choices labor had were between "democratic" capitalism and fascism. The concept of a working-class fight for state power was put into limbo. Any possibility of replacing capitalism with socialism was relegated to a far-off day. Emphasis was focused, instead, on politicking for two-bit reforms under the present system.

Such was the new course that the Kremlin presented for formal ratification at the Seventh Congress of the Third International, which met in August 1935. It was duly rubber-stamped by that body, along with accompanying directives for immediate application of the change in policy by Communist parties throughout the capitalist world.

When the delegates from the United States returned home after the congress, a bit of brainstorming took place. It was not exactly clear to the CP leaders how the new feat in political gymnastics was to be accomplished in this country, but they had to make a start. So they quickly took one obvious step. Their miniscule "red" federation of labor—formed during the "third period"—was liquidated, and workers belonging to the party were told to get back into the AFL post haste.

The top Stalinists then began looking for some way to unite with somebody to form a people's front. An initial move in that direction took the form of a complete turnaround in their attitude on the labor party question. A tentative projection of the switch was presented by William Z. Foster in the October 1935 *Communist*.

"The anti-Fascist mass party should be based on the trade unions," he wrote, "and should include farmers' organizations, the Communist party, Socialist party, state Farmer-Labor parties, veterans' organizations, working women's organizations, workers' and farmers' cooperatives, workers' fraternal societies, tenants' leagues, anti-war societies, groups of intellectuals, etc."

Proceeding in the vein described by Foster, the CP focused for a short time on advocacy of a national labor party as the vehicle for a "broad people's movement." It was to be a peculiar kind of "labor" party, though, with capitalist politicians numbered among its members. That was indicated in the Stalinist platform for the 1935 elections in New York. A key passage stated:

"The hour demands the building of the broadest people's front, uniting workers, farmers, unemployed, professionals, small business men, Protestants, Catholics, Jews, Socialists, Communists, Democrats and Republicans, a people's front, fighting in the interests of the common people, the working people and the poor farmers."

As the CP leaders continued their exhortation about the "anti-Fascist mass party" that the "hour demands," they got themselves quite worked up. By May 14, 1936, the *Daily Worker* was asserting: "Moreover, only such a militant people's front could exert real pressure on Roosevelt and slow down to some extent his retreat before reaction."

Exhortations alone, however, cannot create a movement. The great bulk of the workers, who had many illusions about Franklin D. Roosevelt, were still backing him and the Democratic Party. As a result of the line with which the Stalinists had started, their campaign for a people's front got nowhere at all. Something else had to be tried, especially with national elections coming up in November 1936.

The problem was solved through another handspring. Roosevelt and the Democrats were suddenly proclaimed an "anti-Fascist" force. Earl Browder, the CP's presidential candidate in 1936, campaigned backhandedly for Roosevelt by concentrating his fire on the Republican candidate, Alfred M. Landon. Thereaf-

ter CP politics centered on two interrelated concepts: support of
the Roosevelt administration's New Deal policies and pressure for
a U.S. military alliance with the Soviet Union.

In Minnesota, meanwhile, CP members had been worming
their way into the Farmer-Labor Party. Some managed to join
ward and township clubs. Others got in by way of cultural organizations, language societies, sickness and death benefit associations, and by way of other devices that served as a means of affiliation with the reformist party. Numerous phony setups of the
kind were created for that express purpose.

Once inside the party, the Stalinists pushed their people's front
line. That brought them into collaboration with the more conservative elements in the movement, including career politicians
both in and out of public office. In a single leap the CP had
changed from an ultraleft critic of the FLP into a component of
its right wing.

Undertaking now to serve as the main defenders of reformist
politics, the Stalinists lectured the Socialist Party against allowing the Trotskyists—who had by then entered its ranks—to criticize the Farmer-Labor Party. They did so through a pronounce-
ment issued by the CP in June 1936. Differentiation from the
FLP's reformist program and the conduct of its representatives in
public office was branded an "indiscriminate attack." They urged
the SP to help build a "real Farmer-Labor movement, including
Communists and Socialists and all of the broad progressive
masses." Such a movement, it was asserted, "can accomplish for
the workers here what the French People's Front has gained."
And this claptrap was palmed off as an "Appeal to Reason."

Somewhat later the CP fired another broadside, aimed this time
at the Trotskyist leaders of Local 544. It took the form of a leaflet
entitled "I Accuse," signed by Robert Kelly, which was widely
distributed among trade unionists. His charges implied that Local 544 was being maneuvered into a campaign to discredit the
Benson administration and the Farmer-Labor Party. A hypocriti-
cal plea was then added for "unity of Minneapolis labor."

This slanderous attack was answered at a public rally held in
Local 544's hall. One of the speakers was Ray Dunne, who took
special note of the "I Accuse" authorship. Kelly, he pointed out,
was relatively unknown. The real drafters of the leaflet had to be
such notorious Stalinist wheelhorses as Nat Ross, Harry Mayville, and William Mauseth. Their past conduct in the labor move-

ment had so discredited them, however, that the attack had to be made in the name of some lesser figure whose reputation was not so odious.

Kelly's charges were refuted by the Local 544 leaders and their trade-union allies. The reply, reported in the *Northwest Organizer* of February 25, 1937, can be summarized as follows:

After three years of struggle the Minneapolis labor movement was in its strongest position ever. This progress on the economic front was the keystone of all positive political developments during that period, including FLP election victories. Trade unionists were thus fully entitled to be critical of Farmer-Laborites in public office when their policies were considered wrong.

In contrast, the Stalinists had played a disruptive role during the 1934 Teamster strikes, and at that time they had labeled Governor Olson as the main enemy. Since then, however, they had proclaimed undying love for the FLP. To facilitate that switch in line, they were now resorting to lies against political opponents in order to cover up their own past mistakes and criminal adventures. The true union builders were being pictured by the CP as betrayers of labor. Trade-union issues were being confused with political issues so as to make workers think that a reformist political party could solve their economic problems. This was done, the rebuttal added, to use Minneapolis labor as a tool in the diplomatic service of the national and international Stalinist leaders.

In and of itself this episode, like the previous one concerning the Socialist Party, was not momentous. As will be seen, however, it did serve as a herald of what was to become a bitter and prolonged conflict within the reformist political movement.

By that time the CP had penetrated deeply into the Farmer-Labor Party. The process had been facilitated by two factors: use of paper organizations to achieve extensive representation within the party and help from careerists willing to cooperate in a multiclass people's front. On this basis the Stalinists were attaining a controlling influence at the top levels of city and state bodies, and they were using their position to run things with an iron hand.

Such was the situation as preparations were made for the June 1937 city elections in Minneapolis. A nominating convention was duly convened at which a cut-and-dried slate of FLP candidates was presented. Heading the list was Kenneth Haycraft,

who had served against the Teamsters in 1934 as a lieutenant in
the National Guard. The delegates were urged to endorse him for
mayor, and the convention had been rigged to do just that. Affiliated trade unions were allowed the barest possible minimum of
representation while, in ironic contrast, the place was crawling
with delegates from Stalinist front organizations.

As a result, labor opposition to the whole ploy developed right
then and there. In the sharp dispute that followed, it became obvious that potential existed for a deep cleavage in the party. So the
CP operators and their right-wing collaborators opted to give
themselves a little more time to maneuver into a stronger position
before the showdown. Accordingly, the gathering was temporarily adjourned with all issues remaining undecided.

After this episode a permanent trade-union caucus was formed
and began taking steps to recruit allies in the FLP generally. Influential AFL officials then pressed to have the caucus push for
the nomination of Thomas E. Latimer, the incumbent mayor, as
the FLP's candidate for reelection. It was a miserable choice indeed, considering his strikebreaking record in office. Local 544
tried to get the caucus to pick a candidate whose reputation was
not so obnoxious, but to no avail.

In the given situation, however, the fight actually ran much
deeper than the question of choosing a ticket. A radicalizing
working class was trying to battle the capitalists at the trade-
union and political levels. On both fronts these efforts had run up
against CP sabotage. Workers holding reformist views were
supporting the FLP in an attempt to win governmental control
away from the Democrats and Republicans; and they were now
confronted with a Stalinist plot to take over the FLP, so as to
convert it into an agency for crude political collaboration with the
capitalists.

Sensing the inherent rottenness of the line being foisted upon
them, the workers became aroused. As far as they were concerned
the FLP was their party, irrespective of misconduct in public
office by its elected representatives. They wanted the organization improved so as to become a more effective weapon against
the boss class. But they were not about to stand still for factional
maneuvers that could only run it into the ground.

These deeper aspects of the developing conflict were outlined in
the *Northwest Organizer* of March 18, 1937. Care was taken in
the presentation to avoid any implication that political reformism

had basic merit. The FLP could never be anything but a party of reform, the union paper said. Hence it could never ultimately solve the economic and political problems of the working class. But those facts didn't constitute a license for a group with ulterior political motives to try and seize control and direction of the party. The fight then going on, the article concluded, was one to decide whether the FLP would function in the interests of its members, or if it would be turned over to political adventurism.

Although the Trotskyists backed trade-union opposition to the Stalinist raid on the FLP, no political responsibility could be taken for the proposed nomination of strikebreaker Latimer for mayor. In a broad sense the necessary differentiation could be made through Socialist Party action in the electoral arena. Within the unions, though, the problem was more complex.

It was not realistic to seek official labor support of an SP ticket, not even in the case of a militant union like Local 544. With relatively few exceptions, the workers were not sufficiently advanced in their political development to be ready for such a step. There would be no serious objection to an SP campaign as such. But an effort to secure formal union endorsement of SP candidates would have been interpreted as yet another factional move against the FLP, paralleling the CP assault. Therefore, official action by Local 544 had to remain within the framework of the reformist political movement.

Those were the circumstances in which the next stage of the conflict began to unfold. The "official" FLP nominating convention was reconvened on March 14, 1937. It was boycotted by the trade unionists and their allies, who held a separate convention on the same day. Selection of rival tickets resulted, along with the adoption of separate platforms.

Haycraft was nominated for mayor at the "official" session and Latimer at the labor-sponsored gathering. Trotskyists in Local 544's delegation, who had objected to the choice of Latimer, decided not to formally record their opposition to his nomination. It was not deemed an issue over which a rupture should be precipitated in the trade-union ranks. At the same time, however, the delegates were informed that the Socialist Party reserved the right to put forward its own ticket in the city elections.

Immediately afterward the Stalinists spread rumors around the SP nationally that in Minneapolis the Trotskyists had put the party on record in support of a strikebreaker, who was opposing the FLP mayoralty candidate. Prompt action to spike the lie was taken by national leaders of the Trotskyist forces within the SP. The result was reported in the May 1, 1937, issue of *Labor Action,* official organ of the Western Federation of the Socialist Party. At the time the paper was edited by James P. Cannon, the central founding leader of this country's Trotskyist movement. The report follows in full:

"Stalinist slanders that the Socialists of Minneapolis were supporting strike-breaker Latimer for mayor in connection with the municipal elections were given a thumping refutation by a special investigating committee appointed by the National Executive Committee of the Socialist party.

"The Committee composed of Andrew Biemiller of Wisconsin, Harry W. Laidler of New York, and Francis Heisler of Illinois made a thorough investigation of the charges and interviewed all parties involved in the dispute.

"Their unanimous report declares that all the Socialist comrades present at the so-called 'rump convention' were there as regularly elected trade union delegates, and that they then and there made the statement that the Socialist party reserved the right to run its own candidate in the mayoralty campaign.

"Many of the largest and most militant Minneapolis unions flatly refused to participate in the so-called regular convention at which the Stalinists supported Haycraft, a strike-breaker, for mayor.

"This session of the Farmer-Labor party at which a candidate for mayor was to be nominated had been packed in the time-honored Communist Party manner, with delegates from the Macedonian Singing Society, the Ukrainian Workers' Club, and so on and on. Bona fide unions like Local 544 of the General Drivers' Union with a membership of more than 5,000 were represented at the regular convention by five delegates, while the many C.P. controlled outfits with 300 members or less would have three affiliated locals with fifteen delegates and three 'non-affiliated' with nine delegates. The 'rump convention' was not called by Socialists, but Socialists participated in it as was their duty to do as elected delegates from their trade unions which objected to the Stalinist version of democracy.

"Mr. Haycraft, backed by the Stalinists, was the officer of the National Guard who arrested leading union members during the famous Minneapolis truck drivers' strike.

"The Socialist party has decided, and the National Executive

Committee has ratified the decision, to run Vincent R. Dunne as the Socialist candidate for Mayor of Minneapolis.

"A thorough-going campaign will be waged on the basis of revolutionary Socialist tactics and program."

As *Labor Action* had assured its readers, Ray Dunne used his candidacy to deal with key aspects of the class struggle. He explained the differences between the reformist movement in Minnesota and a revolutionary socialist party, as well as the reasons why only the latter could fully represent labor's interests. Nailing down basic issues in the FLP controversy, he called for united trade-union action in support of working-class democracy and workers' rights.

Public campaigns had also been launched behind the rival candidacies of Haycraft and Latimer, and right from the start cynical maneuvers against labor were carried out by the "official" FLP. The state executive committee intervened arbitrarily and dictatorially to endorse Haycraft. This action flaunted local autonomy; it was a step toward machine rule, which was being substituted for the more democratic process within such a movement of settling party disputes over nominations through primary elections. Thanks in no small part to bureaucratic interference of this kind, Haycraft edged out Latimer when the primaries took place in mid-May. The ballot count was 25,551 to 25,315, a difference of 236 votes.

Final elections followed early in June. This time Haycraft's chief opponent was the Republican nominee, George E. Leach, a political neanderthal who held a brigadier general's commission in the National Guard. In this crucial contest, efforts were made by the trade unionists to close ranks with the rest of the FLP in support of Haycraft. But so much damage had already been done by the Stalinist right-wing cabal in the movement that the necessary mass support could not be mustered at the polls. Leach won the election.

After just two years of Farmer-Labor incumbency, the capitalist ruling class again had direct political control over the mayor's office.

It was a harsh setback for labor, one that would seem to have made clear, even to the Stalinists, that they had gone way too far and that it was now imperative for them to back off from their disruptive course. But simple logic of the kind had become incomprehensible to the people's front zealots. They were about to take another step that would serve to compound their felony.

8. Factionalism Gone Wild

Pushing recklessly ahead, as though the Haycraft fiasco was of no real significance, the Communist Party continued its factional drive for control over the Farmer-Labor Party. Dangers of inflicting further injury upon the workers were dismissed as secondary. It was deemed imperative, at all hazards, to carry out Kremlin directives for creation of a people's front.

The strong opposition encountered within the trade unions was viewed simply as an obstacle to be surmounted. To the CP strategists the solution lay in finding a means to split the opposition. They expected to derive twin benefits from this: trade-union resistance to the Stalinist line in the FLP would be undermined; and workers who could be maneuvered into precipitating the desired rupture within labor's ranks would then become subject to manipulation into support of CP objectives generally.

To achieve those ends the Minneapolis Stalinists set out to abuse the Congress of Industrial Organizations, which was playing a constructive role nationally. Their conduct toward the CIO could only harm the working class.

Apparently they had begun shaping plans for such action soon after the CIO was suspended from the American Federation of Labor in 1936. Their basic aim had nothing to do with the advancement of industrial unionism. Primarily, they intended to use the CIO locally to build a trade-union base from which to press forward with their people's front line. That step now appeared more important than ever to them, because of the labor opposition that had developed to application of their line within the Farmer-Labor Party. So the Stalinists decided that the time had come to attack the state AFL in its Minneapolis stronghold.

There was no justification whatever for the steps they pro-

ceeded to take, as a sketch of the prevailing objective conditions
will show.

At that time a few small CIO units were already present in the
city, existing mainly within the garment and printing industries. These local unions had previously belonged to the AFL, before the national organizations to which they were affiliated
joined in founding the new industrial union movement. After
they became part of the CIO, good relations had continued to prevail between them and the unions remaining in the AFL, and no
local jurisdictional disputes had resulted from the national AFL-
CIO split. Cooperation between the two formations had extended,
moreover, into the fight then going on within the Farmer-Labor
Party.

Under those circumstances no valid reason existed for exceptional CIO organizational activity in Minneapolis. That view
had, in fact, been indicated earlier by the national CIO leaders.
They knew that—in those days—the city had none of the major
industrial plants, which was where their organizing efforts were
concentrated; and they had no desire to compete with the AFL
outside that sphere. For that reason, the CIO officials had turned
down local 574's request for affiliation, made in 1936 after its expulsion from the International Brotherhood of Teamsters.

Subsequently the General Drivers Union won its fight with
Tobin. Under a new charter, as Local 544, it was reinstated into
the IBT and thereby into the AFL. That, in turn, gave rise to a
new labor upsurge within the city, through which the workers
generally were becoming quite well organized; apart from the few
exceptions noted above, they belonged to the AFL.

Disruption of these forces through contrived use of the CIO as a
splitting instrument could only play into the hands of the bosses,
as had been the outcome of the turmoil already generated within
the Farmer-Labor Party. But considerations of that nature were
brushed aside by the Stalinists. Their only concern was to pick
the best place to begin the raid on the AFL. They needed to find a
situation where CP cadres would be able to wield significant influence, and they needed to cook up a way to affiliate the splitters
with the CIO. As they saw it, both requirements could be met by
starting on machinists' locals with AFL ties. Stalinists were present in those organizations to precipitate the split; and workers
pulled out of the AFL could be put into the CIO United Electrical
Workers Union, which was under CP control nationally.

The target of this scheme was the AFL's International Association of Machinists (IAM). It had three units in the Minneapolis area. Oldest among them was Local 382, formed in 1927. During its first years the local had been able to do little more than organize groups of workers in small machine shops around the city. Then it got a powerful stimulus from the Teamster victory in 1934. A campaign followed to bring mechanics at all major garages and automobile sales agencies into the local and, through a strike called early in 1935, the bosses were compelled to sign a union contract.

During the same period a charter was issued to establish Local 1313 for ornamental iron workers. They, too, had to wage a hard-fought struggle before recognition was won from the employers.

Later in 1935 the Minneapolis-Moline Power Implement Company was organized by Local 382. At the Minneapolis plant the entire production force of over one thousand was taken in on an industrial union basis. The firm then signed a union agreement without forcing the workers into a strike. After that, Local 1037 was chartered to begin recruitment of workers at the company's plant in the suburb of Hopkins.

By mid-1937 the three IAM locals had been built up to a combined membership of about six thousand.

A number of CP members had been in and around the machinists' movement for several years. The most influential, in trade-union terms, was William Mauseth. He and his close associates had played it cool during the "third period" so as to avoid jeopardizing their standing within the IAM. As a result they were still more or less on the sidelines when the auto mechanics' strike occurred early in 1935. It was the General Drivers' leadership that played the key role in making the action effective in the face of stiff opposition from the Citizens Alliance.

By the time of the ornamental iron walkout a few months later—which coincided with the people's front turn—the CP had begun to change its trade-union line. Mauseth and Company tried to seize de facto control over Local 1313's leadership. But years of CP sectarianism and ultraleftism had so isolated them from the labor movement that they could not rally the broad support needed to fight off Latimer's strikebreaking attack. Once again, it had remained for the Teamsters and progressive AFL unions to step into the breach and carry the action through to victory.

Now, two years later, reciprocity for this union-building solidar-

ity was to come in typical Stalinist fashion—through the sowing
of divisions in the working class for unprincipled reasons.

There could be no other reason for the course taken by the CP,
because the machinists in Minneapolis didn't need to go over to
the CIO in order to organize along industrial lines. Unlike most
AFL unions, they had not been forced into a narrow craft setup.
In the spring of 1937 the IAM's general executive board had authorized the machinist locals to take in molders, iron workers,
sheet-metal operators, etc., on an industry-wide basis. Militants
within the city's AFL movement had helped to protect the IAM
locals from raids by other unions claiming jurisdiction over those
crafts.

Nor could a changeover to the CIO be justified as a way to organize the unorganized. That objective was legitimately put forward as a key aim of the new industrial union formation nationally; it didn't apply to Minneapolis, where a great majority of the
workers, including machinists, were already organized into the
AFL. Under these circumstances, a shift to the CIO would actually serve to disorganize the organized by creating an unwarranted
rupture in the trade-union ranks.

Still another difficulty would arise from such a move. The IAM
locals held signed agreements with the employers, made under
the AFL. Those contracts would be endangered by a switch in
affiliation to the CIO. This would provide the bosses with an alibi
for a renewed fight on the union.

With the Stalinists hard put to find a plausible excuse for their
intended course, the top AFL bureaucrats proceeded to give them
a handle to grab hold of. When the CIO unions were first suspended from the AFL, the action had been ignored in Minneapolis. The Central Labor Union (CLU), composed of delegates from
AFL affiliates in the city, had allowed the local CIO units to
continue their participation in its deliberations. In July 1937,
however, AFL President William Green sent down orders to
exclude the CIO delegates from the CLU, and a majority of the
body voted to obey his instructions.

The Communist Party was thereby handed a pretext to claim
that the CLU had precipitated a split in the city's labor movement. After that it didn't take long for the raid on the AFL to
begin. Near the end of August, rigged meetings were staged at
which Locals 382, 1037, and 1313 voted to disaffiliate from the
IAM and apply for CIO charters.

Not only had a step been taken that was to plunge the trade-union movement into a bitter internal struggle, but it had been initiated less than two months after the Farmer-Labor Party defeat in Minneapolis city elections, for which the Stalinists had also been largely responsible.

Immediately after the three locals voted to go CIO, the national IAM officials gave the raiders yet another propaganda boost. They launched a red-baiting attack on Mauseth and his cohorts. That didn't wash in Minneapolis, where smears of the kind against labor militants had been used frequently by the Citizens Alliance since 1934. But it enabled the CP to focus attention on the unprincipled nature of such tactics, thereby avoiding discussion of the real issues in the conflict.

Matters were then made worse by top officers of the AFL craft setup who held formal jurisdiction over the molders. They demanded that workers recently organized into the IAM be turned over to them. That enabled the raiders to pose as the true defenders of industrial unionism and to claim that industry-wide organizational forms could be maintained only by breaking with the AFL. Pointing to an added incentive, they talked of lower monthly dues in the United Electrical workers.

By this time AFL members throughout the city were up in arms. There was anger about the raid on the IAM and disgust over the blunders made by top labor officials. It was plain for all to see that the real problems did not center on the special interests of craft-minded bureaucrats; that the bureaucrats' interests should not be put first; and that nothing but further damage could result from red-baiting.

As the *Northwest Organizer* pointed out, what had become involved was not a simple AFL-CIO issue. It was not even an industrial union issue. For self-seeking purposes, the Stalinists had set out to mislead and cheat the IAM membership. Their main aim was to split the Minneapolis labor movement, and that objective would not serve the interests of workers in either the AFL or the CIO. Actually, it constituted a crime against one of the most militant and best organized union movements anywhere in the country.

The Teamster paper also raised a demand addressed to the national AFL. There had to be guarantees, it asserted, that the machinist locals would be allowed to continue as united, all-inclusive metal-trades formations. That view was shared by the Central

Labor Union, and concrete discussion of the subject was arranged with top IAM officials who had come to the city. A CLU committee, headed by Ray Dunne of Local 544, was selected for the purpose. The talks that followed resulted in assurance by the IAM general executive board that organization on an industrial basis would be continued in Minneapolis.

Because of the fast-moving developments, a good deal of confusion had arisen among rank-and-file machinists. Many were still on the fence concerning the split. They needed above all to receive objective clarification of the facts, and that was exactly what the CP wanted to avoid. Toward that end, they used claques to disrupt membership meetings of the machinists—speakers favoring the split policy were cheered and those opposing it were booed. Similarly, on the larger trade-union arena, all possible means were employed to divert attention from the real issues. Teamster criticism of the splitters course, for instance, drew fake counter-charges that the CIO was being "red-baited," a well-known and often-used Stalinist trick.

Attempts to suppress the truth were soon followed by acts of outright intimidation. Gangs of sluggers were organized to deal violently with opponents of the CP line. They proceeded to beat up small, isolated groups of IAM supporters in garages and machine shops, which resulted in serious injury to several trade unionists.

Among those in the strongarm bands were good militants who had been duped by the Stalinist clique. Addressing itself to these misguided workers, the *Northwest Organizer* sought to reason with them. It began by calling attention to things they were not doing. Namely, they were not fighting the bosses for higher wages; they were not carrying on a struggle for better working conditions; and they were not spreading the gospel of union solidarity.

Instead, the Teamster paper continued, they were behaving irresponsibly towards the welfare of union machinists and the entire Minneapolis labor movement. By raiding an established AFL union they were not advancing the CIO's legitimate interests; they were giving it a bad name in the city. In fact, no one was helped by their conduct except the bosses, who welcomed seeing a union torn by splits.

The CP responded to such criticism by extending the raids to other AFL unions. Among them were locals in the woodenware industry, flour and cereal mills, city and county services, and the trucking industry. In one case a dozen drivers in Local 544's jurisdiction were signed up in what was alleged to be a unit of the United Auto Workers, a major CIO affiliate. They worked for a small outfit that delivered box lunches, and their boss had quickly entered into a contract with the "UAW." It called for a weekly wage of $18, whereas the going rate established by Local 544 was $33.20. When the discrepancy was called to the drivers' attention they said they were glad to change union affiliation, because the $18 deal had been cooked up with the employer behind their backs.

Reacting strongly to moves of this nature, the Teamsters Joint Council held a special rally to mobilize its defense against the raiders. A statement was issued pledging continued support to legitimate CIO efforts to organize the unorganized. At the same time, however, it was made clear that attempts by an unprincipled clique to disrupt Teamster locals would be firmly opposed. "No one is going to wreck our movement," the council declared.

To show that the assertion was no idle boast, a special detachment had already been organized among Local 544 members. It consisted of workers with considerable experience in defending picket lines against the cops. At the first opportunity this force gave the CP-led goons a large dose of their own medicine, which caused the bullying tactics to subside rather quickly.

The CP hacks then raised a hue and cry about "Teamster terror." They were answered through an editorial in the September 30, 1937, *Northwest Organizer.* Appropriately headed "The Art of Upside-Down," it caught the essence of Stalinist methods in the following passage:

"We see the Mauseth crowd, in the name of industrial unionism, seek to split up an industrial union. We see these people talk of unity, only to disrupt in practice. We see them cry out against civil war in the movement, when they, and they only, are responsible for the present situation. We see them come out, oh so boldly, against beating up workers, when they themselves began practicing this very thing."

At this juncture the AFL State Federation of Labor held its annual convention. A year earlier the federation had adopted a resolution backing the CIO position and calling for its reinstatement into the AFL. Now, however, the Stalinist raiders had caused enmity toward the CIO in general, and a warlike mood prevailed at the gathering. As a result it took an objective effort, led by Local 544's delegation, to restore a correct sense of balance. After that had been accomplished, the convention voted to again call on the national AFL to recognize the need for industrial unionism. The delegates also decided that friendly relations should be maintained with legitimate CIO unions in the state.

A few weeks later, collective bargaining elections were held at the two Moline plants involved in the raid on the IAM. The splitters had been issued a CIO charter through the CP controlled Electrical Workers Union for use in that situation. At the Minneapolis plant the new CIO setup won the election and became the official bargaining agent. But it was too weak to make a comparable bid at the Moline plant in Hopkins, where IAM Local 1037 won the bargaining rights.

Before long, however, the Stalinists were to profit from an IAM weakness in the Hopkins situation. The officers of Local 1037 failed to keep on top of grievances. They also neglected to promote attendance at union meetings and keep the workers up to date on general developments. Such derelictions enabled the Mauseth gang to grab onto dissatisfied IAM militants and use them as puppets. In the end, a majority of the workers were won over to United Electrical Workers Local 1138, and the IAM was frozen out of the plant.

By this time it was clear that the raid on the Minneapolis AFL had developed into a conflict of indefinite duration. That made it necessary to gear the Central Labor Union for combat action. The process began when the regular election of CLU officers came up early in 1938. Some of the incumbents were Stalinist fellow travelers, who had used their positions to aid and abet the disruption being carried out in the name of the CIO. They were swept out of office in the balloting and replaced by new officers opposed to the splitters.

As the next move to cope with the complex situation that had arisen, the CLU formed an ad hoc leading body called the Policy Committee. It consisted of two delegates from the CLU itself and two more from each of the trade councils in the building, printing, and trucking industries—a total of eight. One of the delegates was Carl Skoglund of Local 544. He played a key role in charting the basic course set by the committee to handle the knotty problems it was to face.

Essentially the Policy Committee had three main functions.

These were to promote support for legitimate unions—both AFL and CIO—engaged in conflicts with the bosses; to handle jurisdictional disputes between AFL unions; and to deal with difficulties caused by the Stalinist disrupters.

Concerning the last function, need for firm steps arose in the spring of 1938. The existing IAM contracts in the garage industry were about to expire and new ones had to be negotiated. Now, however, there were rival unions involved: IAM Local 382 and United Electrical Workers Local 1140, affiliated with the CIO. Between them they represented over six-hundred workers in forty-three shops.

These workers were entitled to have their rights and interests protected, and the AFL Policy Committee sought to do just that. It recommended joint negotiations with the employers through a committee of two each from IAM Local 382, CIO Local 1140, and the Policy Committee. A further proposal was made that industry-wide elections be held, with the union getting a majority of the votes to become the representative of all the workers in enforcing the contract. At the same time the right of any workers to belong to either union was not to be impaired.

IAM Local 382 at first accepted the recommendation. Then it switched positions and tried to open independent negotiations with the bosses. At that point the matter was brought before the Central Labor Union itself, which voted to demand that Local 382 abide by the procedure advocated by the Policy Committee.

But that time CIO Local 1140 had decided to reject both joint negotiations and industry-wide elections. The CP strategists obviously wanted no part of any arrangement that might overcome the split they had precipitated.

In view of Local 1140's attitude, the Policy Committee next helped the IAM representatives open their own negotiations with the garage bosses. Nothing came of it, however, because the union split had given the employers a cocky feeling that they could win any fight that might develop. So the IAM struck the industry, with solid AFL support.

Two days later both the employers and the Stalinists had been brought into line. Joint negotiations took place, as the Policy Committee had originally recommended, and a compromise was reached on a new working agreement. On the issue of bargaining representation, the CIO negotiators still tried to hold out for separate elections in each individual garage. But they had to back off from that stand and agree to industry-wide balloting. Ironically enough, the CIO won the contest by a close vote of 355 to 305.

Many of the mechanics who voted CIO probably didn't know that they were subjecting themselves to a new twist in people's front policy. The CP had recently gone on record against "unauthorized" strikes: that is, workers' struggles conducted without permission from the trade-union bureaucrats.

Although the Stalinists were putting much time and effort into raids on the AFL, they had not neglected their factional activities in the Farmer-Labor Party. In fact the two lines of endeavor were in some respects being synthesized. That had already been shown by a new kind of attack on Local 544. In February 1938 a leaflet was put out over the signature of Douglas Raze, a member of the local, and copies were mailed to Teamster units throughout the state. Purporting to speak for an "Organized Teamsters Farmer-Labor Committee," Raze charged that:

"Our union is looked upon with suspicion and mistrust by many honest members of trade unions all over the state. It has been used to oppose the policies of the Farmer-Labor Party and to split it and weaken it. And all this has been done by a small group of anti-Farmer-Labor leaders who have done all these things in the name of our entire membership. . . .

"For the last year the brothers Dunne and the hangers-on who follow the so-called political philosophy of Trotsky have more and more revealed themselves as opposed to the Farmer-Labor party and principles. . . .

"Who gave them the right to use our paper, the *Organizer,* to attack the Farmer-Labor Party, to take underhanded potshots at Governor Benson and the Farmer-Labor administration, to vilify President Roosevelt and every decent progressive proposal that we union members believe in. . . ?

"We Farmer-Laborites in the drivers unions demand that the Dunne brothers and the rest of their hand picked clique either abide by the manifest wishes of the great majority of our membership—or get out."

This smear was answered by officers of Local 544 at a general membership meeting. They challenged Raze, who was present, to verify his charges with facts. Declining to do so, he confined his remarks to vague generalities when he took the floor. Since Raze was obviously fronting for the CP—which had only recently used the CIO for an attempted raid on the Teamsters—the union members gave him scant heed. His slanders were rejected as just another unprincipled attack on the local.

During the same period a new maneuver was undertaken in the FLP as well. By then the CP had Governor Benson more or less sewed up factionally. He was a small-town banker and tin-horn politician with large personal ambitions. But he controlled no significant force that could serve as a base for the advancement of his political career. Thus he became natural prey for the Stalinists, who proceeded to give him a buildup in order to use him as a pliant tool. One of the dividends from this tactic had already been realized in Minneapolis. Pretending to speak as an "industrial union sympathizer," the governor had used his high office to propagandize in support of the split attack designed to carve a caricature of the CIO out of the city's AFL movement.

As matters now stood, though, Benson's renomination as the Farmer-Labor Party's gubernatorial candidate in the 1938 elections was not a sure thing. He was being challenged in the primaries by Hjalmer Petersen. As lieutenant governor, Petersen had filled the state's top executive post for a few months after Floyd Olson died in 1936. Through this fluke he now enjoyed a degree of prestige as a one-time governor, and that tended to impair somewhat the advantage Benson had as the present holder of the office. In addition, Petersen was attacking the incumbent governor for the way he supported Stalinist tactics in the FLP.

As usual, the CP reacted to the attack by accusing Petersen of "red-baiting." But that alone could not offset the threat to Benson in the primaries, so efforts were launched to make a drastic change in the organizational rules of the FLP.

The *New Leader,* a Farmer-Labor paper, was used for the purpose. In its issue of January 22, 1938, revision of the party's constitution was called for to provide what amounted to a gag law. New clauses were recommended to require that all local units support candidates endorsed by leading party bodies, to forbid the backing of candidates who lacked such "official" sanction, and to make violation of those stipulations grounds for the revocation of unit charters.

The Communist Party's aim, of course, was to intimidate FLP units supporting Petersen in the primaries by threatening them with the danger of being disaffiliated. In their factional view, insistence on freedom of action in a primary contest—so as to test the democratic character of "official" decisions in the reformist party—should be made a crime.

As it turned out, Petersen himself pretty much solved the Stalinists' problem concerning the primaries, thereby obviating their immediate need for repressive organizational measures. Petersen tried to out-do the Benson-CP wing of the party in moving to the right. He not only called for FLP collaboration with the Democrats, as did Benson, but advocated extension of the policy to the Republicans. On top of that, Petersen made an outright bid for support from the industrial overlords. Since all this was alien and hostile to the vital interests of the workers and small farmers, the FLP rank and file began to turn away from him. That left little doubt that Benson could win renomination as the party's candidate for governor.

In those circumstances, general attention became more fully concentrated on issues related to the Farmer-Labor election platform. To many trade unionists, the main problem was to reverse the party's growing tendency to link itself with the openly reactionary policies now being followed by the Roosevelt administration. In Minneapolis the AFL Central Labor Union adopted two key resolutions intended to serve that purpose. One called upon the FLP to speak out against Roosevelt's preparations to plunge the country into the world war that was drawing near. The other advocated a plank in the party's election platform demanding that the war funds be used to provide adequate relief for jobless workers and union wages on the New Deal's "made work" projects.

Then, on March 25, 1938, the FLP state convention opened. As quickly became evident, it had been rigged in advance to give labor a fast shuffle. The main voting power was apportioned toward clubs, township bodies, and Stalinist paper organizations. Trade unions, in contrast, were limited to a single vote apiece. With the CP-Benson clique in control, the party was transformed still further into a Minnesota section of the national Democratic machine.

° Because of Petersen's even more reactionary line, general agreement was nevertheless reached by the delegates to support Benson in both the primaries and the fall elections. After the convention the Minneapolis Teamsters Joint Council's attitude on this point was outlined in the *Northwest Organizer*. With reaction everywhere rearing its head, the paper said, support would be given to the FLP as against the capitalist parties. But that backing would not be uncritical, because of serious defects in the party's platform. As before, the Teamster organ added, the primary weapon of organized labor would remain organized labor itself.

The Stalinists, on the other hand, continued during the election campaign in their efforts to transform the FLP into a people's front. They sought more and more openly to identify the party completely with the New Deal. Because of this, it became increasingly difficult for voters to distinguish their line from Petersen's, as was shown when Benson was able to defeat him in the primaries by only a narrow margin.

This squeaker proved to be the herald of a really harsh experience for the darling of the Stalinists. Through the primaries it had been determined only that Benson was the unquestioned FLP nominee for governor. He still had to face stiff opposition in the November elections from his Republican opponent, Harold E. Stassen, who was strongly backed by the ruling class.

During the campaign, Stassen acted under the guidance of political sharpies hired by the capitalists. They had been keeping close track of shifting political moods among the masses, probing for tricky angles whereby mass discontent could be channeled into support of reactionary political objectives. In this way a script had been prepared for the Republican candidate, which he obediently followed.

From the outset, Stassen assumed a deceptive posture as a supporter of constructive economic and social reforms. In casting himself as a critic of the status quo, however, he sought to conceal the fact that he was opposing the Farmer-Labor Party from the right. No hint was given that his real aim was to move against everything progressive in the state of Minnesota.

In carrying out such a line the Republicans were helped by the failure of the New Deal to overcome serious difficulties that severe economic depression had inflicted upon the toilers. That default had by this time generated widespread discontent with Roosevelt's domestic policies. It followed, therefore, that candidates for public office identifying themselves with the New Deal were bound to run into serious trouble. And that was precisely the kind of political dead-end into which the Farmer-Labor Party was being manipulated by the Stalinists.

Frustrated by the current FLP policy, many who had previously supported the party became passive and disoriented. As election day neared, a large number decided to cast their votes on the simple premise that nothing would be lost by helping to turn the proven rascals out of their seats of power. As far as they could tell, Stassen was at least against the status quo; and since he was relatively new to the political scene they had no basis to judge from past experience how he, as an individual, might perform in public office. For those reasons many gave him the benefit of the doubt, at what was to prove great cost to both the Farmer-Labor Party and the trade unions.

In the 1936 gubernatorial elections, Benson had rolled up a plurality of some 250,000 votes, the largest up to then in the state's history. This time, however, the situation was reversed. Stassen was elected governor by an equally big margin. In two years time the FLP had lost around a half-million supporters in the state.

Credit for that negative achievement belonged in large measure to the Stalinists. Three years earlier they had set out to transform the reformist political movement into a Kremlin-designed people's front, freely swinging their factional hatchets in the process. Since then, the Farmer-Labor Party had suffered two major defeats: first in Minneapolis, and now on a statewide scale. Once again, the ruling class had taken direct control of the two main executive offices in Minnesota's governmental structure, and the workers would have to pay dearly for it.

As might be expected, setbacks experienced by the working class—for which the Communist Party bore heavy responsibility—were not confined to one state alone. Comparable difficulties had arisen throughout the country.

9. Changes in National Trends

Minnesota's unique political situation gave rise to a somewhat distorted view of the national policy followed by the Stalinists. Superficially it might appear that they had some interest in maintaining the organizational independence of the Farmer-Labor Party. But nothing could have been further from the truth. Efforts to tie the FLP to New Deal politics represented only their immediate objective. The basic aim was to liquidate it into the Democratic Party.

Since the people's front turn, the Communist Party had become opposed to any kind of working-class break with the Democrats. Full attention now centered on mobilizing all-out support for Roosevelt, the purpose being to press for a U.S.-Soviet compact against Hitler as a reward.

Proceeding accordingly, the Stalinists resisted leftward trends within the working class. In doing so they committed acts of factional mayhem against those who opposed their line; and as a means of carrying out that policy, they sought to establish blocs and form alliances with other class-collaborationist tendencies in the labor movement.

In this connection Earl Browder, then head of the Communist Party, announced a desire to cooperate with the Socialist Party. He clearly had two things in mind. The SP had been recruiting young workers, students, and intellectuals. Once in the party they crystallized into a left wing moving toward revolutionary positions. This was a course the Stalinists opposed. Browder naturally wanted to intervene for the purpose of checking this leftward development. In the process, he hoped to draw the party's right wing into support of people's front politics.

Not long after Browder's move the Trotskyists entered the Socialist Party in a body, the aim being to counteract pressures

from the right and to help the left wing evolve into a
revolutionary-socialist formation. A sharp conflict followed.

It erupted when the Norman Thomas wing, succumbing to Stalinist influence, used the authority of the SP's national executive
committee to arbitrarily withdraw the party's mayoralty candidate during the 1937 New York City elections. Support was given,
instead, to Fiorello La Guardia, a Republican running on a fusion
ticket.

When the left wing spoke out against this people's front tactic,
a bureaucratic attack was launched against it. The Thomasites
used their majority in the party to conduct a heresy hunt against
the revolutionaries, demanding in effect that they take a loyalty
oath. Party units that refused to knuckle under had their charters
suspended and entire state units were reorganized. In Minnesota,
for example, the Minneapolis, St. Paul, and Austin branches, em-
bracing over two-hundred left-wing socialists, had their charters
lifted. These high-handed tactics resulted, of course, in a deep-
going split.

At the beginning of 1938, a convention of the left-wing forces
was held in Chicago. A big majority among the delegates and
visitors consisted of experienced trade unionists. Trotskyists who
had entered the SP, and militants who were "native" to it, were
represented in about equal numbers. This meant that in a bit under two years the revolutionary-socialist forces had been doubled.

The Chicago convention proclaimed the launching of the Socialist Workers Party and adopted a program in full conformity
with the established principles of the world Trotskyist movement.

For several months previously, the founding cadres of the new
party had concentrated on the struggle within the Socialist Party.
Week in and week out they had fought to win the revolutionists in
its ranks, leaving only the reformists for the Thomasites. That
task had required much discussion of Marxist fundamentals.
Consequently, attention to current nuances in the political evolution of the working class had been somewhat neglected.

In those circumstances the Socialist Workers Party was not
ready at the time of the Chicago convention either to make a full
appraisal of changing objective conditions, or to work out tactical
readjustments needed to meet new problems that had arisen. The
delegates merely reaffirmed the existing Trotskyist position
against the advocacy of a labor party. Before long, however, more
extensive attention was given to the question, and help in doing

so was received from Leon Trotsky, the central leader of the Fourth International, which was also founded in 1938. As a first step toward reaching the necessary decisions, preceding developments in the class struggle had to be reviewed and reassessed.

When the economic depression of the 1930s first set in, the workers found themselves caught in a crisis of organization and leadership. Only a tiny percentage of the labor force was unionized, and those were entangled in a web of narrowly conceived craft setups. Even worse, the structure was dominated by capitalist-minded bureaucrats, who had neither the will nor the ability to initiate and direct a fight in defense of labor's interests.

Faced with this leadership default, the workers gradually began to act spontaneously, often through ad hoc formations. Struggles conducted in that manner were either ignored or sabotaged by the top AFL hacks. Their conduct aroused anger and disgust within the rank and file, thereby opening the way for radicals to emerge as leaders of substantial bodies of workers. Three militant strikes resulted during 1934—in Minneapolis, San Francisco, and Toledo—all of which were won. Those dramatic successes drew national attention, with dual effects. Workers in basic industry became inspired to press strongly for trade-union action; to retain bureaucratic control over the rebellious masses, John L. Lewis took the lead in establishing the CIO as a medium through which to conduct an organizational drive.

Once the CIO arose, the basic industries quickly became organized in advanced industrial form. A wave of struggles developed that were unprecedented in U.S. history, both in scope and revolutionary implications.

During these conflicts a new phenomenon appeared—the sit-down strike—a device through which the workers occupied struck plants and, where necessary, turned them into bastions of defense against strikebreaking attacks. The sit-down technique was used as early as November 1935 by the Akron rubber workers. From there it spread to other industries, reaching a climax in a massive battle against the huge General Motors Corporation.

Spontaneous actions of this kind broke out at various GM plants in the fall of 1936. As they continued to spread, Lewis intervened with a request to hold off until the top CIO officials could get ready to lead a fight in the auto industry. His plea was ignored. In January 1937 the workers went ahead on their own to completely tie up GM. Flint, Michigan, where the corporation had

giant installations, became the focal point of the struggle. Once
they had occupied the plants in that city, the auto unionists selected a broad strike committee to lead the sit-down and then prepared for a siege. Management soon made an attempt to have the
strikers ousted by military force. The workers responded to this
threat by using the company's machinery and supplies to manu-
facture weapons of defense. Confronted with the certainty that a
military assault would bring on a bloody conflict, the Michigan
authorities decided not to use the National Guard, as had been
planned. After that, on February 11, 1937, General Motors made a
contract settlement with the CIO.

It was a tremendous victory. Labor's heavy batallions in basic
industry had brought a hitherto "all-powerful" monopoly corporation to its knees. In the process, the workers had not only put an
end to GM's open-shop tyranny of the past; once aroused in
struggle, they had also ignored ruling-class preachments that
capitalist property was "sacred" and taken over company facilities to advance the union cause. They had thereby given an impressive demonstration of the inherent revolutionary capacity of
the working class.

By and large the workers' earlier problem of getting themselves
organized at the trade-union level had now been overcome. The
crisis of leadership still existed, however, with the result that effective use of labor's power remained obstructed. A demonstration of the grave handicaps resulting from that unsolved problem
was about to occur in the steel industry.

Following the CIO triumph in auto, the U.S. Steel Corporation,
a vast monopoly complex with an odious strikebreaking record, decided not to engage the aroused workers in battle, signing a union
contract in March 1937 without a fight. The CIO proceeded to
take on five of the next-largest corporations in the industry.
These outfits, which acted collectively in labor relations, were
known as "Little Steel." They refused to deal with the union, and
all five were struck in May of that year. The result was an immediate halt in production, as the workers gave massive support to
the walkout.

In this case, however, the bosses persisted in demanding that
their government crush the strike by force and violence. Capitalist politicians in various seats of power then ordered police assaults upon the strikers in several cities. The most vicious took
place on Memorial Day 1937 at the Republic Steel plant in South

Chicago when cops fired upon a peaceful mass demonstration outside the plant, killing ten workers and wounding scores.

Instead of helping to mobilize labor as a whole to defend the steel strikers against the murderous assault, as was his duty, Lewis appealed to the federal government to save the situation for the union. Roosevelt answered the plea with a quotation from Shakespeare. "A plague on both your houses," he replied, acting as though he stood impartially above the class conflict. But the cold fact was that sections of the capitalist governmental structure, over which Roosevelt presided as chief magistrate, were killing and maiming workers whose interests he pretended to represent.

Lewis complained bitterly about this insolent repudiation of the strikers. But he stopped short of breaking politically with the hypocrite in the White House and once again failed to initiate effective trade-union action in defense of labor's rights. As a result of this leadership default, the steel workers suffered a costly defeat and, less directly, the entire working class received a harsh setback.

Just a few weeks earlier, labor momentum had been raised to a new high by the successful fight in auto. There, the workers themselves, acting without permission from the CIO hierarchy, had taken the initiative in class combat. During the struggle they had prepared their own defenses when the capitalists threatened to use force and violence against them, instinctively declining to entrust their fate to "friendly" capitalist politicians. And their methods had enabled them to win. In steel, on the other hand, the top CIO officials—who had exercised full command of the action from the start—pursued the opposite course. They not only failed to make advance preparations for union defense against strike-breaking attacks, but during the test of battle they did little more than plead with their capitalist political "allies" for help against such assaults. That bankrupt policy caused the fight in steel to be lost, and the defeat thrust the combat momentum of the workers generally back into low gear.

This adverse development had to be taken into account by the Socialist Workers Party in reappraising its tactical line. Earlier, the possibility had been left open that the working class might be able to make a direct leap to revolutionary politics, skipping the reformist political stage. Among the considerations involved was anticipation of fierce capitalist resistance to the CIO. That had now come about, at least in the steel industry, and Roosevelt's conduct during the clash had presented compelling evidence of the need for the workers to break with capitalist politics and form their own mass party. Unfortunately, though, the revolutionary socialists were not strong enough in numbers to intervene effectively in the conflict, either during or after the Little Steel strike. Consequently, the defeat suffered by the workers had only negative political effects. It caused a loss of class-struggle momentum in the industrial sphere, which contributed significantly to the blocking of labor's political radicalization.

During the same general period, working-class setbacks abroad were also having untoward effects in this country. Promising revolutionary situations, such as those that had arisen in France and Spain, were being scuttled by the Browders and Thomases, the Lewises and Tobins of Western Europe. Workers in the United States were thus deprived of the inspiration that victorious revolutions across the Atlantic would have imparted to them. If labor breakthroughs of the kind had actually occurred, workers here would surely have been further impelled toward their own independent political course as a class, despite episodic defeats in trade-union struggles.

As matters stood, however, the labor upsurge had been held within the confines of pure-and-simple trade-union action. Sporadic struggles over immediate issues continued, but at a greatly reduced tempo and under the increasingly firm control of the bureaucratic hierarchies in the CIO and AFL.

Another basic factor contributing to this outcome was the capitalists' ability as a class to make a concession here and there to the masses. That was the cheapest and safest course for them, since they could not be sure of the outcome if they tried to suppress the entire labor upsurge by force and violence. Within certain limits, moreover, they had enough fat on their corporate bones to take such steps without cutting too seriously into their profit margins. Acting on such premises, the ruling class allowed Roosevelt to put through restricted "social security" measures as a gesture to the masses in general; and in industrial conflicts the bosses yielded to their employees on some points, giving up no more than was absolutely necessary.

Without such concessions, stingy though they were, the capitalists would have been hard put to hold the masses in check very long. The slowdown in the class struggle after the CIO defeat in

Little Steel would in that case have been short-lived, soon to be followed by another general upsurge. But with union demands being met to a limited extent by the ruling class, it became possible to perpetuate illusions that the workers could eventually solve their problems through piecemeal reforms under the existing system. That, in turn, enabled Roosevelt's lackeys within the labor movement to prevent a working-class advance toward a revolutionary political course and keep the trade unions tied to capitalist politics.

Foremost among these misleaders of labor—in terms of the key positions they occupied—were the business-unionist type of bureaucrats, who officially presided over the existing mass organizations of the workers. With rare exceptions, they were hesitant to use even the elementary weapon of economic strikes, to say nothing of challenging the boss class politically. Consequently, the union ranks were to a large degree prevented from addressing the capitalists in the only language they understood, the language of power.

John L. Lewis, for example, did little more in this respect than accommodate himself to mass actions thrust upon him by the insurgent CIO ranks. After the 1937 fight with General Motors, for example, he opposed further resort to sit-down strikes. It is also important to recall that he took a leading part in quickly tying the new-born CIO to political support for Roosevelt and the Democratic Party. To reinforce his capacity to impose the policies of business unionism, Lewis postponed until October 1938 the holding of a constitutional convention of the CIO. That is, it took place only after things had been rigged so as to assure bureaucratic control over the organization.

Although the business unionists had been able to retain official domination over the workers' mass organizations during the upsurge of the class struggle, they had needed major assistance from misleaders in the radical movement in order to do so. Backing of the kind had come mainly from two distinct tendencies, the Stalinists and the social democrats. These tendencies were distinguishable primarily in the sense that they served different agencies. The Stalinists, of course, were obedient to Kremlin dictates. The social democrats, on the other hand, were Stalinophobes who nurtured such hostility toward the Soviet Union that they usually acted as sympathizers of its opponents, including the U.S. imperialists. Both of these groupings, however, had become reformists to their bones, which enabled them to cooperate, more or less, in helping the business unionists put over their class-collaborationist political line.

The extreme right wing of the social democrats had split from the Socialist Party late in 1935 when the young militants, who were later to become Trotskyists, began to join the party in growing numbers. The splitters then formed the Social Democratic Federation, which quickly became an outright supporter of Roosevelt. Those social democrats who remained in the SP maintained formal opposition to the Democratic Party by running Norman Thomas for president. But their stance was largely a fraud. In the last analysis they, too, were reformists in their basic outlook. That was shown, for example, by the way in which members of both the Thomas group and the SDF became integrated into the trade-union bureaucracy.

A parallel course of cooperation with the business unionists was followed by the Stalinists. When the CIO upsurge began, the Communist Party had significant worker cadres, along with numbers of students and intellectuals, with which to intervene nationally in the new movement. It also had a daily paper at its disposal, as well as a battery of organizers and political agitators. Using this machine, the Stalinists approached the radicalizing workers in the guise of left-wingers, and they got a substantial response. Such acceptance was due in no small part to their relationship with the Soviet Union, which had the respect of many workers. These factors enabled the CP to recruit extensively and build up substantial formations within the CIO. So strong was its foothold, in fact, that constructive use of the advantage could in all likelihood have led to creation of a mass revolutionary party.

Stalinism being what it is, however, that influence was used to corrupt honest trade-union militants and to disorient the workers. Such a course naturally helped the CP gain favor among the top CIO bureaucrats, including Lewis, who allowed it to dominate restricted sections of the organization. Taking devious advantage of this opportunity, the Stalinists proceeded to pump their people's front poison into the industrial-union movement.

According to their gospel, the country had suddenly become polarized along nonclass political lines between "progressives" and "reactionaries." To serve "progress," they urged labor to support Roosevelt in both his domestic policies and his preparations for war. On top of that, they urged that the incumbent president be perpetuated in office. At the 1938 CIO convention, for instance, the Stalinist delegates introduced a resolution to put the union on record—two years in advance of the 1940 presidential election—in favor of a third term for the arrogant patrician who had publicly sneered at the steel workers. That proved to be too much for Lewis, who at least wanted to use the affair as a bargaining point in dealing with Roosevelt. As presiding officer, Lewis simply ruled the Stalinist resolution out of order.

Viewing the situation as a whole, a combination of factors—ranging from capitalist economic and social concessions to misleadership and outright treachery in the workers' movement—had operated to keep trade-union policy within the norms of class collaborationism. Independent labor political action had been blocked, and the working class remained entrapped in capitalist politics, primarily through the Democratic Party. Everything had been neatly handled by the ruling powers and their reformist lackeys. Everything, that is, except basic flaws in the nation's social fabric, which continued to cause mass discontent and generate struggle moods.

In mid-1937, around the time the strike in Little Steel was broken, another economic downturn set in. Within a few months the slump in industrial production reached a low point close to that of the preceding crisis. Millions lost their jobs, many for at least the second time in the decade, and material gains achieved through trade-union action were largely wiped out. Events themselves had demonstrated anew that purely economic struggles were not adequate for the solution of even the most immediate problems facing the workers.

Roosevelt's action in the face of the new crisis provided a further lesson. This time there was no pretense of taking exceptional measures to alleviate the plight of the jobless. Instead, federal appropriations for public relief were held down, as though stable employment existed. At the same time, government spending for military hardware was increased, using the pretext that it would stimulate industry and provide jobs. The reality was that economic improvements resulting from increased arms production would be merely a by-product of the main capitalist objective, which was to gear the country for war.

Parallel with the military buildup, measures were initiated through both the legislative and executive branches of government to provide more extensive means for repressing opposition to ruling-class policy. Among other things, this meant that power generated by the working class through the trade unions would now be stymied in new, subtle ways, thanks to the capitalists' unchallenged control over the governmental apparatus.

These overtones of the 1937-38 economic slump caused many workers to revise their political views. This was especially true within the CIO, where rank-and-file sentiment for the creation of a labor party began to mount. Evidence was thus accumulating of growing opposition to the narrow concepts of business union-ism, which meant that prospects for expansion of revolutionary influence within the mass movement were getting brighter.

To intervene effectively, however, it was clear that the Socialist Workers Party would have to modify its tactical lines on the labor party question. To meet that need, consideration of the required adjustments was initiated in the spring of 1938, when a delega-tion of SWP leaders—Jim Cannon, Ray Dunne, and Max Shachtman—discussed the subject with Leon Trotsky. The talks were held in Mexico where he then lived.

First on the agenda was a reevaluation of the course followed up to that point in the labor upsurge. As Trotsky noted, it had been correct at an earlier stage not to favor development of a national labor party, with the reformist connotations that would be involved. It had not been clear then just how the process of radicalization would unfold concretely, and the relatively swift organization of a mass revolutionary party had not been ex-cluded as a theoretical possibility. But subsequent events had shown that two interrelated factors served to prevent such a development: the CIO movement had arisen with unanticipated rapidity and power; and the revolutionary party had not been able to recruit CIO militants at the rate and on the scale needed to gain effective leadership influence among the mass of indus-trial workers.

This disproportion—between the growth rate of the trade unions on one side and that of the revolutionary movement on the other—had given rise to the need for a turn in policy. The vanguard was simply too weak numerically to guide the CIO directly onto the revolutionary political road. It was necessary, therefore, to make a detour. The time had come to support the development of a more elementary form of independent working-class political action, namely, formation of a labor party based on the trade unions.

A change of this kind did not signify any modification of basic principles. Whether or not to advocate formation of a labor party was merely a tactical question, which could be decided either way, as the concrete political situation dictated. Such flexibility in tactics was both permissible and advisable, so long as a fundamental requirement was met: the action taken had to serve revolutionary strategy. That is, it had to lead in the direction of a working-class struggle for power. So the SWP was careful from the outset to stress the need for adoption of an anticapitalist program by the proposed labor party.

At the same time it was recognized that a party based on the trade unions would most likely assume reformist colorations in the first phase of its existence. In that case, political radicalization of the working class would have to develop over two stages. An organizational break with the capitalist parties would first have to be accomplished, and then—after the workers had created their own party—a campaign could be waged to revolutionize its program.

Even though reformist illusions could be expected to predominate when a national labor party first appeared, the very existence of such a movement would in itself represent an implicitly anticapitalist development. For one thing, the latter characteristic would be a natural consequence of the party's working-class composition. In addition, organized labor would begin to act in a more unified manner and on a higher plane. The workers would start to generalize their needs in a systematic way and direct their demands in political form at the capitalist class as a whole. That step would not only constitute a meaningful advance beyond pure-and-simple trade unionism; it would also create receptivity to revolutionary policies, which would be oriented toward a working-class struggle for governmental control in order to reorganize society on a socialist basis.

For those reasons, the SWP concluded that questions of program should not be made a decisive criterion for support of a labor party during its formative phase. The main thing at the start was to promote a trade-union break with the capitalist political machine. Therefore, it was decided that the minimum requisites for support of labor candidates on the electoral arena would be that they represent a significant part of the working class and that their campaigns in no way be tied in with capitalist politics. Given the fulfillment of those requirements, labor representatives running for public office would be backed, as against their Democratic and Republican opponents.

In shaping this policy, note was taken of the conditional aspects of such support where matters of program were concerned. Reformist shortcomings in the platforms of labor candidates had to be openly criticized in a fraternal tone, and it was necessary to counterpose a programmatic line based on a class-struggle outlook.

Objectives of this nature could be achieved during the formative period through critical support of labor candidates. But once a labor party was established, new complications had to be expected. These could range from reformist blocs with capitalist politicians to right-wing attacks on revolutionary supporters of the new mass party. Such developments were bound to produce internal polarizations. In that case revolutionaries would back the more progressive tendencies within the party. In doing so, however, the half-way character of the progressives' political development would be criticized in an effort to help them advance toward a rounded class-struggle outlook.

Close attention would have to be paid to the problem of maintaining trade-union hegemony within the labor party. Otherwise the reformist bureaucrats would gang up with liberal politicians to usurp dictatorial control over the movement, so as to use it in ways that harmed the working class. If that happened, the organization would remain a labor party in composition only. In practice, it would come to act more and more like a capitalist party with respect to policies the bureaucrats sought to carry out.

In combating these possible trends to the right, the revolutionary party would most likely have to enter the electoral arena in its own name and for its own purposes on some occasions. It followed that, once a labor party had become a living reality, need for changes in the policy of critical support would arise. Situations could be expected to develop in which the SWP would run either a partial or full slate of candidates for public office despite the existence of a labor ticket. In that way questions of program could be more effectively stressed, and matters related to the issue of workers' democracy could be brought out into the open.

On a related point, concerning direct revolutionary activity within a labor party, it was decided that SWP members could join such a movement as individuals wherever the step appeared to be in order.

A somewhat different aspect of the general problem was also considered. It can be expected that once the conscious reformists have been forced into the framework of an independent labor party, they would attempt—on the basis of their bankrupt line—to substitute electoral action for all other kinds of mass opposition to capitalist policy. Such a caper would have to be resisted by counterposing the need to synthesize the parliamentary and extra-parliamentary forms of activity. Each of these forms would need to be used so as to give increased vigor to the other on an interacting basis. In that way an advance toward the overturn of capitalist rule could be developed to the point where the workers and their allies would be ready to launch an all-out fight for power.

During that unfolding process an organized left wing, polarized initially around immediate issues in the class struggle, could grow quite rapidly. Under the impact of experiences in class conflicts, members of that broad left wing could in numerous instances evolve toward understanding and accepting the full socialist program. Finally, in one or another organizational form, determined by the specific circumstances, a mass revolutionary party could be built. Then, and only then, would the insurgent millions have developed a leadership formation capable of guiding them into decisive revolutionary action to abolish the outlived capitalist system.

Such were the general lines along which the Socialist Workers Party leadership, acting in consultation with Trotsky, shaped tentative proposals for a change in tactics on the labor party question. After that preliminary work had been done, the recommendations were submitted for internal party discussion. Then, following deliberation of the matter for a considerable time, a referendum was taken in the fall of 1938. Some party members voted against the policy change, mistakenly believing it unprincipled to call for the formation of any party but a revolutionary party. However, the revised tactical course was approved by a substantial majority, and advocacy of a national labor party based on the trade unions became official SWP policy.

Shortly after the new tactical course was ratified, the SWP's appraisal of changing mass attitudes was confirmed in a quite dramatic way. This took place in the November 1938 elections, which involved congressional and state posts. Throughout the northern strip of states, where the main CIO forces were concentrated, New Dealers were turned out of office. Nationally the Democrats lost twelve governorships, eight posts in the U.S. Senate, and about eighty congressional seats.

Just two years before, in the 1936 presidential elections, the Roosevelt party had rolled up an unprecedented majority. Now the New Deal wave was breaking up on the rocks of social crisis.

Scourged by poverty, insecurity, unemployment, and the threat of war, the masses were becoming disillusioned with the faker who presided in Washington. The millions without jobs could see no merit in his policies, and neither could many others who had employment of a kind. Those in the trade-union ranks who still supported New Deal candidates usually did so in a rather passive manner, showing little enthusiasm about it.

If a mass party of labor had existed nationally, and if it had offered a positive alternative to Roosevelt's line, it would no doubt have gotten heavy support at the polls in 1938. But as matters stood there was no alternative of this kind toward which the voters could turn. So the Republicans became beneficiaries of the widespread discontent, garnering support that was in many cases thrown their way simply as a means of expressing dissatisfaction with current governmental policy. There could be no other realistic explanation of the sharp rise in the Republican vote, since no basis existed for assuming a general turn toward confidence in the party of Herbert Hoover, who had been president when the depression first struck the country.

It was in these same elections that the Farmer-Labor Party— which the Stalinist-Benson clique had identified with the New Deal—lost the governship to the Republicans in Minnesota. That particular debacle caused factional warfare inside the FLP to grow increasingly bitter. Before describing that situation, however, an account should be given of new antilabor moves by the capitalists that were to further intensify the class struggle throughout the state.

RULING-CLASS OFFENSIVE

Local 544's Union Defense Guard: "This situation called for prompt countermeasures. So Local 544, acting with customary decisiveness, answered the threat by organizing a union defense guard during August 1938."

10. Fink Suit

When the national economy again began to slump in mid-1937, the employers sought to use the changed situation as the basis for an offensive against organized labor. Their immediate aim was to thrust the main burden of the new crisis upon the workers. They felt emboldened in that course because the downturn in production tended to blunt somewhat the combativity of the trade-union ranks.

In Minneapolis this antilabor drive was directed by the Associated Industries, a capitalist organization that had replaced the hated Citizens Alliance in January 1937. The central target was General Drivers Union, Local 544. It was singled out because it constituted a labor powerhouse that imparted strength to all the city's trade unions and to Teamster locals throughout the region. The capitalists wanted desperately to weaken Local 544 so as to undermine the fighting capacity of those unions.

They were confident, moreover, that they had gained a political edge over labor. George E. Leach, a Republican, had just been elected mayor of the city, replacing a Farmer-Laborite. This gave the ruling class more direct control over the local government and greater facility in using it for antiunion purposes.

Instead of precipitating a head-on clash, the Associated Industries began the offensive with a flanking move. When Local 544's contracts came up for renewal in the summer of 1937, the trucking bosses stalled in the negotiations. Meanwhile, their counterparts in next-door St. Paul sought to impose cut-rate settlement terms on the weaker Teamster Local 120 in that city. The bosses appeared to anticipate that a basis could thereby be laid to hold down wages in Minneapolis, which would represent a victory over the strong Teamster movement there.

Local 544 upset their scheme by striking one segment of the

trucking employers and dangling the threat of an expanded walkout over the others. In that way it was able to force through contract renewals setting new highs in wage scales. This accomplishment inspired Local 120, in turn, to go on strike for comparable pay rates. Local 544 gave all-out support to the St. Paul union, and its fight was won as well.

Thus the plot hatched by the Associated Industries died aborning. Instead of losing ground, the Minneapolis Teamsters Joint Council, of which Local 544 was a part, continued to make gains for an increasing number of workers. By the year's end it reported a membership of well over 17,000. Its official organ, the *Northwest Organizer,* had expanded its readership at an even faster rate, having attained a circulation of some 27,000. At the same time, fresh impetus had been imparted to the Teamsters' expansion drive throughout the area; and during 1938 the IBT won a uniform, eleven-state contract for over-the-road drivers.

The latter achievement was especially significant. At that time the labor movement had been more or less thrust on the defensive because of the recurrence of deep economic depression. In those circumstances the sweeping over-the-road victory dramatically illustrated the unusual nature of the rise in Teamster power, a development that had resulted primarily from class-struggle concepts introduced into the movement by the Trotskyists.

While such gains were being registered, however, Local 544 also had to fight almost continuously to preserve its strength. At every opportunity the Minneapolis ruling class moved viciously to deal blows to the unions, and it didn't take long for the next one to fall.

On November 17, 1937, Patrick J. Corcoran, head of the Minneapolis Teamsters Joint Council, was brutally murdered by unknown assailants. The capitalist press launched an insidious propaganda campaign seeking to link Pat's death with alleged "gangsterism and racketeering" in the labor movement. The aim was to sow division and demoralization in the movement and, if possible, to contrive a legal frame-up against the leaders of Local 544.

Abetting the boss class for their own factional reasons, the Stalinists joined in the smear attempt. The November 23, 1937, issue of their paper, the *Daily Worker,* carried a story falsely asserting that within the city there was "rising popular indignation against disclosures that racketeering and gangsterism imported into the labor movement here and linked with the Trotsky-ites in the leadership of the Drivers Union has been at the root of the killing."

Lies and slanders of the kind spread by the capitalists and echoed by the Stalinists were emphatically repudiated in trade-union circles. The Board of Union Business Agents, representing the city's entire AFL movement, adopted a resolution that declared: "Every attempt to attribute the murder of Corcoran to forces inside the labor movement . . . constitutes a foul slander on the bona-fide labor movement and its martyred officer, and shields the real murderers and the dark forces behind them."

Having failed in their cynical attempt to use Pat's tragedy as a device to get the workers fighting among themselves, the bosses eased up in their propaganda offensive around that issue. But as Miles Dunne (who replaced Corcoran in office) pointed out, it was necessary for labor to close ranks because a new, determined employer fight against the unions could be expected.

His prediction was soon borne out. On February 16, 1938, a suit was filed in district court against the officers of Local 544 by five alleged members of the organization.

They charged that the union officials imposed unauthorized fines upon the membership, made unauthorized expenditures, appropriated large sums of money for their own use, paid themselves exorbitant salaries, gave no accounting of their handling of union finances, and intimidated the rank and file. On policy issues, they claimed that unemployment relief had been secured from the city for undeserving people and that the union had conspired in restraint of trade.

The court was asked to tie up Local 544's funds, supervise a financial accounting, appoint a receiver to take over the union, ban "illegal" picketing, and proscribe actions that "intimidate and coerce non-union drivers and owners."

As can be seen, the stand taken on matters of policy was utterly alien to trade unionism. So the action quickly became known throughout the labor movement as the "fink suit."

All the plaintiffs—John M. Asplund, Edward Corbett, Robert Fischer, John D. Ryan, and Adolph Svenddal—were individual owner-operators of trucks. During the depression, the auto corporations sought to promote sales by urging workers to purchase a rig, as a means of buying themselves a job. This stimulated the rise of the owner-operator category. The trend was given further impetus by trucking firms that found it profitable in many cases to hire owner-operators rather than rely entirely upon use of their own fleets. This type of operation had assumed major dimensions in the industry, and it presented a problem to the IBT.

The big trucking outfits sought to feed illusions that owner-operators could eventually become small fleet owners, provided they looked upon themselves as part of the business. The employers' object, of course, was primarily to pit such individuals against the fleet drivers in an effort to prevent unionization of the work force. If the move was to be blocked, a counter strategy based on the realities of the situation was needed.

Local 544 had met the threat by developing a special tactic concerning owner-operators. Those owning one truck, who did their own driving, were approached as fellow workers and asked to join the organization. Local 544 helped them secure union pay as drivers, plus the cost of operation of their equipment. Since the response was good, a special unit was set up in the local for these individuals, known as the independent truck-owners section. Significant progress was made thereafter in defending the interests of this category of drivers, who became good union members; but as the fink suit showed, the bosses were still able to find some among them who could be used as tools.

Once the suit had been filed, a quick check was made to determine the membership standing of the plaintiffs. It was found that four had recently come to the union office and prepaid monthly dues for a considerable period so as to create an appearance of membership in good standing. The fifth plaintiff, Ryan, had no claim whatever to union membership when the court action was instituted.

It was soon learned, moreover, that all five were members of a so-called Minnesota Mutual Truck Owners Association, Local 1. That outfit, in turn, was part of a broader structure known as the "Associated Council of Independent Unions." The chief organizers of this company-union layout were F. L. Taylor and E. T. Lee, a pair of rightist political adventurers. They got out a paper, *Independent Labor News,* which proclaimed it was "Dedicated to co-operation between labor and business, and employee and employer." What that meant was shown by the pincers movement "Local 1" was undertaking against Local 544, seeking to raid its independent truck-owners section on the one hand and dragging the union's officers into court on the other.

Behind all this stood the Associated Industries, which was obviously financing the whole thing. The finks were represented, for instance, by Arthur H. Anderson, an expensive lawyer often used by the employers. Further evidence as to the real authors of the attack was soon contributed by Mayor Leach. He admitted publicly, as reported in the February 24, 1938, *Northwest Organizer* that he had talked about the case "when men with union cards and small truck owners have come to my office."

Having failed to undermine Local 544 through other forms of attack, the bosses were now trying to disrupt it by means of a contrived internal dispute. They hoped to reap several benefits from the effort. The specific objectives were to paralyze the union financially, gain access to its membership lists, lay hold of minutes and other important data, cripple the organization's fighting power, and in the process set a precedent whereby judges could remove officers from any union and replace them with court appointees. By making an alleged financial scandal central to the attack, the capitalist strategists were plainly seeking to revive the smear campaign about "racketeering." This was evidently being done both to conceal their real aims and, if possible, to alienate the union's allies from it.

So far as an examination of the union's accounts was concerned, there was nothing to hide. All its transactions had been made for legitimate purposes. Regular financial reports had been given at general membership meetings. In short, there had been nothing shady about the handling of any aspect of the organization's affairs.

But that wasn't the fundamental issue involved. The suit cut across the principle that only trade unionists should be allowed to look at the union's records. Members of a boss-sponsored rival movement, who masqueraded as loyal members of Local 544, were now seeking an accounting for antilabor purposes. A vigorous effort had to be made to fight them off in order to show that boss agents couldn't gain easy access to internal union information. Otherwise the process could be repeated again and again, keeping the local in a state of constant turmoil and setting a precedent for easy attacks on other trade unions.

These considerations were quickly grasped by AFL members throughout the city. Both the Teamsters Joint Council and the Central Labor Union voted unanimously to back Local 544 and to provide help in retaining legal counsel. From then on the union's

case was handled by three experienced labor lawyers: Gilbert
Carlson, John Goldie, and Tom Kochelmocker.

Preparations for a vigorous defense campaign had been completed none too soon. Before long a move was made by Anderson,
the plaintiffs' lawyer, to seize all the books and records of Local
544. He contended that he couldn't prepare his case without
access to the union's ledgers, minutes, documents, correspondence, etc. This step showed that no substantive basis had in
reality existed for the accusations made when the suit was first
filed. It also demonstrated that the legal action had been intended from the outset as a device through which to launch a
fishing expedition into the local's internal affairs.

Anderson's caper was accompanied by reports in the daily
papers that the bosses were forming a broad united front and
raising a $385,000 war chest to put over their antilabor program.
The new formation was given the innocent-sounding name of
"Minneapolis Civic Council." But the same old gang of labor
haters, who ran the Associated Industries, still had full charge of
the operation.

There could no longer be any question that a serious threat
was posed by the new ruling-class offensive, and the labor movement quickly put its defense campaign into high gear. A mass
rally was held on April 11, sponsored by the Central Labor
Union, the Building Trades Council, the Teamsters Joint Council
and the Allied Printing Trades Council. Over 12,000 workers
turned out for the affair, filling the big municipal auditorium. The
keynote was: "Make and keep Minneapolis a union town."

John Boscoe of the printers, who chaired the rally, set the tone
when he said that labor's chief aim was to smash the new open-
shop drive. Roy Wier, organizer for the Central Labor Union,
declared: "Today we're the best organized city in America." In
1933, he recalled, there were only 28,000 AFL members in the city,
whereas by 1938, the total had risen to almost 60,000; and it was
against this entire force that the boss slander about union "gangsterism and racketeering" was directed. Robley D. Cramer, editor
of the *Labor Review,* called for all-out support to Local 544,
asserting that it constituted "the shock troops of the Minneapolis
labor movement."

With labor thus mobilized, the legal battle was soon joined.
Toward the end of April the fink suit came before Judge Frank E.
Reed in district court. Local 544 argued for immediate dismissal

of the case, pointing out that it violated the rule that members of a voluntary, unincorporated association must first exhaust all avenues of relief within their own organization. The Teamsters Joint Council backed up the argument, contending that—as the appellate tribunal of Local 544—it should have been approached by the plaintiffs before they applied to the courts. The union lawyers also stressed that since the individuals bringing the suit were members of a hostile organization and had recruited for it, they could not possibly be acting in good faith.

The latter consideration alone should have convinced an impartial tribunal that the suit deserved to be thrown out. But Reed, who was a notorious labor hater, brushed aside the union contentions. He allowed the case to stand and granted the defense nothing more than a brief stay in order to prepare further argument.

At that juncture yet another tragedy struck the Teamsters. William S. Brown, the president of Local 544, was shot to death on May 25, 1938. The killing was attributed to Arnold Johnson, a member of the union staff, who confessed to the act and told where the body could be found. Brown and Johnson had worked together a good part of the time and had been close friends, so no other reason could be found for the senseless act than temporary insanity. Others on the staff recalled, in fact, that Johnson had appeared distressed at times, and he was possibly suffering from nervous strain due to tension and overwork.

A grand jury investigation followed, during which rumors were leaked to the press in a manner designed to smear the leaders of Local 544. But no basis could be found for a frame-up against others, and Johnson was finally indicted for the killing of Brown. In the trial, the prosecutor acted as though the union's executive board, not Johnson, was in the prisoner's dock. That crooked line was reflected in the newspaper accounts, day by day, until the case went to the jury. In the end, Johnson was found not guilty, the jurors apparently having accepted the defense plea that he was in a mental fog at the time of the murder. The case was thus left open for further use against the union, if the prosecutor could find an angle, but that proved to be impossible.

By this time the slanderous assault on Local 544 extended far beyond the tactics used in connection with the judicial proceedings. A new clamor to rid the labor movement of "gangsters and racketeers" was raised in the boss press. The Stalinists again

joined in the onslaught, and a preacher, Rev. George Mecklenburg of the Wesley Methodist Episcopal Church, also got into the
act.

When the union movement called Mecklenburg's hand, he
agreed to a public debate with Ray Dunne. It took place on the
preacher's turf, where the two argued the question, "Minneapolis
Labor Racketeering: Fact or Fancy?" Highlights of the confrontation were reported in the June 30 *Northwest Organizer*.

Dunne spoke first, making the following main points: "Over a
four-year period, Minneapolis employers have been forced to give
wage increases to the drivers amounting to more than five-
million dollars. Have these employers a reason to attack our
union? Some employers are desperate, they are trying to get out
from under the weight of organized labor. . . . The drive today is
being carried on under the slogan: Free the labor movement from
gangsters and racketeers. Under this guise the employers are
making the attack on unionism."

In rebuttal Mecklenburg contended: "Labor is gouging capital.
It is piracy, buccaneering. I say to labor: 'You have to take the
initiative and clean up.'"

Dunne then demanded names, dates, and facts about the so-
called "racketeering," and at that point Mecklenburg retreated
into the mumbo jumbo of the church. The information was given
to him "in the confidence of the confessional," he answered, so he
could not divulge the source.

As the propaganda offensive against Local 544 mounted in
intensity, Taylor and Lee moved to expand their company-union
activities. Attempts were made to start back-to-work movements
against strikes in the garment and woodworking industries. A
fink "Local 15" began to operate in collusion with the bosses in
the gasoline filling station field; and it was announced that the
recruitment drive of the "Independent Unions" would be
broadened to include "carpenters, plumbers, brick layers, decora-
tors, mechanics, truck owners, truck drivers, helpers, laborers."

If anything was needed to convince the whole AFL of the city
that it faced a serious threat, these developments certainly did
the trick. Other unions could see that they, too, were being set up
for fink suits. A clamor for more highly organized defensive
action resulted, and the Central Labor Union responded by forming a special committee to direct the fight against the company-
union gang.

Then, on July 28, 1938, Judge Reed issued a sweeping order against Local 544. The union was instructed to turn over everything conceivable to the attorney for the five who had sued its officers—correspondence, membership lists, financial records, executive-board minutes, etc.

The Teamsters immediately challenged Reed's decision in a public statement, which called labor's attention to the dire implications of the action. Unless the ruling was overturned, the statement emphasized, the bosses could plant stoolpigeons in any union and bring suit for a financial accounting. The result would be that the courts could give the bosses full access to every written record of the organization.

With the backing of the Central Labor Union, Reed's order was appealed to the Minnesota supreme court. That body refused to review the lower court's decision. But it did hold that, since the action was "of a comprehensive and blanket nature," Local 544 had a right to ask that the original order be modified.

Seizing upon this handle for whatever it might be worth, the union won a partial change in Reed's decision. He made a new ruling that inspection of the books and records would be held up "until such time as it appears to the trial judge that such inspection is advisable." A long period of legal maneuvering then followed before the case finally came to trial under circumstances that will be described in the next volume of this work.

During the interim, however, the Teamsters were subjected to further attacks of a no less vicious kind.

11. Silver Shirt Threat

Clashes between capital and labor in times of social crisis tend to stimulate activity among political demagogues with a fascist mentality. They anticipate that intensification of the class struggle will cause sections of the ruling class to turn away from parliamentary democracy and its methods of rule, and resort to fascism as the way to hold on to state power and protect special privilege. Each of the aspirants hopes, moreover, to be chosen as the "fuehrer" to lead the terrorist movement needed for the murderous assault on the working class that accompanies such a turn in policy.

Several of these would-be Hitlers had, in fact, come forward in this country in the early 1930s, but they made little headway in the period marked by the stormy rise of the CIO. Then, during 1937-38, the situation began to change. A second deep economic slump developed, marking the collapse of Roosevelt's New Deal. Social contradictions in general grew sharper, as the ruling class prepared to plunge the country into the impending imperialist war. The bureaucratic misleaders in the trade unions failed to guide the workers toward a meaningful course for coping with difficulties caused by these developments—formation of an independent labor party. And in those circumstances significant numbers of demoralized middle-class elements in the cities, impoverished farmers, and to a certain extent unemployed workers fell prey to ultraright hucksters.

As a result various profascist groups that had sprung up earlier began to recruit quite rapidly, and they received a parallel increase in financial backing from wealthy antilabor interests. Emboldened by this new support, they became more aggressive, as well as more provocative. In some instances these outfits organized uniformed bands of storm troopers, which were drilled openly; and whether uniformed or not, thugs of that type were mobilized to launch terror campaigns, initially directed at the most vulnerable targets, but aimed basically at organized labor.

Jewish people were among the first to be attacked. As in Nazi Germany, they were made scapegoats in an effort to intensify anti-Semitic prejudices against them, the primary object being to sow division in the working class. But they weren't the only victims.

Lone worker-militants were waylaid and beaten in New York and other eastern cities. Street meetings of left-wing groups were broken up. In Jersey City the notorious Mayor Frank Hague engineered hoodlum assaults on union meetings and picket lines; and in New Orleans a Teamster strike was crushed by vigilantes. As the latter events showed, the ultraright forces that were engaged in these terrorist acts on behalf of the capitalists were rapidly zeroing in on their main target—the mass organizations of the working class.

One of these profascist groups, the Silver Shirts of America, was of special concern to General Drivers Union, Local 544. It was started in 1932 by William Dudley Pelley, who opened a headquarters in Asheville, North Carolina, and published a weekly organ called *Liberation*. Tacitly conceding jurisdiction over the major cities to other ultrarightists, Pelley centered his efforts on the towns and countryside of the farming areas. Although little was achieved in that sphere during the first years, the Silver Shirts had at last begun to make gains.

Apparently this caused a section of the boss class in Minneapolis to become interested in the movement; and Pelley was encouraged to send one of his aides, Roy Zachary, to the city in the summer of 1938 to launch an organizing drive. Two Silver Shirt rallies followed in quick succession, on July 29 and August 2, at the Royal Arcanum hall. These affairs were closed to the public, admission being by invitation only.

Despite the secrecy, the Teamsters hád gotten wind of Zachary's arrival in town and had kept him under close scrutiny. Knowledge of the planned rallies was gained beforehand, making it possible to arrange a way to get reliable intelligence as to what happened.

Thus it became known immediately that Zachary's main theme had been to call for a vigilante attack on the headquarters of Local 544.

It was also learned that literature was passed out at both

meetings inviting the participants to join F.L. Taylor's "Associated Council of Independent Unions." Taylor, by the way, had already shown his fascist inclinations a few weeks earlier when he set out to form a vigilante force under the name "Minnesota Minute Men." So it was perfectly natural for him to hook up with the Silver Shirts when they moved in.

A short time later another ominous fact was revealed by Rabbi Gordon, a religious opponent of fascism, who had also been keeping track of Zachary's doings. Gordon announced that George K. Belden, head of the Associated Industries, had attended both Silver Shirt rallies. When questioned about this by the press, Belden told a reporter for the *Minnesota Leader:* "I am in sympathy with getting rid of racketeers. . . ."

Taken as a whole, these developments added up to a dire threat against the Teamsters. The fink union, which had dragged Local 544 into court, was now tied in with the Silver Shirts; Belden's role showed that the employers were directly involved in the new antiunion plot; and talk of an armed raid on the Teamster headquarters was in the air.

This situation called for prompt countermeasures. So Local 544, acting with its customary decisiveness, answered the threat by organizing a union defense guard during August 1938.

Formation of the guard was reported in the *Northwest Organizer,* and a press release announcing the step was handed to the daily papers, which gave it prominent mention. The new body's functions were described in the report as "defense of the union's picket lines, headquarters and members against anti-labor violence." Through this action the local served public notice that it would take care of its own defense, putting no misplaced reliance on the police for protection.

The union leaders were fully aware that capitalist politicians in seats of power not only tend to wink at fascist hooliganism; they often encourage and abet such extralegal attacks on workers. Not only that. Their minions, the police, condone and protect fascist activities, become members of such movements and, when open violence is used against the trade unions, usually look the other way. Such had been the conduct of capitalist "forces of law and order" in Germany, Italy, and other places; history taught that the situation would be no different in the United States.

An iron necessity was thus imposed upon the workers. If they were to defend themselves, they had to use their own organizations for the purpose. In that respect Local 544's pioneer action in forming a union defense guard not only served its own needs; the step blazed a trail for trade unionists everywhere in the country.

Conceptually, the guard was not envisaged as the narrow formation of a single union. It was viewed rather as the nucleus around which to build the broadest possible united defense movement. From the outset, efforts were made to involve other unions in the project. It was expected that time and events could also make it possible to extend the united front to include the unemployed, minority peoples, youth—all potential victims of the fascists, vigilantes, or other reactionaries.

For these reasons the defense formation was not made an official part of Local 544. Instead, it was initiated by leading members of the local, acting with the approval of the general membership. A spontaneous recruitment process was set into motion through a series of meetings with groups of workers. In this way the main base of the guard was quickly established by the General Drivers; and after that its ranks were gradually extended to include members of other unions in the city that approved the idea.

The guard was in no sense an elite body. It was simply a businesslike formation open to any active union member. The only requirements for inclusion in its ranks were readiness to defend the unions from attack, willingness to take the necessary training for that purpose, and acceptance of the democratic discipline required in a combat unit. Moreover, its activities were conducted only with the consent of the membership of the trade unions involved, and under their control.

As in the case of Local 544 itself, the guard functioned democratically in its internal affairs. Steps taken to carry out its assigned tasks were decided through open discussion and majority vote. This procedure was also used in selecting leaders who were to have command authority during any combat.

Ray Rainbolt of the Local 544 staff was elected commander in chief of the defense formation. He had impressive credentials. Besides his extensive know-how in leading trade-union struggles, he had acquired considerable military knowledge during earlier hitches in the U.S. army.

Those chosen as lower-ranking officers had likewise proven themselves in the class struggle and won recognition as secondary union leaders. Similarly, in the case of the guard's rank and file, all had been battle tested to one extent or another in strike actions. Taking the body as a whole, there were numerous military veterans with various abilities developed in the armed forces. Among them were former sharpshooters, machine gunners, tank operators, and so on. Quite a few had been noncommissioned officers. One had been a signal corps officer and still another an officer in the German army.

Structurally, the body was divided into small units to facilitate rapid mobilization in the event of a surprise attack on the union movement. Squads of five were the norm, with a member of each squad being designated captain. In a relatively short time the force thus organized was built up to about 600.

Members of the guard were issued small lapel emblems bearing the legend "544 UDG," which they were encouraged to wear at all times. When on duty they used large armbands prominently marked "544 Union Defense Guard" to identify themselves. This designation was readily accepted by those from other unions who were part of the formation, because they realized that use of the prestigious number 544 gave the name added meaning.

The organization raised its own funds—for purchases of equipment and to meet general expenses—by sponsoring dances and other social affairs. Part of this money was used to buy two .22 caliber target pistols and two .22 caliber rifles to give guard members a way to improve their ability to shoot straight. Regular practice sessions were then held for that purpose. In addition, periodic drills were scheduled to provide training in defensive tactics.

Members of the guard were not armed by the unions, since in the given circumstances that would have made them vulnerable to police frame-ups. But many of them had guns of their own at home, which were used to hunt game; and those could quickly have been picked up if needed to fight off an armed attack by Silver Shirt thugs.

At the drill sessions, lectures were given on tactics used in the past by antilabor vigilantes in this country and fascists abroad. Discussions were then held to work out defensive measures to meet attacks of the kind.

An intelligence department was also set up. Its task was to keep a lookout for fascist and anti-Semitic literature and activities, fink propaganda, and the like. One particular episode graphically illustrated the breadth of the intelligence arm, as well as the guard's effectiveness in action. It came about when the Silver Shirts attempted to hold another rally, to be addressed by Pelley himself.

On the day of the scheduled affair a cab driver delivered Pelley to a residence in the city's silk-stocking district. The driver immediately reported this to Rainbolt, who telephoned the place and warned that Pelley would run into trouble if he went ahead. To show he was not bluffing, Rainbolt led a section of the union guard to Calhoun Hall, where the rally was to be held that night. Arrival of the union forces caused the audience to leave in a hurry, and the demagogue never did show up. Then, around midnight, another cab driver called Rainbolt to report that he had just dumped Pelley at the Milwaukee depot in time to catch a night train to Chicago.

Following that incident the Teamsters took a step calculated to throw a further scare into the would-be union busters. It came in the form of a special notice printed on the front page of the *Northwest Organizer* of September 29, 1938. The notice instructed all captains of the defense guard to have their squads up to full strength forthwith and to be prepared to mobilize them, ready for action, on short notice.

The move seemed to have the desired effect, for the Silver Shirts transferred their next meeting to the neighboring city of St. Paul. It was held on October 28 at the Minnehaha Hall, and the place was well guarded by cops. Zachary was the main speaker. As reported in the newspapers the next morning, he boasted:

"Leaders of 544 have said we cannot hold meetings in Minneapolis, but we shall hold them, with the aid of the police. The police know that some day they'll need our support and that's why they're supporting us now."

Zachary's line was taken seriously by the Teamsters for several reasons. More could have been involved in the St. Paul affair than a mere effort to boost the sagging morale of the profascist elements by holding a successful meeting. Part of the scheme could also have been to bring pressure upon the Minneapolis authorities to provide them with comparable police protection in that city as well. If so, Associated Industries was in all likelihood involved in the maneuver.

Acting on such assumptions, the high command of the union

defense guard decided to put on a public show of force. The aim was twofold: to make it plain to one and all that the Silver Shirts were not going to operate in Minneapolis without a serious fight and, simultaneously, to test the guard's efficiency in the course of such a demonstration.

Toward those ends an emergency mobilization of the defense formation was called on one hour's notice. Only three people knew what was up. As part of the test all others were left with the impression that a real crisis had developed. By the designated assembly time, just sixty minutes after the call first went out, about 300 members of the guard had turned out ready for action— an impressive performance.

The mobilization took place on a vacant plot of land in the center of the city, so a lot of people would see what was going on. Once the men were assembled there, Rainbolt explained that it had been a practice operation to give yet another warning to the Silver Shirts and their supporters among the employers. A clinical discussion was then held about the results of the test.

Since all kinds of personal plans for the evening had been rudely upset, a bit of entertainment was in order by way of compensation. So the guard was marched in a long column— armbands prominently displayed—to a downtown burlesque theater, where a block of seats had been reserved.

As for the ultrarightists, they appeared to have gotten the union's message loud and clear. Zachary made no further attempts to hold rallies in Minneapolis; fascist propaganda tapered off; and after a time it became evident that the Silver Shirt organizing drive in the city had been discontinued altogether.

Despite this favorable turn in the situation, the union defense guard was maintained as a form of insurance against any resurgence of the fascist threat. But the nature of its activities underwent a change. Target practice and drill sessions were tapered off. Gradually the guard's functions shifted mainly to monitoring union picnics and other large social gatherings. Through occasional public displays of this kind the antilabor forces were reminded of the continued existence of the defense formation.

On balance, Local 544 had not only warded off another capitalist attack. The experience with the Silver Shirts had given

many of its members a better understanding of the need for
workers' self-defense, and the best militants had gained deeper
insight into the laws of class struggle.

*   *   *

It should be noted, however, that the internal union picture was
not entirely rosy. During this same period a new trend had arisen
in the ranks of the local, one that was to persist thereafter. Basically, its roots could be traced to the uneven development of class
consciousness within the organization.

Despite the intensity of the 1934 fight with the bosses, some
veterans of that conflict had failed to advance beyond the most
elementary trade-union outlook. Similar limitations were also to
be found among strata recruited into the local at subsequent
times. From this it followed that workers falling into such a general category would tend to hold certain basic views, positive and
negative, in common. For instance, they believed in the General
Drivers Union; they valued the power it wielded on their behalf
within industry; and they seemed to feel that a permanent means
had been established through which to achieve uninterrupted, if
gradual, improvement in their living standards.

What these workers failed to grasp was that so long as Local
544 really served their interests the bosses would keep trying to
cripple it. Therefore, when attacks on the local kept occurring,
they began to think that the cause might lie in something the
leadership was doing wrong. This meant that the malicious propaganda about "gangsterism and racketeering" was beginning to
get to them, if only subliminally. On top of that, antileadership
sentiments were encouraged by opportunists in the union, who
were looking for reasons to campaign for executive posts. In July
1938, this combination of factors led to the formation of a "Committee of 15" within the organization. A platform was issued by
the group on the basis of which candidates were run for office in
the December 1938 union elections. Two of the planks summed up
the essence of the outlook put forward. One of these directly reflected the impact of capitalist propaganda in connection with
the fink suit. It asserted:

"WE DEMAND that a representative group of rank and file
members be elected annually to constitute a control board whose
activities shall be restricted to reviewing the general policy of the

executive board, the activities of the individual members of the staff, officers and organizers or business agents in regard to organizing work, their expense accounts and the general financial management of the affairs of the Union. This board shall be considered the 'supreme court' of the Union, but shall have no power over strike action, jurisdictional decisions, collective bargaining agreements or individual grievances, but may suspend staff officers within the sixty day period preceding the annual elections."

Another key plank showed the group's sensitivity to the red-baiting that enemies of the union had repeatedly directed at its leaders. That plank declared:

"WE DEMAND that the personal political activities of all present officers be divorced from their official duties as representatives of the Local. In the past the officials in question have misused the prestige of their office and the power of their authority, together with actual negligence of routine duties in pursuit of political policies inimical to the best interests of the organization. We believe these charges to be truly self-evident on the basis of the political creed known to be professed by those involved."

If anything was "truly self-evident" it was not the red-baiting allegations, but rather what the line advocated in those planks really meant—debasement of the leadership structure into a contradictory jumble that would render the union headless, thereby undermining its fighting power; and exclusion of politically class-conscious workers from official roles, thus opening the way for a switch to "statesmanlike" collaboration with the bosses.

As against such a bankrupt course, the incumbent leadership called for continuation of the class-struggle policies and democratic internal structure through which Local 544 had developed its vitality.

Campaigns were conducted around those opposing viewpoints, after which the dispute came before the membership for decision. That step took the form of union elections, which were held on December 22-23, 1938. Five posts were involved in the contest: president, vice-president, recording secretary, secretary-treasurer, and one trustee (two of the three trustees still had unexpired terms to serve).

The "Committee of 15" ran four candidates: R.F. Hornig for president, Frank McArdle for vice-president, Harold Haynes for recording secretary, and Pete Harris for trustee. The office of secretary-treasurer was contested by Douglas Raze, who fronted for the Stalinists and had no connection with the "Committee of 15."

Officers of the union running for reelection included Carl Skoglund, president; Grant Dunne, recording secretary; Farrell Dobbs, secretary-treasurer; and Kelly Postal, trustee. The incumbent vice-president, Jack Smith, who had been an officer of former "Local 500," asked to be retired from activity due to ill health. He nominated George Frosig, who had been vice-president of former Local 574, as his replacement. The two trustees whose terms had not yet expired were Miles Dunne and Nick Wagner.

When the returns came in, the "Committee of 15's" candidates had received 32 percent of all votes cast; Raze had gotten 148 out of 1,217 ballots cast for secretary-treasurer; and the slate of Skoglund, Frosig, Grant Dunne, Dobbs, and Postal had won the election by an overall tally of about two to one.

A few months later Tobin appointed me to his staff of general organizers. Immediately thereafter, on May 8, 1939, Local 544 held a special election in which Kelly Postal was selected to replace me as secretary-treasurer, and Curt Zander was chosen to fill the trusteeship vacated by Postal.

By then the Associated Industries—having come a cropper in the Silver Shirt adventure—had opened still another assault on the union. This time the presence of a Republican at the head of the state government was used for the purpose.

12. Slave Labor Law

What happened next in Minnesota was related in a sense to legislation previously adopted at the federal level. In 1935 President Roosevelt had signed into law the Wagner Labor Relations Act, which required employers to bargain with trade unions representing a majority of their employees. This directive was not as altruistic as it might appear on the surface. Primarily, it was designed to help assure that the insurgent masses of hitherto unorganized workers would come under the domination of AFL (and later CIO) officials with a class-collaborationist outlook.

As a further means of curbing rank-and-file militancy, the law also established a National Labor Relations Board. Its key purpose was to mediate industrial conflicts, and that function was generally carried out in tricky ways that proved costly to the workers. In addition, a category termed "unfair labor practices" was introduced. Ostensibly, charges of that nature were to be directed only at the bosses, but it didn't take long in practice for such accusations to be leveled against organized labor as well.

This piece of legerdemain was hailed by trade-union bureaucrats throughout the country as "Labor's Magna Charta." Like the authors of the Wagner Act, they hoped it would enable them to steer the workers away from self-reliant action and toward dependence on the capitalist government. For similar reasons the trade-union hierarchy also backed various moves toward adoption of supplementary labor laws at the state level, which were intended to further regulate the class struggle.

In Minnesota, however, no progress had been made in passing supplementary laws, for several reasons. A strong left wing existed in the AFL, built around the powerful Minneapolis Teamsters, which had been able to block efforts by right-wing union officials to press for state laws controlling worker-employer relations. Besides that, for several years up to 1938, one or another Farmer-Labor governor had presided over the state. Such reformist politicians, being especially subject to pressure from the trade unions, couldn't afford to play around with labor laws that were strongly opposed within the AFL; and that factor had served, in turn, to deter conservative legislators from taking serious steps to initiate similar measures.

But the situation changed after Harold E. Stassen won the governorship in November 1938. Once again the employers had full control over the state's key executive post, as well as increased strength in the legislature. With that fresh advantage, they immediately proceeded to use the legislative arm of their ruling structure to fasten new legal shackles on the trade unions.

A hint of what was to come had, in fact, been given by Stassen during the election campaign. He had promised in a most demagogic way that, once in office, he would give Minnesota "the most outstanding labor relations bill in the country." At that particular juncture, one of his immediate aims had been to win support from right-wing union officials, who yearned for such a measure. As events were to show, he got more from some of them than simple help in the elections.

The proposed bill was not made public until early in March 1939, at which time it was introduced into the lower house of the legislature. The sponsors of record were H.E. Vance and Helmer Myre, who posed as representatives of farming interests. Relying on such figures as front runners, the capitalist propagandists tried to create the image of a "farm bloc" demanding stiff legislation to impose controls on the trade unions. Stassen joined in the deception by pretending that his support of the projected law resulted from strong rural pressures.

Before long, several facts came to light, showing the true score: "farmer" Myre was found to be an ex-sheriff of Albert Lea, Minnesota; actual farmers on the committee to which the bill was first sent were outnumbered nineteen to four by nonfarmers; and the formal sponsors let it slip that the Associated Industries of Minneapolis had helped draft the measure.

If any doubts remained as to who had concocted the Vance-Myre bill, those were readily cleared up by a study of the basic line. It bore the unmistakable imprint of capitalist sharpies well schooled in fighting organized labor.

The initial draft contained a clause that would outlaw the

closed shop and other forms of compulsory trade-union membership. Parallel with that, authorization would be given for the
bosses to foster company unions. They could "extend to their employees the privilege of using existing facilities including places
for meetings, bulletin space, the use of typewriters and duplicat-
ing machines, occasional stenographic assistance and other facilities."

Another set of provisions called for a "labor relations board"
with authority to regulate strikes. It would be empowered to determine the "appropriate bargaining unit," conduct secret balloting
where a strike vote was to be taken, pass judgment as to what
workers would be entitled to vote, and decide whether a true majority had approved a walkout. Strikes for union recognition
would be declared illegal, as would those called for "any other
reason than for modification of wages or other conditions of employment where the strike is to take place." None but employees
of a struck plant would be allowed to picket, and secondary boy-
cotts would be proscribed.

Echoing the fink suit against Local 544, the bill would empower
the "labor relations board" to summon any person, together with
"books, records, correspondence, documents or other evidence in
obedience to subpoena of the board."

Yet another provision was aimed directly at the Teamsters. It
would be declared an "unfair labor practice" for anyone to "interfere in any way with the movement of articles of commerce by
motor vehicles or teams upon public roads, alleys and highways
in the state."

Taken as a whole, the Vance-Myre bill constituted a serious
threat to the labor movement. An attempt was in the making to
restore the open shop in industry by legislative fiat; the workers'
right to strike was under attack, as was the principle of broad
labor solidarity in industrial conflicts; and the groundwork was
being laid for governmental intrusion into the internal affairs of
trade unions.

As the *Northwest Organizer* observed editorially: "This is the
sort of measure that an all-powerful conquering army of enemy
invaders forces down the throats of a conquered people."

It didn't take long for similar views to become widespread.
Once the details of the projected legislation were revealed,
aroused trade unionists began to speak of it as Stassen's "Slave
Labor Law." In this atmosphere the Minneapolis Teamsters took

the initiative in calling for a special statewide AFL convention to organize a campaign against the new capitalist plot. An official decision was quickly made to convene such a gathering on April 3, 1938, in St. Paul.

Help in the fight was also secured from militant farmers, who saw a threat to their own organizations in the move against labor. With financial help from the trade unions, they circulated throughout rural areas of the state to explain the real intent of the outrage being perpetrated by the Stassen administration. Their audiences proved receptive, and a heavy flow of telegrams, letters, and resolutions of protest soon poured into the offices of legislators.

As objections to the Vance-Myre bill continued to mount, it was hurriedly passed in the lower house with few changes. The vote was eighty-five to thirty-seven. That tactical advantage was then used by the capitalists as the peg for a countercampaign to split the opposition. Hints were dropped that the senate would consider "constructive" amendments to the measure, a move calculated to influence right-wingers in the trade unions. They were simultaneously being wooed and threatened. Through cooperation with the Stassen administration, it was suggested, they could secure modifications of the projected law. On the other hand, the house vote implied that, in case they fail to take such a "statesmanlike" view, Stassen had good prospects of ramming the measure through the senate in whatever form he chose.

In fact, a few amendments would not alter the bill's repressive character. It had to be rejected in every aspect if labor's interests were to be defended. But it was precisely on that point that a rub developed, resulting from the changed form in which the boss class had launched the new offensive.

When the fink suit was filed earlier against Local 544, it was generally opposed by AFL bureaucrats. They saw the move as a threat to their own positions within the trade unions; and in helping the local under attack, they were merely protecting themselves. Similarly, in the case of the Silver Shirt threat, a danger had arisen of extralegal assaults intended to cripple and, if possible, destroy labor formations. In this situation, the right-wingers had little alternative but to condone the steps taken by the Teamsters to block the move.

Matters were different when it came to legislation regulating worker-employer relations. Union officials holding class-collaborationist views not only tend to welcome laws of this kind, but they often press for them. In fact, right-wingers in the Minnesota AFL had already fashioned their own version of such a measure, which they called a "little Wagner Act." Its essential aim was to secure governmental help in dealing with the bosses, substituting that for reliance on use of the union power within industry.

That being the case, the right-wingers were not about to demand that the state government impose no controls whatever upon organized labor. They were ready, instead, to bargain with the capitalist politicians over the extent to which union activities would be regulated and, if anything, Stassen's carrot-and-club tactics made them more eager than ever to do so.

It was in those circumstances that the special convention of the AFL State Federation of Labor met on April 3. Almost eight-hundred delegates were present, an unusually heavy turnout. Speaking from the floor, many spelled out the features of the Vance-Myre bill to which they vigorously objected. Proposals were advanced to organize a mass march on the statehouse and to call a general protest strike if the bill was passed by the senate.

When the vote was taken, however, the line of the right-wing machine prevailed. As a matter of form, endorsement of the "little Wagner Act" was first reiterated. Then the main decision was rammed through. The federation officers were instructed "to press for amendments in the Senate which will eliminate . . . objectionable features [of the Vance-Myre bill] and bring about enactment of an equitable labor relations Act."

Following the special AFL convention, the senate made a few concessions to trade-union criticisms before passing the Stassen-backed measure in its final form on April 19. But it remained a viciously antilabor device, as a sketch of the main provisions will show.

No one could be compelled to join a labor organization.

Strikes in violation of a working agreement with an employer were declared an "unfair labor practice." In the walkouts that were to be permitted, a majority of those engaged in picketing had to be employees of the struck firm. At plants where no strike was in progress, protest actions could not involve more than one picket at each entrance. Sit-down strikes were banned outright.

In all cases, unions had to give ten days' advance notice of a desire to negotiate with the employers. Another ten days' notice was then required if the workers decided to go on strike, which made a total of twenty days before a walkout could begin. That, of course, gave the bosses time to prepare strikebreaking measures.

The governor was to appoint a state labor conciliator to mediate worker-employer disputes. If the conciliator decided that an industrial conflict was "affected with a public interest," the governor was to name a commission of three to investigate the matter. Hearings were then to be held by the commission, and that body had thirty days in which to make a public report on the controversy. During the thirty-day "waiting period" the union was forbidden to strike.

It was declared unlawful to interfere with "free and uninterrupted use of public roads" or to obstruct "ingress to and egress from" any place of business. An even more specific stricture was included to protect scab trucking. That clause prohibited interference with a vehicle or driver "when neither is party to a strike."

As a final ironic touch, court injunctions were authorized against unions engaged in "unfair labor practices" and in cases where an unlawful act was "threatened."

With the amended Vance-Myre bill put through the legislature on a basis highly favorable to the ruling class, Governor Stassen immediately signed it into law. In doing so, he declared over the radio: "I will stand back of this law with the full strength of the state government."

Next the governor appointed a state labor conciliator to administer the new measure. He chose a right-wing labor official for the post, Lloyd J. Haney, president of the St. Paul typographical union. Haney, incidentally, had campaigned for Stassen in 1938.

At that juncture the Associated Industries set out to intensify the antilabor offensive in Minneapolis. An energetic drive was launched to bring new members into its front organization, the "Civic Council," so as to broaden its base of operations. Propaganda moves were also undertaken to refurbish the tarnished image of the company-union setup, the "Associated Council of Independent Unions." The employers counted on using such instrumentalities in taking full advantage of the newly enacted Slave Labor Law. In addition, their strategists expected to be aided by the rightward drift of the Roosevelt administration, which was busily preparing for war.

These developments were taken up editorially in the *Northwest*

Organizer of May 4, 1939. The capitalists were about to step up their slander campaign against militant trade unionism, the Teamster paper predicted. Under that cover they would set into motion a many-sided attack. Their aims would be to whittle away at the unions, one by one; divide the labor movement; isolate their victims; and thereby to gradually weaken the organized working class of the city so that their goals could be reached without triggering a big flare-up. In the end, the editorial said, the bosses hoped to break the power of the union movement and achieve a lowering of wages to pre-1934 levels.

The cogency of this prediction was widely recognized by Minneapolis trade unionists. Such was the case even among middle-of-the-road AFL officials, who had class-collaborationist leanings. They had been impressed by the progress made since 1934 through militant union action, and they didn't want the employers to regain the upper hand.

As a result, there was a big response when a meeting of the executive boards of AFL locals in the city was called on April 30. Over five hundred union officials attended, practically all of them ready to continue the fight against the Slave Labor Law.

A resolution was passed by the gathering, which stated: "We declare ourselves unalterably opposed to this law." In addition, a motion by Miles Dunne of the Teamsters was adopted, demanding that President Robert Olson and Secretary George Lawson of the AFL State Federation of Labor also speak out against the measure. As the motion showed, there was considerable anger against Olson and Lawson. They had not only said nothing about the final version of the Vance-Myre bill; they had also failed to criticize Haney for accepting the job of administering the new antilabor law.

As for Haney's conduct, one passage in the above resolution put the meeting on record as being "opposed to any and all members of trade unions acting in the capacity of Administrator of the Minnesota Labor Relations Act or in any manner lending aid to the Republican attempt to smash the Minnesota trade union movement."

Shortly afterward the capitalists made their opening move. As was to be expected, Local 544 was the target. With many of the local's contracts about to come up for renewal, it submitted proposals for improved terms. In the talks that followed, the trucking bosses took an arrogant and hostile attitude. They rejected the union demands out of hand and presented counterproposals calling for slashes in wages.

Faced with this situation, Local 544 called a special membership meeting to prepare for battle. Among the guest speakers was R.D. Cramer, the editor of *Labor Review*. He told the assembled truck drivers: "We are not the only ones to recognize your power. The employers recognize it, too, and seek a new club from the Stassen administration to smash you and the trade-union movement. The employers got such a club from Stassen—the Stassen Slave Act."

Ray Dunne spoke for the leadership of the local. Referring to the new antilabor weapon, he told the membership: "We are going to observe the law in the way it deserves to be observed." The workers, perceiving exactly what he meant, responded with thunderous applause.

From the outset the conflict focused on the transfer industry where the union contract expired on May 31. Repeated attempts to open meaningful negotiations failed, and on June 7 Local 544 filed the required ten day's notice of its intention to call a strike. Haney and Stassen did the expected thing, holding the dispute to be "affected with a public interest"; a commission was then appointed to sit on the matter for thirty days. Those named to the body were Thomas McCabe, a Duluth lawyer; William Gurnee, secretary of the St. Paul College of Law; and A.P. Blair, an officer of the Duluth Brewery Workers Union. All three had campaigned for Stassen's election.

The union quickly initiated countersteps. Its attorneys, Gilbert Carlson and John Goldie, took the matter to court in an effort to have the "public interest" ruling nullified. At the same time, another special meeting was called to rally general membership support of the embattled transfer workers. A motion to give the executive board authority to strike the transfer industry was put to a vote at the gathering, and a secret ballot was deliberately taken so the bosses would not misread the workers' sentiments. The motion carried 1,053 to 103.

While this was going on, the AFL forces, acting collectively, brought pressure on Stassen for an interpretation of the new law concerning employer violations of working agreements. The unions argued that such violations should be termed an "unfair labor practice" and in those cases labor should be exempted from giving notice before calling a strike. Attorney general Burnquist ruled, however, that "violation of a collective bargaining agreement by an employer in Minnesota is not an unfair labor practice under the terms of the state labor relations act, unless the employer institutes a lockout. Even if the employer involved is known to have violated the agreement, a union must give ten days' notice of a strike." In other words, the bosses could tear union contracts to shreds and the Stassen administration would still try to protect them from strike action.

A similar attitude was shown in the court's response to Local 544's appeal on the "public interest" issue. Judge Luther Youngdahl held that the transfer dispute involved the "public welfare," and that Stassen was justified in throwing it into his hand-picked commission for thirty days.

During this compulsory "waiting period," the local carefully proceeded to follow Tobin's rules concerning official IBT approval of a strike. A double purpose was intended: by securing such formal sanction, the danger of Tobin getting out of line in the tricky situation would be minimized; it would also be a way of showing the bosses that they were up against solid union forces.

The move proved successful on both counts. On June 30 a letter was received endorsing a strike of the transfer industry in the name of the IBT's general executive board. Backing of the kind, incidentally, was unprecedented in the history of the Trotskyist-led local's relations with Tobin. It appeared to reflect the impact on him of the successful over-the-road campaign in which the Minneapolis General Drivers Union had played a key part.

News of Tobin's action had an effect on many of the city's trucking bosses. They began to realize that Stassen's law could do little more than postpone the day when they would have to face the union in battle. As a result, some two-hundred employers outside the transfer sphere decided to renew their contracts with Local 544 on terms that provided gains for the workers involved. That development gave the local a propaganda edge over the transfer companies. Moreover, if they decided to force a prolonged strike, support from union members who would still be working could enable the transfer drivers to hang tough indefinitely.

On July 5 Stassen's commission made its public report on that particular dispute. The commissioners came out in support of the transfer firms' request that the work week be shortened from forty-eight to forty-four hours, with no change in hourly pay. In an attempt to justify this wage reduction, they claimed that the cost of living was declining, an argument that was patently false. What really motivated the employers' proposal for a cut in hours and weekly pay was the continuing slump in production.

Local 544 flatly rejected the commission's report. Then, on July 7, the union pulled out the workers at Pratts Express and Security Warehouse. Action was confined only to those two of the fifty-seven outfits involved, so as to test whether the rest of the bosses could be shown that the Teamsters meant business without having to take all the transfer workers off the job. The message got through, and contract renewals were soon obtained throughout the industry without need of a more extensive walkout.

The settlement provided that the work week would gradually be shortened from forty-eight to about forty-five hours, and hourly wage rates were to be correspondingly increased so that there would be no cut in take-home pay. Various gains were made on other matters as well, including for the first time the granting of paid vacations to the workers.

Considering all the complex factors involved, it was a significant victory for the union movement and a heavy blow to the hopes of the Associated Industries.

By then the St. Paul unions were having their own troubles with the Slave Labor Law. Being traditionally conservative, they had at first been inclined to accept the measure and simply try to live with it. Before long, however, fresh experiences caused that attitude to change. Once the law was passed the bosses had become tougher than ever in resisting labor demands and more prone to flout existing working agreements. In that situation, the unions found themselves handicapped by curtailment of the right to strike and picket. As a consequence the St. Paul Trades and Labor Assembly, the city's AFL central body, voted in July to condemn the new law in all respects.

Another convention of the AFL State Federation of Labor, convened in Duluth on September 11, showed that this mood had become even more widespread. A report calling for nothing more than amendment of the Stassen law was presented to the gathering by a majority of the legislative committee. That position was opposed by a minority of the committee, for whom Gene Larson of Minneapolis Milk Drivers Local 471 was the reporter. Larson called for outright repeal of the law. In the debate that followed, both the president and secretary of the federation defended the majority report. A vote was then taken in which the nine-hundred delegates overrode the official machine. By an overwhelming majority, they demanded that the law be repealed.

The federation officials failed, however, to continue the fight in the spirit of the convention decision. Instead, they maneuvered to change the policy and, after a time, managed to shift the main emphasis back toward efforts to have the law amended.

Meanwhile, the harsh line of the Stassen administration had produced significant repercussions on yet another front. Trade unionists within the Farmer-Labor Party became more opposed than ever to the policies that had contributed to the party's loss of the governorship in 1938. This caused increased determination to break the grip of the Stalinist–right-wing bloc that had grabbed control of the reformist political movement, and important new developments ensued.

13. FLP Rift Widens

Before describing the new political developments in Minnesota it would be helpful to review the main outlines of the earlier situation. During the first years of the working-class upsurge in the 1930s, the Trotskyists did not advocate the formation of a labor party, due to the reformist connotations involved. Allowance was made, instead, for the possibility that the workers might be able to make a direct leap to revolutionary politics in the course of their intensive struggles against the boss class.

Application of that national line was partially modified in Minnesota, however, in view of the existence of the Farmer-Labor Party. The FLP, which was based on mass support among the workers and small farmers, had broken organizationally with the capitalist two-party system. In the process, it had displaced the Democrats as the main opponent of the Republicans in state politics.

In those circumstances the Trotskyists decided that Farmer-Labor Party candidates could be backed at the polls against their capitalist opponents. But this support was given critically in so far as programmatic questions were concerned. The workers were cautioned that defense of their class interests could not be safely entrusted to reformists holding public office. They were urged to rely primarily on their own strength. This required that they build strong trade unions, shape their policy on the basis of class struggle realities, and develop a combat party that they could truly call their own.

Programmatically, the FLP fell far short of being a party of the kind the workers needed. Its basic line centered on a call for reforms under the existing system, to be achieved in a gradual and orderly manner through parliamentary action alone. Emphasis was placed accordingly on the substitution of reformist politics for class-struggle actions. As interpreted by FLP representatives in public office, implementation of that policy required blocs with liberal capitalist politicians on a statewide scale, along with support of the Roosevelt Democrats nationally. The fact that such a course violated the interests of the workers and small farmers was ignored. The official line was carried out by a machine consisting in large part of lawyers, small-town bankers, and other business people who were ambitious to develop a political career for themselves through the reformist movement.

These characteristics of the Farmer-Labor Party fit right in with the needs of the Stalinists, who had set out to capture it after their people's front turn in 1935. Their aims were to intensify the FLP's ties with Roosevelt's New Deal and ultimately to transform it into the Minnesota section of the national Democratic Party.

The Communist Party was aided in those respects by the pro-Democratic line that had already been instituted in an oblique way by Floyd Olson, the state's first Farmer-Labor governor. Olson had set up "all-party committees," which gave Democratic politicians an influential place within the FLP's ruling structure and thus cleared the way for Roosevelt to take a "neutral" stand concerning Minnesota politics. In the 1936 campaign, for example, withdrawal of the Democratic candidate for governor in Minnesota had been traded for FLP support of Roosevelt's candidacy for reelection as president.

After that, the Stalinists grabbed onto Olson's policy, seeking to apply it in a more open, ever more flagrant manner. At the same time they initiated crass attempts to impose dictatorial machine rule within the FLP as a means of suppressing opposition to their liquidationist course. On both counts they got considerable help from right-wingers in the party, who shared their class-collaborationist outlook.

Resistance to such policies and methods soon arose among trade unions affiliated with the Farmer-Labor Party. The opposition centered in Minneapolis, where an open clash occurred during the 1937 city elections. As outlined earlier, this clash developed when the Communist Party hacks and their right-wing allies rigged a city convention to nominate a handpicked ticket and adopt a people's front platform. The trade unionists, who balked at that insolent treatment, held their own convention, nominating a separate slate of candidates and drafting a labor platform for the elections. With rival tickets entered in the primaries, the FLP's state executive committee flaunted local autonomy by backing the "official" candidates against those supported by the trade unions. In that confused situation the Republicans were able to get George E. Leach elected mayor in the final balloting, thereby dealing labor a severe political setback.

Instead of learning a lesson in principled politics from this experience, the bloc of the right wing and Stalinists continued on the same disruptive course in preparing for the 1938 gubernatorial election. As a result, the internal FLP conflict became even more intense.

Such was the political climate in Minnesota when the Socialist Workers Party made its 1938 turn on the labor party question (for the broad reasons stated in a previous chapter). That change in line permitted SWP members in the Teamsters to emphasize several aspects of the problems involved in building a labor party, a step that has since been advocated consistently by revolutionary socialists in this country. Because an independent party basing itself on workers and farmers already existed in the state, tactical problems that arose went considerably beyond the matter of critical support at the polls. Both the nature of the reformist formation and the essential character of its program had to be dealt with.

As Marxists have repeatedly stressed, the concept of building a two-class party of the FLP type is basically false. Superficially, the workers and farmers within its ranks appeared to have equal standing and influence. In reality, however, the middle-class ideology engendered by the farmers—who are economically petty proprietors—tended to dominate the movement, blocking the development of an anticapitalist outlook by the wage workers. That is why a mass political organization, which aims to oppose the capitalist parties, must be based primarily upon the trade unions. Only with that solid class footing can a meaningful political alliance of workers and farmers, along with other victims of capitalist exploitation, be created; that is, a massive political movement acting under the leadership of the most decisive social force, the working class. It also follows that, once such a formation can be established, objective potential develops for the shaping of a programmatic course leading toward a struggle for state power by labor and its allies.

Steps toward those desired ends could be initiated around the Farmer-Labor Party on the basis that, in the last analysis, it rested chiefly on trade-union support. A campaign was therefore in order to achieve a correspondingly dominant voice for organized labor within the movement. Basically, that meant a fight for the workers to have democratic control over the mass party and for the adoption of a class-struggle program that would serve their interests.

As noted above, an incipient labor rebellion against the Stalinist–right-wing machine in the FLP had, in fact, already loomed in Minneapolis during the 1937 city elections. In the resulting polarizations a new, amorphous political movement had taken preliminary shape. It consisted in the main of the trade-union caucus that ran its own slate of candidates in the 1937 primaries, acting with the help of some middle-class allies. An opportunity had thus arisen for revolutionaries to intervene in the situation with the object of pressing for the development of an appropriate form of labor party. That step, of course, involved taking sides with the workers in the factional struggle within the FLP and helping them to move toward independent political action rooted in class-struggle concepts.

Proceeding accordingly, the Socialist Workers Party addressed an open letter to Elmer Benson, the FLP candidate for reelection as governor, prior to the November 1938 elections. It contained the following warning: "The truth is that the Farmer-Labor Party is in danger of mortal defeat at the hands of reaction, unless the workers and farmers can be armed with a program which will spur them to the utmost efforts to achieve victory."

The SWP letter advocated two key steps to overcome the existing danger: make a clean break with Roosevelt's New Deal, which had become widely discredited in the eyes of the toilers; and throw the full weight of the FLP into a campaign to form a national labor party.

Both the warning and the policy recommendations were disregarded, however, by the political hacks dictating the official line of the Farmer-Labor Party. In spite of everything, they persisted in identifying the organization with the program of the Roosevelt Democrats. That false course served to bewilder many thousands of workers and farmers, who became easy prey for the Republicans. As a result, Benson was overwhelmingly defeated at the polls by Harold E. Stassen, the gubernatorial candidate of the ruling class. That harsh setback caused further intensification of the factional polarizations taking place within the FLP.

An analysis of this situation was presented in the November 17 *Northwest Organizer:* "The one glaring fact that emerges from the election returns of November 8th is that the masses, seeing their economic status unimproved after six years of the New Deal, were determined to turn their present rulers out of office. . . .

"The tendency that has made rapid headway in the Farmer-Labor Party in the last two years—to become the Minnesota section of the New Deal and to resist control by the workers' and farmers' organizations—toppled the FLP to the ground. . . .

"Many months ago the unions here had protested to the FLP leaders against an organization set-up that removed the power from the economic organizations of the toilers and gave control to the singing societies, the art circles, the ward clubs, the all-party committees and the Communist Party. The unions had sought to urge upon the FLP a real program for housing, for unemployment relief, against war, and against any tie-up with the New Deal. But the Duluth convention rejected the unions' suggestion. . . .

"Only the trade unions can reform the ranks for the sort of political movement that alone will play a role in the future: a movement for real independent labor political action, controlled by the unions, with its policies and leadership shaped by the unions.

"The labor party movement in Minnesota, when it comes back, will come back as part of a national labor party, a party with a democratic regime, a party that has broken cleanly with both old parties, a party that will have the sort of bold answers to the needs of the masses that will win and hold the support of the workers, the farmers, the youth, the lower middle classes."

About a month after the *Northwest Organizer* made the above declaration a new clash between organized labor and the Stalinist–right-wing gang took place at a Hennepin County convention of the FLP. At issue was selection of the county's delegation to an upcoming state conference of the party. The conflict arose over the disproportionate voting strength that the county executive committee gave to ward and township clubs, along with Stalinist paper organizations. The gathering had been packed with a slew of delegates from those setups, while trade-union representation was arbitrarily held to a minimum.

The outfits favored by the party machine were composed of units established on a city ward or rural township basis; they were composed largely of officeholders and their hangers-on. A place had also been found in those formations for hastily rechristened Democratic Party politicians. As for the paper structures fabricated by the Communist Party, they ranged from phony "workers" clubs to "cultural" front groups and consisted mostly of CP members and fellow travelers. One union delegate to the county affair remarked: "There's enough paper in those organizations to print a deluxe edition of *Gone With the Wind*."

When the trade unionists tried to overturn the false criteria used in allowing excessive representation at the gathering from such nonlabor quarters, they were outvoted. Not only that. The Stalinists made an effort to prevent the seating of General Drivers Local 544's delegation, using a technicality for the purpose, but the attempt failed.

With the decision-making power thus rigged against the trade unions, a majority of those selected to represent Hennepin County at the state conference came from ward and township clubs, and from CP front groups. Organized labor, representing thousands of workers, had been subordinated by the party machine to the interests of a clique that spoke for only a few hundred people.

While the Stalinists were pulling off that caper in Hennepin County they received an unexpected blow. Right-wingers in the FLP state committee, with whom the CP had been collaborating, suddenly passed a resolution proposing the expulsion of "Communists" from the organization. The formula they used sought to proscribe affiliation by "any member of the Communist Party and also such other persons as advocate the overthrow of the government by force and violence." A threat was added to revoke the charters of local clubs refusing to carry out the desired expulsions.

In one respect the attack was a farce, since it was launched by politicians who had long been working hand and glove with the Stalinists. Their real objective was to duck responsibility for the disaster into which they had helped lead the Farmer-Labor Party. To do so, they were trying to put the whole blame on the CP. The hypocrisy involved was further underlined by the fact that the "anti-Communist" politicians and the CP hacks remained united in their determination to prevent organized labor from having its rightful voice in the FLP.

As for the attempt to expel the Stalinists, they could sidestep the thrust by simply denying membership in the Communist Party. But there was another, more sinister, aspect to the right-wingers' unprincipled resolution. Its terminology implied that a much broader campaign was intended, which would include red-baiting of trade-union militants within the FLP.

This reactionary move by the state committee was immediately blasted in the *Northwest Organizer.* An explanation was given as to why the Stalinists shouldn't be expelled from the Farmer-Labor Party as "reds." Removal from posts they held in the organization was recommended, though, on different grounds— their pro-Democratic, pro-war, party-wrecking, union-splitting policies. The real answer to the FLP's problem, the Teamster paper stressed, was to put the party under the control of the workers' and farmers' organizations. Meaningful steps could then be taken to repudiate the New Deal and form an alliance with progressive sections of Labor's Non-Partisan League—founded by the CIO—with the aim of building a national labor party.

The high command of the FLP, of course, had no intention of making such a turn in line. That became clear to worker-militants generally when a state convention of the party was convened in St. Paul on January 27, 1939. With the allocation of delegates having been stacked against the unions, the right-wingers were able to block discussion of controversial political questions. They focused, instead, on the Communist Party issue as the central matter before the gathering, exploiting the fact that most delegates had become fed up with Stalinist disruption. Because of that widespread sentiment, a motion was readily passed to bar CP members from the organization. There was no significant follow-through, however, and Stalinists holding FLP posts remained largely untouched.

Since the real issues in dispute had been kept off the convention floor, nothing was done to modify the party's bankrupt line in a way that would attract working-class support. As a consequence, a number of AFL unions dropped out of the Farmer-Labor Party. Their withdrawal, however, did not signify that the workers' organizations were becoming politically apathetic. The action simply reflected the frustrations trade unionists were experiencing at the hands of the party machine. They were opposed to the line that had caused loss of the governorship to the Republicans; they wanted a policy that would come closer to serving their class needs; and they insisted on their right to a meaningful voice in deciding that policy.

Determined to move toward achievement of those aims, the Minneapolis AFL sought a direct political alliance with farm organizations. The effort soon got results within the Farmer-Cooperative-Labor Council that had recently been formed. A special meeting of the council was held in February 1939, at which plans were laid to establish broad collaboration between the different segments of its membership. The session also took an important organizational step. A drive was launched to expand the alliance, numerically and geographically, by setting up volunteer local committees throughout the state, consisting of representatives from farmer, cooperative, and trade-union circles.

It didn't take long for this development to pay off. Thanks to the volunteer committees, rural support was mobilized during the following spring in the campaign against Stassen's Slave Labor Law. In the process, moreover, farmer-militants began to move toward support of the trade unions in the fight against the wrecking crew of the right wing and Stalinists within the Farmer-Labor Party.

The full significance of these trends—which went in the direction of reconstituting the mass political movement as a labor party based on the trade unions—did not become apparent until preparations began for the 1939 city elections in Minneapolis.

On April 2 the FLP held a routine convention in the city to nominate candidates and adopt an election platform. But things didn't go according to plan. Many AFL unions boycotted the affair, and the Stalinists heading the local FLP setup found themselves without an army. In those circumstances they were forced to make a gesture toward organized labor. So the CP generals proposed that a second convention, jointly representative of the FLP and the trade unions, be convened on April 8. As usual, though, their "joint" representation gimmick was a fake. They intended, for example, that an FLP club of twenty members would have five delegates, whereas a union of five-thousand members would be allowed only three delegates.

At that point the Socialist Workers Party put up its own candidate for mayor of Minneapolis. Carlos Hudson was the nominee. There were several reasons for his candidacy, as an SWP statement explained.

Despite growing opposition within the labor movement, the

Stalinists were still trying to promote a people's front election campaign. For that purpose they were again conniving to pack a nominating convention with CP members and fellow travelers. If candidates were chosen on that basis, those selected would not only be advocates of the war-mongering, relief-slashing New Deal; they would be outright opponents of independent working-class political action.

Trade unionists were being repelled from the Farmer-Labor Party by the Stalinist line, the SWP statement added. In fact, the FLP was falling into a state of collapse. Organizationally, its decline threatened to put Minnesota's workers and farmers back where they were some twenty years earlier, when they first concluded that the capitalist political parties offered them no future.

By voting for Hudson, it was urged, the workers could indicate their desire to make a clean break with boss politics and build an independent, nationwide labor party.

Key issues around which labor should mobilize politically were outlined in the SWP's election platform. These included: opposition to any war conducted by a bosses' government; increased direct relief for the unemployed and trade-union wages on "made-work" projects; a $20 billion federal public-works and housing program; operation of the city's idle production facilities under trade-union control; a ban on the use of police against strikers; and the building of union defense guards.

There was yet another aspect to the SWP's action. The statement in support of Hudson's candidacy spelled out—bluntly and clearly—the dangers thrust upon the workers by the Stalinists. It also pointed the way to a solution of the problem through independent political action under labor's leadership. Thus, distribution of the SWP campaign material served both to stimulate initiative among trade-union militants and to reorient them politically, thereby also backing the Trotskyist leaders of Local 544. They were able to press more effectively within labor circles for decisive steps to cope with the FLP situation and, as events quickly showed, a significant change was to result on the local political scene.

On April 8 the joint session of the Farmer-Labor Party and organized labor took place as scheduled. But the CP hacks dominating the local FLP got a surprise. Trade-union representatives came in such numbers that they were able to assert full control over the deliberations. To all intents and purposes the gathering was converted into a labor caucus, one that was ready and able, moreover, to dictate the choice of candidates and write the platform for the city elections. Confronted with this force, the Stalinists had no choice but to appear to go along. So they pretended to agree on a joint labor-FLP ticket, as chosen by the trade-union majority.

T.A. Eide was endorsed as the labor candidate for mayor, and labor nominees were also chosen for the city council and various minor offices. Eide, who had never before participated in an election campaign, had been secretary of the Franklin Cooperative Creamery since 1925.

All nominees were required to pledge that they would abide by the platform drawn up by the trade unions. The main planks were as follows: recognition of labor's right to organize, bargain collectively, strike and picket; provision of adequate unemployment relief; no state or city sales tax. The point about the rights of labor had special cogency since it was already clear at the time that Stassen's new antilabor law would soon be enacted.

After weighing this turn of events, the Socialist Workers Party made a shift in tactics. Hudson's candidacy was withdrawn and critical support was extended to the labor ticket. The considerations involved were explained in a new public announcement.

For the first time in three years the Communist Party had failed to control a labor political convention in Minneapolis. Instead, there had been a welcome resurgence of the trade-union movement on the political field. The action of the union delegates at the April 8 caucus made it possible to salvage the remains of the once-progressive Farmer-Labor movement; a stride had been taken toward labor's political unification in a campaign to drive the Associated Industries from city hall. That was why the SWP had withdrawn its candidate for mayor and urged all workers to vote for the candidates of the April 8 caucus.

This move was made, the announcement continued, without in the least concealing the SWP's basic differences with both the political program and the organizational setup of the labor caucus. The most glaring deficiency in the caucus platform was its failure to speak out against Roosevelt's war policy. It also failed to make clear the next logical step for the unions—creation locally of a labor political league, which should link up with forces working to establish a national labor party. Organizationally, the existing caucus form was too loose a structure. It did not provide the necessary apparatus for holding candidates to their pledges, if elected. That had been a great weakness of the Farmer-Labor Party as well. One of the factors contributing to its crash had been the lack of a way for the trade unions to control persons elected to public office by the FLP.

Attention was also called to the fact that Hudson's withdrawal from the mayoralty race did not set a precedent. The action in no way implied that the SWP would thereafter withdraw its candidates when confronted with candidates of other labor groups. In future cases, the SWP would decide, according to circumstances, whether to file its own candidates or give a measure of critical support to candidates of other labor groups.

In sharp contrast to the principled stand taken by the Socialist Workers Party, the Stalinists proceeded to maneuver factionally against the labor slate chosen at the April 8 session. They wanted desperately to stem the trend away from support to the New Deal. Having already helped to ruin the Farmer-Labor movement with their people's front line, they now set out to scuttle labor's new political upsurge—and their control over the local FLP was used for the purpose.

As a first step, the Stalinists induced Kleve Flakne, a lawyer who had no connection with organized labor, to file for mayor against Eide in the primaries. One of their pitches in that connection was to falsely charge that Eide was "under the thumb of Local 544." The attempt was futile, however, and Flakne was snowed under in the primary balloting.

After losing that round the Communist Party and its fellow travelers launched yet another campaign of sabotage against the trade-union slate. Eide was again the central target. With labor's mayoralty candidate now facing the Republican incumbent, George E. Leach, in the run-off election, he was subjected to a vicious sneak attack. Thousands of leaflets were distributed, mainly in middle-class wards, purporting to "support" Eide in the name of the CP. The leaflets were written, moreover, in a dishonest way implying that the labor campaign was tied to the New Deal. Those tactics served to undermine Eide's standing with the electorate in two ways: the pro–New Deal line of the leaflets tended to weaken his attractive power among workers; and the act of tagging Eide with CP "support" alienated middle-class elements from him.

Since the Communist Party had packed the Farmer-Labor ward clubs with its members and followers, there were few people in those bodies ready to lend active support to the labor campaign. That made the idea of a joint FLP–trade union ticket more of a misnomer than ever. Only a very minor contribution to the collective effort could be expected from within the ward clubs. Therefore, nothing could be gained by the formal inclusion of these outfits in the campaign that would offset the political handicap resulting from the fact that they bore the FLP label, which was becoming a symbol for Stalinist treachery.

In those circumstances it would have been better for organized labor to dissociate itself from the Farmer-Labor Party. But many trade unionists still clung to the hope that the FLP could be resuscitated, and they didn't want to break the long-standing formal relationship. For the same reason they had been unwilling to move toward the building of a permanent labor party organization. Consequently, a temporary campaign apparatus had to be assembled virtually overnight.

There were ample forces at hand for the task. Deep political ferment was spreading within the trade-union ranks under the blows received from both Roosevelt and Stassen; and labor's election policy, inadequate though it was, had a degree of progressiveness that appealed to the politically aroused workers. To illustrate the point, the platform represented a measurable advance over FLP platforms of the 1936–38 period. The labor candidates attacked the Stalinists—without red-baiting them— branding the CP a reactionary force within the workers' movement. There was no advocacy of support to the Roosevelt Democrats, and that stance implied silent rejection of the New Deal. Thanks to the latter factor, especially, the workers reacted enthusiastically to the labor ticket. As a result, trade-union committees soon sprang up in various wards to assume leadership and control of the campaign effort.

In effect, a political confrontation had developed between the trade unions acting as a labor party, on the one side, and what amounted to a Republican-Democratic coalition, on the other.

Big money was put up by the ruling class in support of the Republican ticket. Lies about the labor candidates and distortions of their platform were printed in the boss press. "The preachers," said the *Northwest Organizer*, "led their sheep back to the Leach fold." Democratic "friends of labor," who loathed the idea of a working-class break with capitalist politics, threw curves at the labor campaigners; and the Stalinists chipped in by helping to intensify an antilabor "red" scare among middle-class voters. All in all, it was quite a formidable opposition that the embattled trade unions confronted politically.

The run-off elections took place June 12. With some 157,000 ballots cast for mayor, Leach edged out Eide by only 7,000-odd votes. On a precinct-by-precinct basis, Eide received a majority in the predominantly working-class wards. Leach got the bulk of the middle-class ballots, and the silk-stocking districts voted solidly for him. In other contests, several lesser posts were won by labor candidates, but reaction gained control of the city council for the first time since 1935.

On balance, the narrow margin of the Republican victory signified that labor had made a big comeback after the crushing defeat of the Farmer-Labor Party in the 1938 gubernatorial election. The closeness of the mayoralty race was especially significant, when compared to Benson's loss to Stassen by over 250,000 votes just eight months earlier.

After taking note of these positive aspects of the election outcome, the June 15 *Northwest Organizer* emphasized that the unions were now on the right track. It was necessary, however, to sharpen the political line; to differentiate more clearly from the two boss parties; to carry the labor party idea still deeper into the union movement and the unemployed organizations; and to launch future election campaigns through open conventions.

Concerning the problem of excluding the Communist Party from bureaucratic control over labor politics, the Teamster paper advised, organizational steps were not enough. It was necessary to clarify working-class opposition to the Democratic Party and to Roosevelt's war policy. Those were positions the CP couldn't accept, so they would be blocked from maneuvering their way around trade-union control of labor's political movement.

As for the Stalinists' postelection line, they could hardly restrain themselves from gloating publicly over Eide's defeat. That was shown by their criticism of the labor campaign, which was made in a June 24 statement by the Hennepin County Council of the Communist Party. The statement said that the objectives of the New Deal "were not championed in a sufficiently clear-cut manner by the united front candidates or campaign leadership. . . .

"The campaign was confined almost exclusively to Farmer-Labor and trade union ranks, failing actively to involve liberal church groups, small business men, professionals and other progressive middle class groups. . . .

"The Democratic Party failed to concern itself with or take an active part in the campaign while the Farmer-Labor and trade union forces neglected to solicit its support. . . .

"The record of the Trotskyites clearly reveals what would be the character of the so-called 'Labor' Party which they propose to substitute for the Farmer-Labor Association. It would be an instrument to fight against the New Deal. . . ."

This crooked line was pushed by the Stalinists at a statewide conference of the Farmer-Labor Party held shortly after the Minneapolis elections. They got help from right-wingers, who were equally determined to hamstring independent working-class political action. At the FLP gathering these twin forces rammed through a policy of continued collaboration with the Democrats. Programmatic changes that could draw support from the newly stirring political forces of labor were rejected. So stultified were the proceedings, in fact, that many delegates grew disgusted and walked out of the conference before it adjourned.

The Stalinist–right-wing coalition failed to repair the FLP's political image. In addition, their pro-New Deal line soon became even further discredited when a united front of building-trades mechanics and unemployed workers conducted a national strike against Roosevelt's relief policies, which were becoming increasingly harsh.

PLIGHT OF THE JOBLESS

Part of cavalcade of WPA demonstration on the way from Minneapolis to state capitol in St. Paul during 1939 protest action.

14. Organizing the Unemployed

While preparing this segment of Teamster history I asked Max Geldman, an organizer of the unemployed in the 1930s, for his recollections about conditions and events during that period. One of my questions concerned the prevailing mood among workers who had lost their jobs because of economic depression.

"Let me illustrate," he responded, "what I consider the general reaction of the unemployed to the indignities of being on relief. I'm not speaking here of anger at the authorities, or of militant struggles waged by the jobless. It's the indignity of having to fill out forms and of being interrogated by relief interviewers: such as, how much money do you have, when were you last employed, why do you need relief, etc., etc.?

"On the workers education program, a project developed after the Works Progress Administration was set up by Roosevelt, we used to write and enact plays dealing with the plight of the unemployed. I wrote one which didn't have much of a plot. The opening scene told how Mr. Smith, employed on a good job for years and years, comes home and informs his family he has been laid off and there is no possibility of his being rehired or finding a new job. The next scene has the family gathered in their living room. A woman in a fur coat, note pad and pen in hand, is seated before them and conducting an interview along the lines of the customary abusive treatment received by applicants for public relief. This scene had a devastating effect on every audience before which we played. Those present sobbed, lived again through their own bitter experiences, and hissed and booed our actress relief investigator.

"The mass of unemployed hated the relief setup; resented the indignities they were subjected to; shed tears over their plight; and broke out in angry actions: such as protest demonstrations,

177

sit-ins at state capitals, hunger marches, and raids on food warehouses in which food was expropriated and distributed to the needy."

During the first period of the depression, jobless workers had to depend entirely on Scrooge-like doling out of public relief by local agencies, as described by Max. Then, with the advent of Roosevelt's New Deal in 1933, the federal government instituted a series of relief programs based on "made work." After one program had existed for a time, it was deliberately scrapped and replaced by another. Each such change threw into confusion whatever unemployed organizations had come into existence. The jobless lost at least part of the gains they had made through struggle, and in general they found it necessary to reorganize themselves and begin all over again in their fight with the government.

The third and most extensive of these programs was the Works Progress Administration. Its essential character was outlined by Geldman as follows:

"After the WPA was established the life-style and reaction of the great mass of unemployed differed from the previous period in two main respects. There were feelings of satisfaction at the outset over what they expected would be useful labor; also, gratification at not having to face relief investigators with requests for necessities like clothing, fuel, and other 'extras' beyond food and rent.

"The workers soon found, however, that there was not much satisfaction in working on WPA projects. In the cities they were usually paid $60.50 a month, plus distribution of surplus food products. The wage was less in rural areas, around $40.00 a month in northern states and even lower in the South. Whatever the rate, it was hardly enough to keep body and soul together. Besides, there was little dignity in the assigned work. Here and there something useful was accomplished, like the belt-line road around Minneapolis, or the murals painted by needy artists on post office walls and public buildings; but for the greater part it was unproductive, made-up, busywork.

"Considering the billions spent that could have been used to creative ends, it was like dumping products to maintain high prices and fat profits. The labor power of millions was wasted, so as not to upset the balance of the capitalist system. No wonder the symbol of WPA was a worker leaning on a shovel, and so also was the national song of the unemployed called 'Leaning on a Shovel.'

"How could anyone have any satisfaction in labor that often consisted of one group of workers digging a hole and of another group filling it up?"

Shortly before the WPA came into being, a new formation appeared within the Minneapolis labor movement, one that was to have a significant effect on later mass struggles against Roosevelt's stingy relief policies. In the spring of 1935, General Drivers Local 574 expanded its structure to include an auxiliary unit known as the Federal Workers Section. This unit was especially designed as a vehicle for organization of the unemployed under the local's direct sponsorship. Its creation marked a pioneer step in trade-union activity, and for that reason the way had been carefully prepared during the course of preceding events.

When Local 574 launched its 1934 campaign for bargaining rights in the Minneapolis trucking industry, there was great potential for support from the city's unemployed. The jobless were in a deeply rebellious mood. Generally speaking, they looked upon any struggle against the status quo as their struggle. Some among them were, of course, susceptible to being tricked into serving the bosses as strikebreakers; but that danger could be minimized if organized labor sought to promote united action by the employed and unemployed in defense of their collective interests.

Being conscious of those factors, Trotskyists in the General Drivers' leadership initiated policy measures designed to forge the necessary working-class unity. In effect they were saying to the unemployed: "Help us now to win our battle against the trucking employers, and we will then back your cause with the full power of our union."

Thousands of jobless workers responded to the appeal during the hard-fought trucking strikes that followed. Voluntarily accepting discipline in combat, they stood shoulder-to-shoulder with the strikers in defending picket lines against the cops. Many were arrested before the battle was finally won; scores suffered injury from police clubs and guns; and one of them, John Belor, gave his life for the cause.

A close affinity grew up between the truck drivers and the unemployed. The average Local 574 member thought it only fitting and proper to form the Federal Workers Section, so as to help those who had so loyally backed the union in its time of need.

Since the FWS had only auxiliary status, members of the unit were not accorded voice or vote in regular meetings of the union. There were practical reasons for that restriction. Efforts had been made to get the AFL central body in the city to sponsor a broadly based formation of unemployed, backed officially by the entire union movement. Nothing came of the attempt, however, so Local 574 undertook the full task on its own. All jobless workers were invited into the FWS, whether or not they had previously belonged to one or another trade union. A heterogeneous body was bound to result, which could grow to considerable size. Its incorporation into the local, with full voting rights, would have distorted the basic character of the truck drivers' organization. Problems would have resulted that could only weaken the trade-union base upon which the unemployed movement was to be built, thereby putting the whole project in jeopardy.

Despite the restriction on voting rights thus made necessary, the jobless workers gained a lot from the overall arrangement. Affiliation with a strong trade union gave their movement unprecedented inner stability, a new measure of dynamism, and an enhanced growth rate. In addition, a member of Local 574's executive board, usually Grant Dunne, helped the FWS in dealing with city relief agencies and WPA officials. Such action signified that workers on relief were backed by the full power of the entire local in their clashes with the authorities.

Although the Federal Workers Section functioned under the supervision of the union's executive board, it had full democratic rights in forming an internal structure and in shaping its own policies. The section had its own executive committee and, due to the peculiar needs of the unemployed movement, the committee was viewed as an open-end body to which personnel could be added as circumstances required. There was a steward formation, which consisted mainly of representatives elected on WPA projects. A grievance board was also established and, like all official bodies, it was accountable to the monthly membership meetings of the section.

After a time a special women's division was formed, primarily among workers on a large WPA sewing project. In this connection it should be noted that most of the FWS members were on WPA, mainly workers on labor projects. The section had only scattered influence among unemployed professionals.

An effective leadership was soon consolidated within the section. It consisted of a staff whose members got no pay from the organization; all shifted for themselves economically, living generally on the same plane as the unemployed. The staff members functioned as a team and developed a division of labor accordingly.

Responsibility for political leadership within the section fell primarily upon Max Geldman, who also spoke for it publicly on major occasions. Since his story throws light on the political radicalization of the times, I asked him to provide a sketch of his early life.

"I was born, so I was told," Max said, "in Warsaw, Poland, on May 8, 1905. My parents, although petty-bourgeois in origin, were rebels. My grandfather was one of the last of the feudal baron's Jews. He took care of the baron's varied interests, such as collecting rents, overseeing his lumbering and milling projects. My father and his three brothers worked with my grandfather on those projects, but things got rough when the baron lost his holdings. After that the family split up.

"One of the brothers went to the South Ukraine, where he settled in Odessa. There were also three sisters and they stayed in Poland. Except for one of the sisters, all those who remained in Europe appear to have been caught up in the Nazi exterminations during World War II. The sister who escaped was aided by non-Jewish sympathizers. Somehow she made her way to Paris by way of a kind of underground railroad, where she managed to hide out until the city was later liberated from the Nazis.

"My father, together with his brothers Moisha and Ben, who used the surname Geltman, migrated to America. Ben and my father became needle-trades workers in New York City. Both were members of Local 22 of the International Ladies Garment Workers Union.

"My uncle Benny was an ultraleft radical. Every boss in the industry knew that when Benny was in a shop there would be a strike. Also he participated in atheistic raids on synagogues on Yom Kippur, such as eating ham sandwiches during the most holy period of worship. Unfortunately, he married an orthodox Jewish woman and lived an orthodox life from then on.

"My father was a mild individual, well liked and respected by his associates. He was a good union man, voted for Debs and later Roosevelt. He could not understand my development as a revolutionary. During the struggle between the left and right wings in the garment unions I, as a member of the Young Communist League, participated in left-wing demonstrations in the New York garment district. We were rounded up by the cops and spent a day in jail. My father couldn't understand it. He looked at me, shook his head in bewilderment and remarked: 'I work and my son goes to jail.' As I became more revolutionary, my father became more conservative. On my mother's side there was an uncle who was in the Communist Party underground after Pilsudski took power in Poland. He was imprisoned and died in jail.

"As for my education, I would say the greater part was self-education. I graduated from what was called grammar school up to the eighth grade. I was eight years old when the rest of the family joined my father in New York. We lived on the east side, Eighth Street and Avenue B, on the fourth floor of a tenement building. Later on we moved to Brownsville, a section of Brooklyn. Life was tough in both areas. You learned how to survive, or you didn't.

"After graduating from grammar school I went to work as was expected of the oldest boy in a Jewish family. I worked as an errand boy in a merchandise importing concern. It was customary in that environment to start as errand boy, then advance to shipping clerk and then to salesman. But the firm went broke, and I was left jobless in the midst of the highest point of capitalist prosperity, 1927. The rest of my formal education was a year at night school and two years as a nonmatriculated student in City College.

"My real education was at the main library in New York. There, with others, we studied and then discussed the books we read—Marx, the utopians, literature, anthropology, etc. I was influenced in a radical direction by the hardships my family went through, by the backbreaking labor my father was subjected to as a sewing machine operator. He lost a thumb when a sewing machine needle went through it.

"There was also the influence of my cousins: Herman, who was in the CP underground, and my namesake, Max—both sons of my uncle Moisha Geltman. I joined the Young Communist League in 1927, after experiences in the Passaic textile strike as a volunteer picket and in the struggle to save the lives of Sacco and Vanzetti. In 1928 I was sent by the YCL to do anti-imperialist work in a setup called Citizens Military Training Camps. It was an ill-conceived project. The high point of our intervention was to post leaflets in the camp streets exposing the imperialist nature of the military training given American youth. For what could be gained by such activity, it was a foolhardy and dangerous adventure.

"When I got back from the camp the CP adults and youth were involved in the last stages of an internal party struggle between factions led by Jay Lovestone and William Z. Foster. I was bewildered by the conflict, not understanding the politics of what was going on. The question of Trotsky came up. He was condemned and slandered. I was uneasy, skeptical, but didn't know enough about the situation to take a position. Later—after Trotsky was expelled from the Russian CP, Max Eastman's *The Real Situation in Russia* was published, *The Militant* appeared, and Trotsky's criticism of the draft program of the sixth congress of the Communist International was circulated—I began to get some understanding of what the internal political struggle was all about. But I still remained in the Communist Party. It is difficult to leave an organization that claims to be the party of the international communist revolution.

"At that point I left for Chicago, mainly because I couldn't figure things out. I was in Chicago when the 1929 economic crash hit, working at the Majestic Radio Co. The plant shut down and never reopened. I was unemployed and kept my head above water by last resource work: such as folding advertising circulars, addressing envelopes and then, in the bitter cold winter, distributing advertising material. You couldn't make more than $1.50 a day. It was tough.

"I met Goldy Cooper there. We shared life and participation in the Trotskyist movement from then until her death in 1952. I had left the Communist Party—drifted away in 1929—and joined the Communist League of America in 1930. Goldy joined the CLA in 1931. I became acquainted with the Minneapolis Trotskyists during our seasonal treks to nearby Chaska, Minnesota, Goldy's home town.

"After returning from Chicago to New York I participated in a 1934 hotel strike. Then, for a brief period that year, I was New York organizer for the CLA. In the fall of 1934 I transferred to

Minneapolis and soon thereafter I became involved in the Federal
Workers Section of Local 574."

Geldman shared the central leadership of the FWS with
Edward Palmquist, who chaired the section and had charge of its
general activities. Palmquist typified a particular category of
militants who play a unique role when the mass movement is on
the march. A brief description of his basic traits was provided by
Geldman.

"Ed acted from convictions," Max recalled, "which were based
on events, associations, and loyalties to what seemed just and
right. The most important aim for him was to settle a grievance,
give the authorities hell, and demonstrate the power of the
Teamsters, which was synonymous to him with workers' power.

"Politically, he tended to look upon the Minneapolis scene in
black and white colors. There was us, the union forces, which
basically meant the General Drivers; and then the bosses, the
cops, the relief and WPA administrations, the Stalinists and all
enemies of the union. His greatest strength was his likeness to
the figure in John Reed's *Ten Days That Shook the World,* who
answered all questions by saying he knew only that there were
two classes, the workers and the bosses.

"Ed sometimes had difficulty distinguishing between major
and minor issues. He could go to war, be ready to call a broad
strike, over a worker on relief being denied a bag of coal. His
method of settling grievances was at times crude but often
effective. He would phone a case worker in the relief setup and
say that the needs of a given relief client had better be met, or
he'd make it personal with the case worker, and he meant it. Ed
was proud of the union, proud of the union power. As far as he
was concerned, Minneapolis was our city and the authorities
outside interlopers.

"The FWS membership respected Ed and looked upon him as
their leader—and that he was. Even if I had to argue with him on
occasion over some tactical difference resulting from his
impulsiveness, the good part of our relationship was that we
usually came to agreement and worked well together. On balance,
he was good to have around when the chips were down."

Others on the FWS staff included: Carl Kuehn and George
Viens, who served in the respective positions of secretary and
treasurer; Marvel Scholl, my wife, who together with Viens
concentrated on functions such as fighting for aid to dependent

children and organizing women on a WPA sewing project; also Roy Orgon and Louis White, who handled grievances involving both the city relief system and WPA.

Right after the Federal Workers Section was formed, it began a fight for improvements in the local welfare setup. There were two immediate aims: correction of abusive practices followed by the city authorities; and an increase in the budgets allocated to families on relief.

A series of clashes with relief investigators and their superiors followed, which put an end to the worst abuses they had been heaping upon jobless workers. That accomplishment, in turn, helped to stimulate mass action in the battle for higher family budgets. When the city council held a hearing on the question, the unemployed turned out in force. Not only did they pack the council chamber, but further demonstrations followed in which the determined workers held their ground against the cops.

The militant struggle forced the authorities to expand the food budgets for those on relief. Increased allowances were also granted for rent, clothing, utilities, coal, and medicine. Minneapolis had, in fact, emerged from the confrontation with one of the highest relief budgets of any city in the country.

Still another showdown took place when the WPA was established. Wherever possible, the unemployed were quickly removed from the city's relief rolls and put to work on federal projects. But the WPA paid only $60.50 a month, which was below the budgetary level the city had been compelled to set for relief clients. Hence the transfers meant an automatic cut in income for the workers involved.

As a corrective, the FWS demanded that the city provide supplementary aid for WPA workers, so their income would remain equal to what they would have received if still on direct relief. Although the authorities resisted the demand, mass pressure forced them to grant it. In doing so, however, they insisted that the concession was temporary and would apply only during the winter months. Consequently, as will be seen later, another battle had to be fought before the arrangement was firmed up on a year-round basis.

Electrified by the victories already won, the jobless workers began to join the FWS by the hundreds. So enthusiastic was their response, in fact, that the new, union-sponsored organization was able to move rapidly toward geographic expansion.

Within a few months almost all the existing unemployed formations in rural Hennepin County became affiliated with the FWS. A solid front was thus consolidated against the Board of County Commissioners, as well as the relief authorities in Minneapolis. Not only did that advance strengthen the fight for improved direct relief, it also laid the basis for coordinated action to obtain uniform wages and better conditions on WPA projects throughout the county.

These developments indicated the potential for building a statewide unemployed formation. Steps toward that end were initiated late in 1935. At that point, however, the FWS collided with the Stalinists, who were in the process of turning a political somersault.

In 1931 the Communist Party had begun to establish units called Unemployed Councils. Initially, an ultraleft line, shaped to conform with "third period" Stalinism, was imposed upon those organizations. Adventuristic tactics were used in protest actions on behalf of the unemployed; and dead-end factionalism, camouflaged under the euphemism of "united front from below," was practiced against other tendencies in the mass movement.

Then, during the fall of 1935, the CP started to make its people's front turn, as decreed by the Kremlin. A reversal of policy within the unemployed movement resulted. The Stalinists abandoned their previous ultraleft stance and soon became apologists for Roosevelt's close-fisted relief program. Their organizational tactics were modified, so as to facilitate the shift in line. In Minnesota, steps followed to replace the Unemployed Councils—which had a badly tarnished name—with a new setup, known as the United Relief Workers Association. This outfit made its debut as a Stalinist front at a broad conference held in Ortonville on January 11-12, 1936.

Over thirty unemployed formations and trade unions around the state sent delegates to the Ortonville gathering. Since the organizations involved had never before met in joint conference, it was a milestone for the movement. With the exception of the Stalinists, those in attendance came prepared to concentrate on the development of a militant course of action.

Miles Dunne, a Local 574 leader, gave the keynote address. He proposed three main demands upon government agencies, which had been formulated through previous informal talks. These were: 67½¢ an hour for unskilled labor and the union scale for skilled workers on WPA projects; a thirty-hour week; and worker representation on all relief boards. To fight for those demands, Dunne advocated formation of a loose federation of trade unions and unemployed groups, bound together by a common program. His recommendations were approved by the body, and a follow-up conference was scheduled for February 8–9 in Minneapolis.

A sour note was introduced at Ortonville when the United Relief Workers tried to focus the deliberations on a people's front pitch. The move was backed by a handful of delegates, who represented little beyond the customary assortment of paper organizations used by the CP. But they didn't get very far. The diversion was blocked by a majority vote to table the Stalinist resolution.

As the *Northwest Organizer* said editorially in reviewing the session, the CP's tactics put obstacles in the way of creating an effective formation of unemployed on a statewide scale. If that objective was to be accomplished, the Teamster paper cautioned, a mobilization was needed that would make the projected Minneapolis conference representative of genuine WPA workers' organizations and trade unions. It could not be "a hodge-podge of half-baked intellectuals, political parties, leagues against this and that, and baritones and tenors."

Many seemed to agree with that view, for the representation from legitimate workers' bodies at the February meeting was considerably larger than had been the case at Ortonville. The Stalinists, too, were there in force—paper setups and all—hoping to take charge of the proceedings.

A fight developed right off the bat when the CP tried to put Harold Bean of the United Relief Workers in the chair. Frank Ellis of Austin, Minnesota, leader of an independent packing-house workers union, ran against him. Ellis won and that enabled the delegates to get down to serious business. The following decisions were then reached: to establish a state federation of WPA and relief organizations and trade unions; to set up a central headquarters; to form a broad state executive committee along geographic lines; and to schedule further gatherings at the county level to elect one delegate to the state committee.

Before those plans could be implemented, however, a new national development altered the Minnesota situation. The change resulted from the merger of three organizations—the

National Unemployed League, the Workers Alliance of America, and the Unemployed Councils. A brief review of the background to this event should help explain what was happening.

The National Unemployed League had been launched in 1933 by militants belonging to the American Workers Party. It had since done considerable recruiting, especially in Ohio, Pennsylvania, and West Virginia. Additional strength had been imparted to it politically in 1934, when the American Workers Party combined with the Trotskyists of the Communist League to create the Workers Party. Then, in the spring of 1936, the Workers Party began preparations to enter the Socialist Party, and at that point a question arose concerning the vehicle through which organization of the jobless should be continued.

A separate unemployed structure, the Workers Alliance, had already been established by the Socialist Party. So in the given situation it was decided that the National Unemployed League should be incorporated into the SP-sponsored body, and steps were taken toward that end.

Meantime, the Communist Party—which was maneuvering to draw the social democrats into a people's front orbit—became concerned about the contact Trotskyist cadres were making with young rebels inside the SP-led unemployed formation. For this reason the CP ordered its Unemployed Councils to get in on the merger. A unity convention ensued, early in April 1936, at which the three main tendencies within the mass movement decided to amalgamate their forces in the form of an expanded Workers Alliance of America.

At first glance it might appear that the Trotskyists, social democrats, and Stalinists could now cooperate in leading an effective struggle to defend the jobless workers' interests. But organizational unity did not, in itself, make that possible. More was involved. The formal step of combining into a single body had yet to be accompanied by agreement on basic program. It remained to be decided whether a class-struggle or class-collaborationist policy would prevail, and that key issue became a barrier to consolidation of a united movement.

There was nothing subtle about the conflict over program that followed in Minnesota. The Stalinists immediately set out to entrap the unemployed in people's front politics, using a crude organizational maneuver. Their tactics were designed to gain factional advantage from inclusion of the Unemployed Councils in the national unification. The remnants of that outfit within the state—together with the recently contrived United Relief Workers Association—were unilaterally proclaimed the "Minnesota Workers Alliance." It was a cynical attempt to picture those groups as the only legitimate representatives of the new national formation, the object being to use the workers' desire for a single, powerful organization as a means to establish Stalinist control over the movement.

More specifically, the CP was trying to outflank Local 574's Federal Workers Section and displace it as the main force among the jobless in Minnesota. But that was easier said than done. The FWS—armed with a class-struggle program—had already fought and won several battles against the relief authorities. In doing so it had earned the active support of thousands of needy workers in Minneapolis and Hennepin County as well as the respect and confidence of many depression victims throughout the state.

Besides that, Local 574's unemployed unit had provided significant forces to beef up the picket lines of several trade unions, and help had also been extended in other forms to prevent the bosses from starving out striking workers. In a recent taxi walkout, for example, the FWS had managed to obtain several hundred relief orders from the city authorities, which were then distributed to the strikers at regular intervals for the duration of the conflict. Through such acts of solidarity, it was winning increased backing from employed workers, along with support from the jobless.

All in all, the Federal Workers Section had already developed into an unusually strong unemployed organization with demonstrated vitality.

Then, in the summer of 1936, it received still further impetus when Local 574 was reinstated into the International Brotherhood of Teamsters as Local 544. After that the FWS found new allies among the various local unions in the Minneapolis Teamsters Joint Council, and fruitful relations were developed with two citywide AFL bodies: the Building Trades Council and the Central Labor Union.

This increased support quickly proved most helpful. In August of the same year, the capitalists engineered a new form of attack on the unemployed. They had interrelated objectives in mind: to pare the outlay of tax money for public relief by driving as many workers as possible off the relief rolls; and at the same time to force the victims into a desperate search for jobs, which they would have to accept at scab pay, thereby helping to reduce general wage levels. A campaign directed toward those ends was launched through a capitalist front called the Taxpayers Association, which raised a hue and cry about alleged "chiselers."

Buckling under the pressure, the city authorities decreed that a pauper's oath had to be signed as a prerequisite to receiving public relief. Those refusing to sign were denied further access to the dole, and criminal prosecution was threatened against anyone making a false statement in a relief application. The consequences were terrible for the jobless. Hundreds, who felt compelled to sign the oath so their children could eat, began to live in fear that they might be jailed on some technicality.

A fight against the vicious decree was promptly opened by the Federal Workers Section, acting with strong AFL support. Demonstrations were held and relief stations picketed. So heavy was the mass counterpressure mobilized by labor that the welfare board soon backed off from the new regulation. The workers' victory was made even firmer shortly afterward, when the Minnesota attorney general felt compelled to rule the pauper's oath unconstitutional.

Not much of a role was played by CP-led groups in the fight. As Max Geldman described that aspect of the situation: "The Stalinists, who had limited influence among the unemployed in Minneapolis after 1934, did little more about matters of public relief than present unrealistic demands, accompanied by generally empty threats. Their position was really no better on local WPA projects. On that score, too, the Federal Workers Section was far and away the strongest. Our objective was to have the projects organized like union jobs, and to act in cooperation with skilled workers on WPA, who belonged to AFL building trades locals. And enough headway had been made along those lines to impress upon the authorities that they had better listen to our grievance committees. They knew that we not only represented unskilled WPA laborers; we had strong trade-union backing.

"On WPA, as elsewhere," he continued, "the Stalinists were not concerned with the realities of what could be accomplished for the unemployed. What they really wanted was to find a way to put the FWS in a hole and give themselves organizational advantage. So they launched an adventure, calculated to give a mistaken impression that they were the most militant tendency in the movement. There was ample opportunity for them to do that, for the projects were tinder boxes. It didn't take much agitating to stir the workers into battle, and the Stalinists undertook to profit from that mood to serve their factional aims. They called an irresponsible work stoppage, pretending to champion legitimate grievances that they could not settle and actually didn't care to settle."

The stoppage to which Geldman referred was called by the "Minnesota Workers Alliance" on September 3, 1936. It began on a WPA project at the Minneapolis airport, where some of the workers belonged to the CP-led outfit. Picket detachments were then sent from the airport to other projects in an effort to extend the walkout across all of Minneapolis and Hennepin County.

Neither the FWS nor the building-trades unions had been consulted in advance about the strike, or about the issues to be raised. Yet the Stalinists brazenly demanded that, in support of the action, those organizations pull their members off the projects. To avoid having the CP's ploy lead to a defeat for the workers, that was done. But in taking the step, the FWS forced through a decision to convert the stoppage into a five-day holiday. That move prepared the way for the workers to extricate themselves from the bad situation into which they had been maneuvered.

Not only had the action been precipitated in an utterly irresponsible manner; confusion prevailed as to the nature of the demands. In those adverse circumstances there was no chance to win any significant concessions from the WPA authorities. Instead, a danger existed that an attempt to keep the projects closed down indefinitely could lead to a broken strike. This necessitated the shift from the notion of a prolonged walkout to the concept of limiting the protest action to a fixed period. So compelling was the need for such a change in tactics that even the Stalinists had to agree on the return of all workers to the projects at the end of the five-day period.

Soon after that fiasco, Local 544's unemployed unit made a new organizational move. It was reported in the *Northwest Organizer*, which said in the issue of September 17, 1936: "The matter of the Workers Alliance . . . needs clarification because of the great need for unity on a state and national basis. To further unity the Federal Workers Section has applied to the Workers Alliance of America for a charter on the following basis:

"1. That we do not recognize the present Minnesota Workers Alliance because it is not an effective organizing medium.

"2. That a Minnesota convention of the WAA be held . . . and be limited to unemployed organizations and that representation therein be in direct proportion to the actual present paid up membership. We are informed that these conditions are acceptable."

Concerning the latter point about the conditions being acceptable, Geldman's recollections provide an account of the basis for that assumption, as well as a sketch of background factors involved.

"The Trotskyists considered it essential," he said, "to advocate that unemployed organizations under our influence become part of the newly expanded Workers Alliance of America. We saw it as a potentially progressive movement which could bring significant benefits to the millions of unemployed. In that connection an opportunity would be presented to confront the people's fronters with our class-struggle program on a national scale. Besides, it was a means to counter Stalinist efforts to swallow left-wing militants in the Socialist Party. And we felt that the Federal Workers Section, as the strongest organization we influenced, could play a key role in opposing Stalinist efforts to control the Workers Alliance.

"Our leading people met with David Lasser, national head of the WAA. An understanding was reached that the FWS could affiliate with the national organization and still remain intact under the umbrella of Local 544. It was also agreed that we would cooperate in seeking AFL and CIO endorsement of a united, statewide unemployed organization.

"On that basis the Federal Workers Section agreed to participate in a Minnesota convention of the Workers Alliance, which opened December 12, 1936, in St. Paul.

"We prepared for the convention in Local 544's customary style. As warranted by our numerical strength, the FWS elected about sixty delegates. Carl Skoglund and Grant Dunne were assigned by the Local 544 executive board to assist us. Endorsement of the projected unification of unemployed organizations was obtained from the Minneapolis Central Labor Union. Contributions were then solicited from AFL locals to help finance the penniless FWS delegates. In that way enough cash was raised to charter a bus for their transportation and to assure that they ate regularly while in St. Paul.

"At the same time," Max added, "the Stalinists were making preparations for the affair in their own devious way. They didn't play much of a role in the actual struggles of the unemployed, but they sure knew how to rig the voting at conferences.

"Emergence of the expanded Workers Alliance of America had been a godsend to the Communist Party in Minnesota. The CP proceeded at once to use its connections in the Farmer-Labor Party as a gimmick to form so-called Workers Alliance locals around the state. These were not really unemployed organizations. They were catch-all setups, which embraced farmers, small storekeepers and other tradespeople, along with an occasional lawyer, etc. Such types were used both to beef up Stalinist influence within the FLP and to serve as voting delegates at unemployed gatherings. Most of them were filled with people's front illusions, and one in every so many dreamed of getting elected to public office. Flocks of delegates from that milieu came to St. Paul where the CP was able to manipulate them like puppets on a string."

In rounding out his description of the situation, a few other factors should be noted. Basically, there were two components of organized unemployed in Minnesota. Of these, the Federal Workers Section was by far the largest and most effective. Its ties with the union movement had enabled the FWS to organize the jobless of Hennepin County almost completely, and its influence was growing elsewhere in Minnesota, as well as in neighboring states.

The other component consisted of CP-led outfits in Minneapolis and St. Paul that were relatively small and weak, along with recently formed Workers Alliance locals—of the kind Geldman described—in rural areas of the state. In terms of the number of organizations under their control, the Stalinists had a mechanical edge, but it was the FWS that actually represented a big majority of all the organized unemployed in Minnesota. So, if David Lasser had kept his agreement with Local 544 that representation at the St. Paul convention would be based on the relative size of the formations involved, the CP would have controlled only a minority of the delegates. But it didn't work out that way.

Lasser, who was formally a member of the Socialist Party, had been named to head the Workers Alliance at the time it was originated by the SP. When the Alliance was later expanded through the April 1936 unity convention, he continued on as its principal officer. After that he acted more and more openly as an avid people's fronter, with what seemed a natural liking for the Stalinists.

His partiality for the Communist Party came to the fore in an official WAA ruling concerning the seating of delegates at the St. Paul gathering. It was decreed that voting strength would be based on total dues stamps purchased from the national office since the dates of issue of local charters. That gave the CP-controlled locals a big advantage. They had been paying dues to the WAA for several months, whereas the Federal Workers Section was a new applicant for a charter and had purchased only one month's dues stamps. In that situation, Lasser's tricky ruling gave the Stalinists an artificial voting majority of about three to one against the FWS, although the actual relationship of forces in membership terms was almost the reverse.

There was little opportunity, moreover, for FWS speakers to influence political innocents who had been sucked in by the CP. From the outset the Stalinists and their fellow travelers kept up a drumfire of demagoguery.

As Geldman depicted the scene: "We were drawn into debate on all the people's front topics of the day—antifascist front, support for the New Deal, etc., etc. We were attacked as opponents of unity, as wild extremists. In that way we were blocked off from getting across to the politically backward rural delegates a clear grasp of our program for action. We were unable to make them see the need for a class-struggle policy, statewide unity of the unemployed, and the closest possible alliance with the trade unions. Our proposals on basic line were drowned in demagogic rhetoric about a people's front setup against the corporate monopolies in Minnesota."

Yet there was a certain irony in one outcome of the confrontation to which Max referred. The few decisions made on questions of line stemmed from resolutions submitted by the FWS. These centered on specific demands: for bigger WPA appropriations, higher wages on "made work" projects, etc. Only the FWS had concrete proposals to offer on those matters, and the convention passed them—without dissent.

With agreement having thus been registered on immediate demands around which to mobilize the unemployed for action, it would seem that unity could be achieved. But the Stalinists were determined to keep the Trotskyist-led forces out of the Workers Alliance. Toward that end, they devised a provocation intended to cause the FWS to walk out of the convention, thereby laying itself open to a charge of refusing to cooperate in unifying the unemployed movement.

A slate was brought in by the Stalinists for a state executive board on which they were to have a handpicked majority of two-thirds. Notice was served at the same time that, as a condition for affiliation with the Workers Alliance, the Federal Workers Section would have to submit to the authority of the state board. Instead of walking away in anger, however, the Local 544 unit played it cool. Its delegates simply declined to accept any posts on the rigged state board. In doing so they informed the convention that the FWS remained willing to abide by the WAA constitution; that it would persist in fighting for a democratic regime within the Minnesota section; and that it was ready to take the lead in fighting for the immediate demands which the gathering had unanimously voted to make upon the state and federal governments.

Confronted with that declaration, Lasser and his CP pals had to go through the motions of conducting postconvention negotiations over the question of relations with the FWS. In the discussions that ensued they got around the problem by stiffening the terms for affiliation. A demand was made that the FWS sever its organizational ties with Local 544 and that its membership be scattered into yet-to-be-created neighborhood and WPA locals of the Workers Alliance, functioning under control of the CP-dominated board elected at the St. Paul affair.

Such terms were, of course, unacceptable. Severance of the FWS from Local 544 would have broken the main tie through which unity of the employed and unemployed was being made a reality. The jobless workers would have been thrust, instead, into a political trap that would have made it impossible to conduct a meaningful fight in defense of their interests. For those reasons the negotiations soon led to a definitive split in the movement.

From then on the Workers Alliance found itself doomed to sterility in Minnesota. Apart from an occasional showy adventure over one or another immediate issue, it played no significant role among the unemployed. But it did have an apparatus, which was used to serve the narrow factional interests of the Stalinists. Within the state they converted the Workers Alliance into an instrument to promote their pro-Roosevelt, people's front line; and since that line included factional warfare against the AFL within the Farmer-Labor Party, jobless workers under their influence were unable to secure powerful allies by developing fraternal relations with the AFL movement. That, in turn, made it impossible to build an organization capable of forcing important concessions from the relief authorities.

Local 544's auxiliary unit, on the other hand, continued to gain in size and effectiveness. By June 24, 1937, as reported in the *Northwest Organizer* of that date, the Federal Workers Section had around eight-thousand members on its rolls. Its superiority over the Workers Alliance—in terms of overall fighting capacity—was fully demonstrated when a major battle developed later around demands aimed squarely at the Roosevelt administration.

15. National WPA Strike

"Federal Workers Section of Local 544 Tuesday morning achieved one of the most significant victories in the history of the organization," the *Northwest Organizer* of Thursday April 8, 1937, reported. "After a campaign covering six weeks time the Board of Public Welfare was finally forced to grant the demand of the Federal Workers Section that supplemental aid, which had been granted as a temporary concession during the winter months, be made permanent and continued."

At issue was the question of supplementary city relief for workers drawing WPA wages. On the day of the breakthrough, Ed Palmquist, Max Geldman, and Roy Orgon represented the FWS in the culminating argument with the Minneapolis welfare board. Here is how Geldman remembered the mass actions leading to the victory that had just been won:

"We stormed every session of the welfare board, picketed city hall, organized mass meetings, and mobilized big demonstrations. We held all-night vigils at the homes of Farmer-Labor Party representatives on the board, and we got help from I. G. Scott, a Farmer-Laborite county commissioner, who made a public statement in support of our demand.

"At one point the FWS adopted a resolution declaring that—unless the supplement was granted—the workers would quit WPA and go on the public relief rolls, thus increasing financial pressure on the city. We got backing for this policy from the AFL Central Labor Union.

"In the end we won a year-round supplement for WPA workers, set up on a graduating scale. It started with $9 a month for a

197

family of three and increased for each additional dependent. The supplement began only with the third member of a family. Couples without children got none. But Minnesota families tended to run large, so a great majority on WPA were helped by the provision."

By the following summer, however, jobless workers faced a new problem. An epidemic of WPA layoffs developed as Roosevelt shifted his fiscal policy toward a big increase in military spending. Trying to seize the lead in protesting against the layoffs, the Workers Alliance rushed to schedule a demonstration which turned out to be small and ineffective. General Drivers Local 544, on the other hand, proceeded to organize a massive protest action, one that stood in marked contrast to the fiasco pulled off by the Stalinists the previous September.

Two sections of the local were involved in the action, the Federal Workers and the Independent Truck Owners (ITO). Several hundred members of the latter unit worked on federal projects and for the past two years they had been conducting a running fight against the WPA administrators.

When the WPA was instituted in 1935, individually owned and operated dump trucks were hired to haul dirt on airport and road projects. After thirty days work the owner-operators would be laid off indefinitely and new ones put on the job. One result of that practice was to give the auto corporations a boost, since it helped to stimulate truck sales among jobless workers who could find a way to make a small down payment. Another effect was to impede unionization of such truck drivers, because of the turnover in personnel. The General Drivers managed to organize them, nevertheless, and under the threat of strike action the federal authorities were compelled to cease the "rotation," as they called it, and give the owner-operators steady work on a seniority basis. Payment of union wages to these drivers was also forced through, along with an added sum to cover the cost of operating their trucks.

Now, though, members of both the ITO and the FWS were confronted with a new threat of layoffs. So they combined in calling a two-day protest strike, which began on July 22, 1937. Around ten thousand workers responded to the call, and every project throughout Hennepin County was closed down. The protest was backed by members of building-trades unions working on WPA. The AFL Central Labor Union supported the FWS-ITO demand for bigger WPA job quotas and higher wages; and a joint AFL-FWS committee was formed to follow up on those demands after the two-day protest ended.

By early fall the campaign had not only slowed down the layoffs, but labor pressure had won a 25 percent hike in the city's supplemental aid to those on WPA. On top of that the FWS was soon able to secure raises in both WPA wages and direct relief allowances for workers who were suffering discrimination in rural sections outside Hennepin County.

For an organization that had existed only about two years, the Federal Workers Section had compiled quite a record of accomplishments. These included: prevention of discriminatory practices on the part of relief supervisors; increase in the budgets of families on city relief to more than double the 1934 figures; payment of a city supplement to WPA workers; solid organization of WPA projects in Hennepin County; blocking of attempted wage cuts and arbitrary discharges; and effective handling of workers' grievances on WPA.

In addition the Building Trades Council had been helped to establish a minimum wage of 68¾¢ per hour for common labor on WPA. Various unions had been supported by pickets from the FWS during strikes, and it had fought to get city relief for the workers involved. Some of those unions had then reciprocated with financial aid to Local 544's jobless unit.

Thanks to such money contributions, it had become possible for the FWS to subsidize three of its officers, paying them wages at the WPA level. That enabled them to devote full time to the organization; removed them from any dependence on the relief setup for their own economic needs; and permitted them to function freely in the interests of the membership.

Accomplishments of this kind had not gone unnoticed by the capitalist overlords of the city. They had become increasingly irritated about the amount of money spent for relief and they tried to do something about it. Their stooges rigged a grand jury report calling for "drastic economy in public affairs." Mayor Leach then opened a propaganda assault on the Federal Workers Section, branding it "a racket to take money from the unemployed." His slanderous charge was made not long after the fink suit, described in a previous chapter, was filed against Local 544 in the winter of 1938. Leach's aims were obviously to reinforce the false charges leveled against the union's executive board by the finks and at the same time to extend the smear attack on the organization to include the FWS leaders. But it didn't work.

Organized labor was too powerful in Minneapolis—and too much aware of the value of the Federal Workers Section—for the boss class to get away with the scheme to cripple the unemployed movement. If anything, the jobless workers themselves had even stronger feelings on the subject. Their mood was characterized by Max Geldman in these words:

"Members of the FWS were not just unemployed stiffs. They were union members, wore union buttons, paid union dues (if only 25¢ a month). They had a union to represent them, to fight for them—and they believed in it."

In those circumstances Local 544's auxiliary section had little difficulty fending off the capitalist attack, and it was able before long to extend its activities into yet another sphere. During the depression, young workers had dim prospects of securing meaningful employment. Students, as well, found it tough to get jobs upon their graduation from school, which caused them to coin the ironic phrase, "WPA here we come." As a means of stemming restlessness among these young people, Roosevelt created a National Youth Administration, designed to steer them into the federal "made work" setups.

With an eye on that development, the FWS established a Youth Committee in mid-1938. It was given the responsibility of forming a subdivision composed of young workers and students. Oscar Schoenfeld was designated secretary of the committee; among those who played leading roles in its activities were Peggy Kuehn, Jake Cooper, Oscar Coover, Jr., Don Severson, and Rube Scholl. Together, they developed such an effective recruitment drive that the first major youth rally filled the big Teamster hall.

Those present at the rally adopted the following demands upon the government: WPA projects for youth sixteen to twenty-five, based on their right to work; National Youth Administration benefits to all youth, whether or not their families are on relief; free textbooks in high schools; free tuition in universities; a minimum wage of $15 a month for high school students, $60 for university students; no deduction of youth earnings from the budgets of families on relief; divert all military funds to work relief.

This activity among the youth was paralleled by an intensified controversy over the issue of WPA jobs in general. Persistent

mass pressure for reversal of the layoff trend—coordinated by the
AFL-FWS committee that had recently been formed—was
brought to bear on federal officials. Two conjunctural factors
gave added weight to the workers' demand: unemployment was
mounting because of the new economic slump that had been
developing since 1937, and Roosevelt wanted to avoid alienating
the unemployed voters from the Democratic Party in the
upcoming national elections. In those circumstances labor was
able to win a significant concession. The WPA job quota for
Minnesota was increased by 6,000, raising the state total to
66,000.

Quite soon, though, matters took a turn for the worse. After the
November elections a new federal policy was put into effect, one
that was to become increasingly savage during the following
months. Layoffs were resumed and by the end of December the
Minnesota WPA rolls had been cut back to 64,000. With workers
losing jobs day after day in private industry, this action thrust
the direct relief load toward crisis proportions. In Minneapolis the
situation was rapidly becoming the gravest since the inception of
the WPA.

A mass protest meeting against the layoffs was sponsored by
the Central Labor Union at which the following demands upon
the government were backed, as presented by the Federal
Workers Section: stoppage of WPA layoffs; diversion of military
spending to meet social needs; a $20 billion federal public works
program; appropriation of $25 million by the city and state
governments to finance a housing and public works program; a
local construction program to furnish workers with decent homes;
opening of all idle factories under government operation; a thirty-
hour week in government and private industry with no cut in
pay; union wages on WPA; an immediate 30 percent increase in
all social security benefits; and no abrogation in any way of the
workers' right to strike.

Roosevelt, of course, had an opposite line in mind. He was
tapering off the "pump priming" domestic expenditures of the
New Deal period and preparing to expand the outlay for
armaments. His aims now were to prop up industry with war
orders; to balance the federal budget at the expense of the
unemployed; and in doing so, to pressure the idle component of
the labor force into accepting, on the bosses' terms, any jobs that
might be offered by private industry.

In his January 1939 budget message to Congress the president listed over $2 billion for arms, roughly double the total for the previous year. He was recommending what—up to then— amounted to the largest peacetime military budget in U.S. history.

Concerning money allocated to the WPA, on the other hand, he proposed a drastic cut. For the current fiscal year—from July 1, 1938, to June 30, 1939—a sum of $1.425 billion had been set aside to finance the federal relief program. By January 1939 nearly all of that money had been spent, and Roosevelt was now asking for a supplementary appropriation of only $875 million to cover the remainder of the fiscal year—with $125 million of the sum to be set aside for "emergencies" during the next fiscal period starting July 1, 1939. Then, when Congress acted on the budget, the supplementary appropriation was pared to $725 million. As a result, monthly WPA expenditures were immediately reduced by about one-quarter.

Simultaneously, the WPA administration was revamped under the direction of Colonel Francis Harrington, who proceeded to shave its job rolls. His opening moves were accompanied by an announcement of plans to return full control of public relief to state and local agencies.

As a first step toward that end, some categories of workers were subjected to immediate victimization. Many women were forced off WPA on the grounds that they should seek help from the Aid to Dependent Children program. Members of national minorities got it in the neck on various pretenses. Orders went out to fire foreign-born workers who had not obtained U.S. citizenship, and within a few weeks about forty thousand of them were dropped. Investigations were launched at the same time to determine whether those remaining on WPA had outside sources of income. That step took the form of continual hounding and cross-examination of the workers, including visits to their homes by investigators.

General, indiscriminate layoffs then followed, month in and month out. In October 1938 there had been 3.35 million on WPA. By May 1939 the rolls had been reduced to 2.6 million, and a further cut of 200,000 had been scheduled for June. Almost a million workers had been, or were about to be, dropped from the federal program since the national elections seven months earlier.

Those callous policies were being carried out, moreover, at a time when unemployment, according to trade-union estimates, had again risen to over 11 million; some 300,000 youth had reached employable age during that immediate period; and industrial production had fallen 15 percent below the November 1938 rate.

As though the federal action wasn't harmful enough, state and local authorities began to cut direct relief allowances as workers thrown off WPA applied for such aid. What this overall grinding down of relief measures meant for the jobless was capsuled in a report by the American Association of Social Workers, a body of professionals engaged in relief management. As quoted in the Trotskyist paper, the *Socialist Appeal* of June 20, 1939, that organization fixed the total number of persons dependent on one or another form of public relief at twenty-three million. Aid they received from all sources—federal, state, and local—averaged about 22¢ a day!

Such were the conditions faced by the unemployed when the Workers Alliance held a national "Right to Work" congress in early June in Washington, D.C. As described by an eyewitness in the June 13 *Socialist Appeal*, all proposals submitted to the congress emanated from a behind-the-scenes conference room. Stalinist whips then stampeded the delegates into accepting whatever resolutions were presented.

Eleanor Roosevelt, the president's wife, was invited to address the gathering. In introducing her, David Lasser, the Workers Alliance president, said, "I'm sure that this day is an historic one for the unemployed, the WPA workers, and the underprivileged generally." During her remarks, Mrs. Roosevelt said WPA workers were "government employees" and then declared, "No group that actually works for the government has a right to strike against the government." After her talk the Stalinists pushed their main resolution through the congress. It contained an assertion that "we should form such organizations and clubs as are necessary to rally the utmost support to keep the New Deal in the White House in 1940."

An altogether different stand was taken by the Federal Workers Section. With WPA jobs in Minnesota slashed to about 52,000 by this time—a drop of 14,000 since the previous October, with yet another 2,000 scheduled to get the ax by July 1—the FWS took the initiative in organizing a mass protest. An unemployed formation in St. Paul, known as the Workers Benefit Association, quickly endorsed the action, and mass enthusiasm forced the Workers Alliance leaders in St. Paul and Minneapolis to cooperate. A Joint Action Committee, consisting of representatives from all these organizations, then called a one-day protest holiday on June 2, 1939.

More than five thousand WPA workers, who readily dropped their tools in response to the call, mobilized for a demonstration at the statehouse in St. Paul. Most of the participants from Minneapolis were transported in trucks provided by owner-operators belonging to Local 544. Comprising a motorized parade several miles long, they passed by the Minneapolis WPA office and circled city hall on their way to the capitol. Only about twenty-five workers paraded in the name of the Workers Alliance, partly because a number of them preferred to ride in vehicles carrying FWS slogans.

Banners displayed on the trucks supplied by Local 544 read: "Bread not bullets"—"All war funds to the unemployed"— "Thirty dollars for thirty hours"—"We want rat-proof houses for our children"—"Keep the bull in the stockyards, Stassen, we want jobs"—"Maintain relief standards or we fight."

After the demonstrators reached the capitol in St. Paul a committee of sixteen presented their demands to Governor Stassen. These centered on three key issues: reinstatement of all discharged WPA workers; more WPA jobs at union wages; and the calling of a special session of the state legislature to take action on behalf of the needy jobless.

When Stassen rejected the demands, the committee challenged him to come out on the capitol steps and explain his stand to the demonstrators. He undertook to do so, but such a chorus of boos greeted him that leaders of the demonstration had difficulty in quieting the workers so he could be heard. The jobless were deeply angered by their plight, and they wanted the governor, together with every other public official, to know it.

Similar manifestations of the fighting mood among the unemployed were cropping up elsewhere in the country, usually in a spontaneous way. So the federal government made a phony gesture of appeasement. Layoffs during June were held to 100,000, half the figure previously scheduled, leaving 2.5 million on the WPA rolls nationally.

In the meantime, Roosevelt set Representative Woodrum, one of his Democratic wheelhorses in Congress, to work on a more deceptive whittling job. As chairman of a House appropriations subcommittee, Woodrum pushed through a series of policy recommendations that emanated from the White House. The WPA budget for the fiscal year beginning July 1, 1939, was held down to $1.477 billion—a sum roughly one-third less than was spent on WPA during the previous fiscal year. In conformity with that financial perspective, the bill sponsored by Woodrum contained new devices to hack federal relief spending.

One provision decreed that all who had been on WPA for eighteen months would automatically be removed from the rolls. This harsh step was palmed off as a "rotation" process, under which the workers being dropped had to spend thirty days seeking employment in private industry before they could reapply for "made work" jobs. In reality, though, the pretended thirty-day layoffs were meant to be permanent; and since at least 500,000 workers would fall into that category, it followed that a total of no more than 2 million jobs would be retained out of the 2.5 million. At that point the cumulative layoffs since the fall of 1938 would add up to 1.35 million. And the situation was bound to get even worse because, as this provision indicated, Roosevelt's real aim was to impose a de facto eighteen-month limit on eligibility for WPA employment.

Furthermore, the Woodrum bill abolished the previous government policy of paying the prevailing community wage to skilled workers on federal projects. This meant that, once Congress had passed the bill, organized labor's hard-won protection of union wage standards in the federal relief sphere would be wiped out by a stroke of Roosevelt's pen.

More specifically, it was stipulated that skilled workers would have to put in 130 hours monthly in order to earn the same pay they had previously received for 75 hours. In Minneapolis, for example, this lengthening of hours with no change in total income cut the skilled workers' wage rate from $1.25 to 71¢ an hour, truly a descent into the worst of open-shop conditions. Among other things, this hike in the hours of work laid a practical basis for the firing of many building-trades mechanics from federal projects. For similar purposes the hours of the unskilled were also boosted, from 80 to 130 a month, with a corresponding slash in the hourly wage rate.

Another, no less sinister, aspect of the new relief measure was described in a public statement by Woodrum. As quoted in the June 20 *Socialist Appeal*, he said: "The bill contains restrictions that would strike a body blow at the relief racketeer. There are some organizations that flourish today because they are able to hold it up to the WPA worker that by affiliating with them they will be able to perpetuate his job, as it is called, with the Federal government."

Toward the end of June the Woodrum bill was passed by both houses of Congress, with the foregoing provisions intact. Roosevelt then signed it into law and proceeded at once to impose the lengthening of hours and the consequent cut in wage rates on WPA. What happened right after that was described in a special bulletin by the *Northwest Organizer,* issued July 13, 1939.

"The strike of WPA workers continued to mount and roll across the country like a tidal wave this week," the Teamster paper said, "as fresh thousands of desperate and disgusted workers downed tools and brought the number of men and women on strike close to 500,000 with still more to come out.

"America has never seen such a popular strike. Not even the great nation-wide strike for the eight-hour day in 1886 approached the present strike in numbers. . . .

"American labor defies the yoke of the vicious Roosevelt-Woodrum relief bill. Fighting from coast to coast, AFL, CIO and unemployed organizations followed the lead of New York and Minnesota in a militant thrust against the vicious measure.

"The strike movement began spontaneously throughout the country when workers saw WPA notices posted up which threatened to smash fifty years of union-building at one stroke."

Concerning local developments, the report added: "A spontaneous mass movement against the new Roosevelt-Woodrum Relief Law began last Wednesday in Minneapolis, St. Paul, and Duluth, and quickly grew into a statewide protest political strike enveloping practically all of the fifty thousand WPA workers in the state. . . .

"When the workers returned to their WPA jobs on Wednesday following the July 4 holiday, they were confronted with notices informing them of a lengthening in hours and a cut in wages. Apparently, workers on the State Fair Grounds projects were the first to refuse to work under the new slave provisions. The 160 skilled workers were quickly joined by the bulk of the unskilled men. A series of meetings were held on the grounds, and by noontime all work had ceased. From the Fair Grounds, strikers traveled to all other WPA projects in the Twin Cities. Discontent with the new WPA provisions was so widespread that a word was enough to close down projects. Unorganized workers were fully as eager as their organized brothers and sisters to down tools. . . . On Thursday the movement continued to spread. District WPA Director Richards reported 90 percent of the Minneapolis projects were shut down. . . .

"On Thursday the Minneapolis Building Trades Council met and officially sanctioned the strike, voting to direct its members to stay out until the wage cut was removed by Congress for all workers and appealing to the rest of the WPA workers to join them in the walkout. Friday the Workers Alliance met and voted to endorse the strike. . . . Friday morning the Policy Committee of the Minneapolis Central Labor Union endorsed the stand of the Building Trades Council. Saturday morning at 10 o'clock Local 544's Federal Workers Section met in its strike headquarters at Bryant and 7th Avenue North and officially voted to support the strike. . . .

"Monday morning the Building Trades Council opened an official strike headquarters at the Central Labor Union hall, 18 North Eighth Street. . . . Monday morning at 5 a.m. 544's Committee of Five Hundred turned up at strike headquarters, Seventh and North Bryant, and dispatched squads to all projects with the result that the shutdown was again complete in Minneapolis. . . .

"At 8 o'clock Monday night 5,000 workers attended a mass meeting on the Parade Grounds where leaders of the Joint Action Committee set up by the Building Trades Council, 544's Federal Workers Section and the Workers Alliance, explained the aims of the demonstration and vowed their intentions to make this a fight to the finish.

"The first issue of the *WPA Organizer* issued by the Federal Workers Section's Committee of Five Hundred was distributed at the Parade Grounds. The leaflet called upon Congress to repeal the scab wage bill; to give a job to every able unemployed worker at union wages and conditions by transferring the three billion dollar war appropriation to the unemployed; to open the idle factories under trade union control; and to enact a 20 billion dollar housing and public works program.

"Tuesday morning the strike spread to the extent that two-thirds of the technical and professional workers employed on WPA projects at the University campus joined the walkout."

As this account in the *Northwest Organizer* indicated, the nationwide strike was neither planned in advance nor called by any organization. It simply broke like an unforecast thunderstorm all over the country. By the hundreds of thousands, skilled mechanics and unskilled laborers joined in wrathful protest against the abuses to which they were being subjected.

Turning a deaf ear to this massive demand for justice, Roosevelt threatened the strikers with heavy reprisals. Orders went out from Washington to fire all workers who remained off the federal projects five consecutive days. Local welfare boards were urged to deny them direct relief allowances. At the same time, propaganda was spread about an alleged back-to-work movement. In Minnesota, for instance, the state WPA director, Linus Glotzbach, made false reports that most of the workers were returning to their jobs. The boss press featured his lies in front-page stories, along with other untruths cooked up in editorial offices.

Threats and lies alike were brushed aside by the strikers, whose numbers grew steadily. Within a short time some ten thousand had walked out in Minneapolis, and elsewhere in the country the forces involved in the struggle were similarly expanding.

Due to the spontaneous nature of the walkout, it had assumed a generally unorganized character at the outset. By the second day, though, the AFL building-trades unions had begun to take a hand. One of the first to act was the New York City Building Trades Council, which called an official strike of skilled workers on local WPA projects. AFL unions with members on federal construction jobs soon followed suit in several other cities, and the CIO promised to back them. After that, only one necessary step remained to be taken. In keeping with the strategic needs of the struggle—which had the essential characteristics of a political strike—it was vital for the building-trades unions to link their demands nationally with those of the unskilled workers.

If that was to come about, however, pressure would have to be put on the AFL bureaucrats by the unskilled masses. For that job, a national organization was needed. But as matters stood the only force of such geographical scope was the Workers Alliance of America, which had become Stalinized. Not only was the WAA incapable of taking militant action, but its officials actually played what amounted to a strikebreaking role. Instead of backing the spontaneous walkout, they merely called for a one-day stoppage on WPA projects around the country, deliberately setting a delayed date for the action—July 20. By that time, they seemed to hope, the strike would have folded and they could more gracefully avoid taking a stand against Roosevelt.

In Minneapolis, on the other hand, a firm basis had been laid during previous struggles to press for coordinated action by the trade unions and the unemployed movement. It was no big problem to arrange consultation between the local Building Trades Council and Local 544's unemployed unit. As a result, agreement was quickly reached to combine in demanding restoration of the union wage scale for skilled workers, increased pay for unskilled labor, and jobs for all in both categories. A Joint Action Committee was then established to lead the struggle for those demands.

Locally, the Workers Alliance officials found it impossible to follow their national line of delaying action until July 20. In view of the strikers' militancy, they felt it expedient to formally endorse the walkout. That, in turn, made it possible to draw them, none too willingly, into the Joint Action Committee initiated by the Building Trades Council and the Federal Workers Section.

Picketing was then organized under the direction of the Committee of Five Hundred, which had been formed by the FWS. Apart from a few minor incidents, no difficulty was experienced in keeping the projects closed down. That enabled the strikers to spend considerable time distributing special bulletins, printed by the *Northwest Organizer,* so that the workers generally would have their side of the story. In addition, regular meetings were held to keep everyone informed of developments and to help maintain a staunch fighting spirit.

Before long, Glotzbach, as state WPA director, made a public request to the Minneapolis police for help to reopen the local projects. Immediately thereafter the Joint Action Committee leading the walkout met with him and presented the following demands: no reprisals against any strikers; recognition of the Building Trades Council's right to remain on strike and to picket for union wages; all projects requiring skilled labor to remain closed. A mass rally was then held at which the strikers voted to support those demands, which had been refused by Glotzbach.

As Max Geldman recollected the reasoning behind the Joint Action Committee's course: "FWS policy was that we didn't call a strike on the projects, but we were supporting the walkout officially voted by the building-trades unions. We felt that such a position would help to protect our members from the threat implied in Roosevelt's stand that 'you can't strike against the government,' a dictate that the official labor movement was in a far better situation than us to openly defy. The line that was adopted gave the unskilled laborers a kind of umbrella under which to proceed with the necessary action, and at the same time our support of the building-trades workers served to strengthen trade-union ties with the unemployed movement."

Events were soon to show that there was good cause for the FWS leaders to try as best they could to protect the membership from victimization. On July 13 Attorney General Frank Murphy stated to the press: "There must be no strike against the government of the United States by anyone, anywhere, at any time. . . . Those leaders who have moved to exploit the protests of WPA workers in violation of the federal statutes will be prosecuted."

Murphy added that federal district attorneys had been instructed to keep a close watch on activities of WPA strike leaders. He singled out Minneapolis, especially, as a spot where "evidence of labor racketeering or criminal conspiracy against the nation's relief program" may "result in indictments."

There were several reasons why Minneapolis was getting such close attention from the Roosevelt administration. Through the initiative of the Federal Workers Section, extensive unity had been forged between the employed and unemployed workers of the city. Use of the resultant class power had wrested substantial concessions from the authorities in the WPA sphere and in the allocation of city relief. Those achievements had come to serve, in turn, as beacon lights for the jobless nationally. Labor in Minneapolis was now conducting the most effective strike in the country against the WPA cuts. Small wonder, therefore, that a gang-up against Local 544's auxiliary unit was instituted at all levels of government.

The counterattack began with an attempt to reopen the federal sewing project, organized by the FWS and located at 123 North Second Street. WPA officials telephoned the workers enrolled in the project, a great majority of them women, telling them that they must return to the job or they would be summarily fired.

Then, toward noon on Friday, July 14, the Minneapolis police turned up at the establishment in force. Besides the usual clubs and revolvers, those on foot carried riot guns, and they were backed up by six armored cars. Soon after the cops arrived, a handful of strikebreakers headed for the entrance to the building. At that point the forces of "law and order" launched a tear-gas attack on the pickets and escorted the finks inside.

By the time of the 7:00 P.M. shift change, some five thousand strikers had gathered at the scene, along with about an equal number of sympathizers. They had come to voice a massive protest against the noon attack, but the capitalist authorities were not willing to accord them even that elementary democratic right. Shortly before the scheduled change in shifts, the armored cars were stationed at strategic points, one right in front of the project door. A few minutes later an assault was made on the empty-handed protesters, just as the scabs were being herded out of the building. Moving with the support of a tear-gas barrage, the cops advanced on the assembled demonstrators, firing at them from point-blank range. Even after the crowd broke and ran, the minions of the law continued their shooting and clubbing.

A sixty-year-old jobless worker, Emil Bergstrom, was shot dead. Many were wounded by the flying lead and flailing clubs, including a little girl and a little boy. Seventeen were injured seriously enough to require hospitalization.

Within twenty-four hours of the police riot, an emergency meeting of workers' representatives, qualified to speak for the entire labor movement of the city, adopted a resolution vigorously protesting the unprovoked assault on unarmed strikers. The full text of the resolution was printed in the *Socialist Appeal* of July 21, 1939. Its key passages declared:

"Whereas this tragic attack by police upon workers, innocent bystanders and children present came as a direct result of the actions of the persons and agencies named below, and is not understandable without the policies and actions taken by these persons and agencies,

"Be it resolved: That the combined united labor front of AFL, CIO, Workers Alliance and the Federal Workers Section of Local 544 places direct responsibility and blame for the Minneapolis situation upon:

"1. The present contemptuous and unyielding policy of the Works Progress Administration, national, state and local, as witnessed by the actions of Colonel Harrington toward the legitimate protests of hundreds of thousands of workers in exercise of their constitutional civil rights to strike, to walk out or to picket; and their economic right and duty to make a struggle to live; and proved by inclusion of a five-day firing clause which is in no way mandatory or part of any relief act;

"2. The inflammatory statements and the published orders to the Federal Bureau of Investigation with respect to Minneapolis, which gave to the people of the United States an erroneous impression of the true cause of the WPA protest here as well as elsewhere;

"3. State WPA Administrator Linus Glotzbach, who demanded police action against a majority of WPA workers who are here on strike, in full knowledge of what consequences might follow;

"4. The local Mayor, his Chief of Police, and the admittedly crazed brutality of the Minneapolis police, who acted on orders to fulfill regulations for WPA promulgated from the Federal WPA office;

"And be it further resolved: That this labor movement calls upon the people of the United States to recognize and correct the laws, policies and attitudes upon the part of the above-mentioned agencies which have precipitated this nation-wide problem, and calls upon them to unitedly defeat any prosecution or frame-up attempt as a result of the murderous assaults of the Minneapolis police."

Shortly after the adoption of this angry protest, funeral services were held for Emil Bergstrom at the AFL's central headquarters. Thousands then escorted his remains to the cemetery. Max Geldman gave the memorial address. In the course of his remarks to the strikers, who had come to pay last respects to their martyred class brother, he said:

"Emil Bergstrom will take his place alongside Henry Ness and John Belor [who were murdered by the Minneapolis cops during the 1934 Teamster strike]. . . .

"We must struggle not only to repeal the vicious Woodrum relief bill. We must also build for a society where labor shall not have to ask for relief, where labor may enjoy those blessings which it now produces for others."

At the July 15 meeting, where labor's collective protest against the police attack was adopted, there was one point on which those present were not unanimous. Delegates from the Workers Alliance objected to criticisms of the Roosevelt administration contained in the document. No one was taken by surprise, however. The Stalinists running the WA had been trying unsuccessfully to get motions passed at strike meetings calling for the reelection of Roosevelt in 1940. So their objections were simply overridden and the criticisms of the White House gang remained in the protest resolution.

About the same time, WA President David Lasser paid a brief visit to the city and stated to the boss press that the strike should be called off. Working-class disgust over his conduct was reflected in the July 20 *Northwest Organizer,* which referred to him as "the man who developed an 18-inch tongue by constantly licking the boots of the national administration."

According to the July 16 St. Paul *Pioneer Press,* Lasser also said in a telegram to Roosevelt: "To further avoid shooting innocent people by power drunk reactionaries, and to give Congress opportunity to deliberate relief law changes in atmosphere of calm and reason, we are polling national board Workers Alliance on question temporarily ending all WPA job stoppages in which we are concerned, including suspension one-day national WPA protest planned for July 20. Workers Alliance has never and would not strike against the government."

Lasser was proposing that WA members in Minnesota and elsewhere break ranks in the strike and capitulate to Roosevelt. That finky notion didn't sit well with WA rank-and-filers. A number left the organization locally and went over to the Federal Workers Section. Since the FWS had also been recruiting hundreds of unorganized WPA workers during the heat of combat, it was continuing to gain in strength while the Workers Alliance was growing weaker in Minnesota.

The ruling-class line in the aftermath of the July 14 police assault was indicated by Mayor Leach. He rushed a wire to Washington claiming that the city was "rapidly approaching a revolution" and demanding that Roosevelt send in federal troops. Governor Stassen also tried to divert attention from the outrage that had been committed against the strikers by making a vicious attack over the radio on the whole Minneapolis labor movement.

Both Stassen and Leach were answered in a radio address by John Boscoe, president of the AFL Central Labor Union. He refuted charges that the strikers were being manipulated by a small handful of agitators and explained why the WPA walkout was backed by all sections of the city's working-class movement.

Boscoe asserted that those harming the unemployed were in government, not within organized labor. He also stressed that the cops had deliberately fired on peaceful pickets and pledged that the trade unions would defend any workers who might be subjected to legal frame-ups.

Elsewhere in the country, leadership defaults were taking their toll on the strike movement. In city after city the rebellious WPA workers were being forced back onto the projects and, as a consequence, organized labor in Minneapolis was becoming dangerously isolated in the fight against the federal government. In those circumstances it was necessary for the unskilled workers locally to make a planned retreat. Toward that end, negotiations were arranged between the Joint Action Committee and the WPA authorities. Settlement terms were argued out as follows:

The government waived its ruling that workers absent from their jobs five consecutive days would be fired, agreeing that all who had been removed from the rolls on that basis would be reinstated. An understanding was reached that members of the Building Trades Council would continue their refusal to work on WPA projects until the prevailing union wage was restored; also that they retained the right to picket if attempts were made to use scab labor. Unskilled workers were not to be called upon to go through picket lines. Projects that couldn't be operated without skilled mechanics were to remain closed; and in such cases any unskilled laborers involved were to be transferred to other projects.

Those terms were submitted to the strikers for approval on July 20, 1939—fifteen days after the walkout began. They were ratified at separate meetings of the Building Trades Council, the Federal Workers Section, and the Workers Alliance. After that the unskilled laborers returned to the projects, still showing excellent morale.

But there was one troublesome catch in the settlement. The Joint Action Committee had pressed for a commitment from the government that there would be no reprisals against the strikers, and assurance was refused. Instead, the federal authorities claimed the "right" to require signed affidavits from the strikers attesting that they "have not engaged in illegal activities."

It was an ominous sign.

1939 WPA demonstration at state capitol in St. Paul. Max Geldman (with hand raised) trying to still heckling demonstrators as Governor Stassen (hands in coat pockets) attempts to speak.

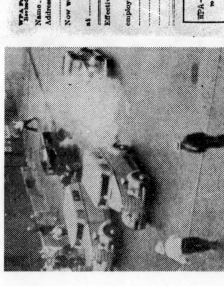

Left: Armored police cars lay down a tear-gas barrage before assault on demonstrators outside Minneapolis WPA sewing project. A worker was killed and several were seriously injured in the July 14, 1939 attack. Right: A sample copy of the notorious pink slips issued by the tens of thousands to workers who were being laid off as Roosevelt moved callously toward liquidation of the WPA.

16. Victims Made to Appear Criminals

As far as the federal authorities were concerned, nothing was settled in Minneapolis. Although the unskilled laborers returned to their WPA jobs, they were still in a fighting mood. The building-trades mechanics were standing firm in their refusal to accept the pay cut. Both categories of workers had been outstandingly militant in defying Roosevelt's ban on strikes against the government. Therefore, it was soon learned, the president had decided to take punitive action against them. His object was to prevent further struggle against liquidation of the federal relief program, and to do that he first had to behead the Federal Workers Section.

Proceeding accordingly, U.S. Attorney General Frank Murphy launched a legal attack on the FWS. It opened right after the workers voted on July 20 to ratify the terms their Joint Action Committee had negotiated with the WPA administrators. Murphy began with public speculation about a "conspiracy" in the local walkout. On that premise he ordered a grand jury investigation "into charges that WPA strikers had interfered with persons wishing to work in Minneapolis and St. Paul."

He also gave the capitalist press a handle for an antilabor smear by making a snide remark that "no labor leaders in Minneapolis or elsewhere have enough influence to prevent my department from doing a thorough job."

Victor E. Anderson, the U.S. district attorney, followed up with an announcement that he was only waiting for a formal FBI report before implementing Murphy's order. During the national WPA strike, FBI agents had been sent into the principal areas of struggle to recruit scabs and gather evidence for prosecution. Their role as labor spies and agents provocateurs was clearly indicated by an account in the Minneapolis *Tribune* of July 24, 1939.

"The Federal Bureau of Investigation agents, about 25 of

217

them," said the capitalist daily, "were in a good position to learn what took place around the sewing project in the series of riots July 14, it was disclosed Sunday. Wearing overalls and other articles of workmen's clothing, the agents, posing as pickets and onlookers, mingled with the crowd surging around the project building. . . . When the shooting and tear gas bombing started, the agents scattered with the rest of the crowd."

On the day this report was published a federal grand jury was convened to "investigate" the Minneapolis strike. As usual, it was rigged against labor. The proceedings were conducted amid great secrecy, except that choice tidbits were leaked to the boss press for sensational headlines.

But what was actually happening became clear enough when the *Tribune* reported: "Witnesses who told about union operations in connection with the strike spent more time in the jury room than did those who told of interference with the workers." Unquestionably, the Federal Workers Section was being singled out as the primary target.

During its proceedings the grand jury called in scores of witnesses, drawn from four broad categories: WPA officials, FBI agents, Minneapolis cops, and workers who had scabbed during the strike.

As an incentive to the flunkies involved in framing up Local 544's unemployed section, Roosevelt chose this time to nominate Linus Glotzbach, the instigator of the July 14 police riot, for promotion from state to regional WPA director. The Minneapolis Central Labor Union protested the nomination, unanimously denouncing Glotzbach as a strikebreaker. But the protest was ignored.

Then, on August 18, the grand jury indicted 103 of the Minneapolis WPA strikers. U.S. Attorney Anderson refused, however, to divulge the names of those involved. Instead, he subpoenaed officers of the Federal Workers Section and the AFL Central Labor Union to appear before the jury, where they were grilled in an effort to trick them into some damaging admission. After that, further indictments were announced, the process continuing until charges had been leveled against a total of 166 workers.

Most were accused of "conspiracy" to deprive the WPA of "workers' services" in violation of the Woodrum law. Several faced frame-up charges arising out of incidents during the strike, and some, it was later found, were named in more than one indictment.

Before long, wholesale arrests began. U.S. deputy marshals barged into the homes of WPA workers at all hours of the night. Because of the secrecy surrounding the indictments, none knew that they, personally, were wanted by the government. Yet the marshals handcuffed the hapless victims and carted them off to jail in a manner intended to give the impression that they were dangerous criminals. This was done, moreover, to the accompaniment of lurid headlines and pictures in the daily boss press.

Over forty workers were grabbed in this manner during the first roundup. Later they were manacled again and marched in a body—accompanied by newspaper photographers—from the jail to the federal court building for bail hearings. Monstrously high bond was then set—a total of more than a quarter-million dollars.

This vicious treatment was denounced by the *Northwest Organizer,* which stressed that the workers' only "crime" was protesting against the layoffs and the terrific cut in WPA wages. If justice were done, the Teamster paper said, those sitting in the prisoners' dock would be government officials and their uniformed thugs, charged with "murder, assault with intent to kill, malicious intent to starve a million families, illegal strikebreaking and conspiracy to defraud the people of the right to life and liberty."

Addressing itself to all trade unionists, the *Northwest Organizer* added editorially: "The federal prosecution of the Minneapolis WPA strikers is a sharp warning to the labor movement of the nation that the national administration is deadly serious about its preparations for war and its campaign to hogtie organized labor. . . . It becomes clearer than ever that the national administration is seizing upon the WPA strike in Minneapolis as a pretext for crippling the powerful local labor movement in preparation for America's entry into the war [which had just broken out in Europe]."

The arrested workers certainly didn't consider themselves criminals. They organized within the Hennepin County jail, where the federal government had put them, and elected Max Geldman as steward. Then they demanded and won the right to hold collective political discussions about the legal attack on the Federal Workers Section.

Food was delivered to them daily by various Teamster locals—milk, fresh fruit, hot evening meals. A huge cake had been made by the bakers' union to celebrate a visit to the city by Tom Mooney. It was sent intact to the jailed WPA workers as a gift from Tom and the union.

Mooney and a second union organizer, Warren K. Billings, had been framed up on murder charges in 1916 after a dynamite explosion at a reactionary "Preparedness Day Parade" in San Francisco, California. The labor movement contended that the explosion had been set off by agents provocateurs, and a long struggle was conducted for release of the two trade unionists. Both were finally pardoned, Mooney on July 7, 1939, when he began the national tour that brought him to Minneapolis. He visited the jailed WPA militants, brought them cartons of cigarettes, and made a speech in solidarity with all class-war prisoners.

As these demonstrations of support to the arrested WPA workers showed, a defense movement was rapidly being constructed. In fact, a legal assault on the strikers had been expected, and a warning of the danger had been raised earlier in the protest resolution adopted right after the July 14 police attack at the WPA sewing project. For that reason the city's AFL movement was generally ready, able, and willing to spring into action in response to Local 544's appeal for help.

When the first indictments were announced, a committee to raise bail funds was chosen. It consisted of representatives from the Central Labor Union, Building Trades Council, Teamsters Joint Council, and Federal Workers Section. Next, a joint meeting of the executive boards of all AFL unions in the city was held. At that session a WPA defense committee was formed, one that could speak authoritatively for the AFL. Two representatives were assigned to the committee by the Central Labor Union, along with two each from the three citywide councils: the Building Trades, Printing Trades, and Teamsters. George Murk, head of the musicians' union, was selected to chair the committee.

With that prestigious body speaking for the defense, it didn't take long to win added support from workers' organizations in the neighboring city of St. Paul. Financial contributions to raise bail and hire lawyers came from local unions in both cities. In addition, volunteers took to the streets selling tags for people to wear expressing solidarity with the defendants. Two things were gained in that way: individual protests against the frame-up were publicly registered and badly needed money was raised.

Three attorneys who specialized in labor cases were retained by the defense committee: Gilbert Carlson, John Goldie, and Tom Kochelmocker. Later, a fourth lawyer, Tom Davis, was added to the defense staff. Davis was among the few surviving populist attorneys who had practiced in frontier days, fighting the railroad and lumber barons. A colorful, impressive figure, he knew all the courtroom tricks and was quite effective in addressing juries. For those reasons he was of special help to the defendants when they went to trial.

The most immediate task, of course, was to post bond for the jailed workers. At the meeting where the broad defense committee was formed, a protest against the exorbitant bail was sent to Roosevelt in the name of 125 AFL locals in Minneapolis. The Minnesota State Federation of Labor and AFL President William Green were induced to join in the complaint. Under this pressure a 75 percent reduction in the bail was obtained, but it was still outrageously high. The defense committee provided bonds for those arrested, with the Central Labor Union putting up its headquarters building as security.

Labor pressure also forced another concession from the White House. Further arrests were being made as new indictments continued to be issued, but they no longer came as a surprise. The names of those charged on one or another count were now being given to the defense committee, which enabled the victims to surrender voluntarily, accompanied by counsel. That process continued until all the indicted workers—166 of them—had been booked and fingerprinted. They were then allowed temporary freedom on bail, pending trial.

Among those arrested were about forty women, mostly workers on the WPA sewing project. Many had children who in some cases had no one else to depend on, and several were over fifty years of age.

Taken as a whole, the *Northwest Organizer* said: "The indicted make up a veritable cross-section of the city's population. There are young men and women who have never known what it is to hold down a job in private industry. There are World War [I] veterans. There are college graduates and there are workers who have toiled from childhood. There are Negroes and Irishmen, there are Jews and Catholics and Christian Scientists and

Seventh Day Adventists. There are veteran union members and persons who for the first time in their lives participated in a strike and a picket line. The one thing in common about all these people is that their economic situation was and is desperate."

At that time oppressed national minorities in Minneapolis— such as Asians, Blacks, Chicanos, Native Americans, and Puerto Ricans—were quite small in numbers. None were then conducting organized civil-rights struggles locally. Insofar as individuals within these groups participated in social conflicts, they acted as members of the working class. Being the last hired and the first fired, however, very few had industrial jobs enabling them to join trade unions and take part in struggles against the bosses. But the situation was somewhat different in the unemployed movement. In terms of percentage, the proportion of national minorities among the jobless was greater than their relative weight in the city's working class. For that reason a significant number of these workers became involved in the WPA strike, and some were now caught in the federal government's legal dragnet.

Organizationally, an overwhelming majority of the WPA defendants adhered to the Federal Workers Section, and a handful belonged to the Workers Alliance. All had been released on bond, except seven members of the Workers Alliance. Those workers, too, were offered help by the AFL-sponsored committee, and it had also asked the Workers Alliance to join in a wholly united defense structure. Both the offer and the request were spurned by the Stalinist leaders of the Alliance, who chose, instead, to initiate a cynical factional maneuver. It took the form of establishing a separate defense committee in the name of the CIO setup that the Communist Party had contrived locally by precipitating an unjustified split in the AFL.

Ralph Helstein, a labor attorney who frequently handled CIO cases, was retained to defend the Workers Alliance members. But so little was done by the CP-rigged defense outfit that Helstein soon complained to the AFL lawyers about the failure of the CIO to give him any meaningful help. The upshot of the situation was described in the September 21 *Northwest Organizer*.

"Tuesday afternoon," the Teamster organ reported, "the Central Labor Union's WPA Defense Committee, through chairman George Murk, issued a press release informing the labor movement of the present status of the defense work, and answering the bold-faced pretensions of the so-called CIO Defense Committee, which is now whining that the Central

Labor Union WPA Defense Committee didn't do right by the
seven Workers Alliance members still in jail.

"The truth is that the Central Labor Union WPA Defense
Committee addressed itself to each Workers Alliance member,
offering its full defense services to these men. The Workers
Alliance members, however, were kept in line by the Communist
Party and rejected the aid of the Central Labor Union, electing
instead to be defended by the CIO Defense Committee. The CIO
has done a lot of talking but so far it hasn't made any concrete
move to come to the aid of these workers who are looking to it for
help."

Murk's press release, printed in the same issue of the Teamster
paper, said in part: "At all times since its inception the AFL-WPA
Defense Committee has offered its full and impartial assistance
and defense services to all WPA strikers indicted. No one has at
any time been denied such assistance for any reason whatsoever." Murk then cited the failure of the CIO committee to act on
behalf of the seven Workers Alliance members still in jail, and
added: "The AFL-WPA Defense Committee has therefore taken
their plight under consideration and is planning steps to provide
them with such proper defense as the CIO Defense Committee
has now clearly shown itself unable or unwilling to provide."

Shortly after that the doubly victimized Workers Alliance
members, embittered by their experience with the Stalinists,
turned to the AFL-sponsored committee for help. Bond was
posted for them, and they finally got out of jail.

A few days later 134 of the indicted workers were ordered to
present themselves en masse before a federal judge for arraign-
ment. It was quite a spectacle, the courtroom jam-packed with the
working-class targets of Roosevelt's vengeance. All pleaded not
guilty, and a series of consultations followed between the
defendants and the labor attorneys to prepare for their appearance in federal court.

Eight of the WPA strikers went to trial on October 2 before
Judge M.M. Joyce. Five were members of the Federal Workers
Section: Richard Connell, Ben Palmer, Carl Pemble, Myron
Phillips, and Leslie Wachter. One, John Marshall, belonged to the
Workers Alliance. The other two, Arnold Mullen and George
Smith, had no organizational affiliation. They had simply joined
in the spontaneous walkout.

Many other workers crowded into the federal building, eager to
lend the defendants their moral support. But most were refused

admittance to the small courtroom. So they packed the corridors, waiting for information about the trial proceedings to be passed to them during the occasional recesses.

Messages of solidarity poured in from trade unions and unemployed formations in all parts of the United States. An appeal for financial support to the WPA defendants was sent out by the Minnesota State Federation of Labor. Word came that the AFL Executive Council had passed a resolution protesting the federal court action in Minneapolis, and the resolution was thereafter used effectively in raising funds for the defense.

On the ruling-class side, care was taken to see that no workers got on the trial jury. It consisted of seven farmers, a realtor, a lumber salesman, a restaurant owner, a hardware dealer, and a former deputy sheriff.

Formally, the jury was to pass judgment on allegations that the defendants had violated the Woodrum law, which made it a crime to "interfere" with WPA workers. Actually, though, the eight—and all other workers indicted—faced court action under the president's decree that "you can't strike against the government." Since the prosecution couldn't twist the facts sufficiently without exposing the antidemocratic character of Roosevelt's dictate, charges of "conspiracy" were leveled against his victims.

Accordingly, the eight were accused of conspiring to intimidate and interfere with WPA workers. But most of them hadn't even known one another until they met during the strike or after being arrested. So it was a "conspiracy" between strangers.

The government based this particular case on a disturbance that occurred on a WPA research project at the University of Minnesota. A scab, Philip Slaughter, had pulled a knife on the pickets. In the scuffle to disarm him that followed, he stabbed one of the defendants, Myron Phillips. Typically, the knife wielder had been allowed to go scot-free, while those he had attacked were being prosecuted by U.S. District Attorney Anderson. The prosecutor made a crude attempt to falsely cast the strikers as the aggressors by putting a couple of finks on the witness stand to testify that the defendants had bullied them.

All five of the FWS members—Richard Connell, Ben Palmer, Carl Pemble, Myron Phillips, and Leslie Wachter—were convicted of "intimidation" and of "interference" with WPA workers. With the exception of Palmer, they were also found guilty of "conspiring" to violate the Woodrum law. John Marshall, Arnold

Mullen, and Gordon Smith were acquitted. The judge then announced that passing of sentence would be temporarily postponed.

The boss press, of course, gloated over the convictions. But intense anger was widely manifested within the working class. During the court proceedings, a defense witness asserted from the stand: "This whole trial is a joke." Agreeing wholeheartedly with his sarcastic remark, workers on the projects said after the convictions: "We are all conspirators."

A second trial followed immediately in Judge Joyce's court. Once again there was not a single worker on the jury. It was composed entirely of business people and well-off farmers, most of whom were from outside Minneapolis. This time there were four defendants—Charles Connors, Milton McLean, Charles Moore, and William Riley—who had been caught up in the attack on the Federal Workers Section. All faced charges similar to those in the first trial. To buttress its case, the government alleged that they had committed various specific acts. Connors, for example, was accused of assaulting a scab. He was a Black worker, who defended his conduct with the terse explanation: "He made an insulting reference to my race."

Connors, McLean, and Riley were convicted of "conspiracy" and "overt" acts in the picketing of WPA projects. Moore was found not guilty. After the jury had rendered its verdict the judge announced that sentences would be handed down later.

Prosecutor Anderson next sought to hold a mass trial of ninety defendants. He argued that since all had participated in the picketing of the WPA sewing project they had been lumped together by the federal grand jury in one "conspiracy" indictment. The defense countered the move with a fight to have separate trials of these workers. In the end, Judge Joyce ruled that twenty-five of them would be tried as a group, and the new proceedings began in his court on October 30.

It was not only in Minneapolis, incidentally, that the federal government's attack on militant workers was growing in intensity. During this same week the frame-up trial of the seven Teamster organizers, described in the opening chapter, had begun in Sioux City, Iowa.

Defendants in the third Minneapolis WPA case included fourteen women and eleven men. They were: Margaret Schoenfeld, Pearl Richards, Ida Dunlap, Eddie Alberts, Victor Nicholas,

Ralph Core, Max Geldman, Harriet Munson, Minnie Kohn, Myrtle Squarcello, Sigrid Ansuma, Anna Wisdom, Oscar Schoenfeld, Frank Stevens, Ed Palmquist, Floyd Hurley, Leslie Wachter, Stella Ross, Lois Viens, Dorothy Green, Bertha Gates, George Totino, Marie Morgan, Nellie Wallbridge, and Charles Grider.

Among them were central leaders of the Federal Workers Section, including a number of its outstanding activists, and all but one of the twenty-five were members of the FWS. The situation of the women was described by Marvel Scholl, who had transferred to Omaha, Nebraska, in the spring of 1939. In a column written from Omaha for the *Northwest Organizer,* headed "One Woman to Another," Marvel said:

"Next week when Federal Judge Joyce's court reconvenes, a group of our sex is coming to trial on the WPA thing. I would like to talk about these women, today. To tell you something about them as persons and unionists. Knowing them, working with them, taught many of us that women can be as good 'union men' as any member of the male sex. A little less than two years ago the women on WPA began to realize that unless they did something about their own status, they would be left far behind the men. Most women on WPA are mothers, left alone to take care of their children. Unlike the men, they had not only to work on WPA, but they had also to maintain their homes, keep their children clean and in school, keep them fed and well.

"In other words, they had a double job. It might have been easier, from a purely physical point of view, had most of them stayed on direct relief or mothers' aid—but women are no more ready and willing to take something for nothing than are the opposite sex. They clamored for and got jobs, sewing, cleaning, assisting in the hospitals, clerical work—anything at which they could work to earn money.

"Working on huge projects, under supervisors who were prone to give favors to favorites, made a group of these WPA women workers realize that unless they organized they were lost. So they organized. They won new and better conditions for all the workers. They took care of their members, called on them when they were ill, helped them get relief when they couldn't work, helped them get back their job when laid off, assisted them to do better work when they were in danger of losing those jobs because maybe sewing wasn't something they had been born to do—got parents of workers on Old Age Assistance—aided mothers to get Aid to Dependent Children when it was no longer possible for them to go on with the double job.

"In other words, these women took upon their own shoulders the cares and tribulations of many hundreds of families. Took those burdens willingly, their only compensation the knowledge that somebody else's life was a little less burdensome than it had been. They worked tirelessly, completely forgetting themselves in their efforts to help the other fellow.

"Next week several of these women come to trial. They are charged with 'conspiracy.' They face almost certain conviction. If these women—if any of the WPA workers who stand convicted or are in danger of being convicted—if they are guilty, then so is every man and woman in the United States who has ever dared to stand up for his or her own ideals; who has ever struck out against oppression; who has ever believed that this is a free country.

"They are charged with 'conspiracy' because they believed in the Golden Rule which tells us to 'do unto others as you would be done by.' If 'conspiracy' is helping your fellow man to a better life; if 'conspiracy' is putting bread into the mouths of hungry children and old people; if 'conspiracy' is giving your all with never a thought for yourself, then they stand convicted. They are real women. They make me proud to be a woman!"

The fate of these women about whom Marvel had written so eloquently, and that of the men involved, was now to be decided by a jury stacked against them. During the proceedings the defense lawyers forced an admission from the authorities concerning the nature of the panel from which the jurors had been picked. The panel consisted of people recommended by county attorneys, clerks of state district courts, probate court judges, the Minneapolis Junior Chamber of Commerce, and a small-town postmaster, as well as some whose names had been taken from rural telephone books.

Sitting on the trial jury selected from that panel were five farmers, a filling-station owner, an accountant, a road-grader operator, a salesman, a garage owner, a housewife, and a nonunion carpenter. All but one were from outside Minneapolis. To intensify their bias against organized labor, the prosecution sought throughout the trial to pump hatred of the WPA strikers into them.

Toward that end it was repeatedly stressed that the defendants had been on the picket line outside the WPA sewing project on July 14. FBI agents lurking in the vicinity had spotted them and turned their names over to the grand jury. Among other charges, they had been indicted for "interfering" with the scabs that the cops herded into the building. Only a handful of the workers employed on the sewing project had finked. The prosecutor used this fact to contend that the bulk of those who stayed out had been "intimidated" through a "conspiracy" on the part of the defendants.

Ever since the police assault on the sewing-project pickets, the boss press had been trying to depict the strikers as violent aggressors against whom the cops were merely trying to protect the scabs. Now, in federal court, those responsible for the July 14 outrage played the role of accusers, and the victims sat in the prisoners' dock.

In an effort to show that the violence had been precipitated by the strikers, Anderson put "loyal" workers from the sewing project on the witness stand. While waiting to be called they sat in the corridor outside the courtroom, talking with FBI agents, and the coaching given them showed through when they testified. Their stories were too good, too pat, to be true. On top of that the defense was able to demonstrate that their identifications of specific individuals was largely a fake.

A double row of seats had been allotted to the big group of defendants. While the finks were testifying they switched chairs from time to time. This caused the witnesses, who had evidently been told where one or another defendant was seated, to make mistake after mistake in attempting identifications.

Some appeared to be acting under strain. Their demeanor, no doubt, reflected pressure from the authorities, probably threats that failure to cooperate would cost them their WPA jobs. Despite everything, two of these witnesses reversed the planned stories when they took the stand and had to confront the defendants. They said there had been no threats against them, that the picketing had been peaceful.

There were others, however, who showed the characteristics of outright stoolpigeons and paid strikebreakers. For instance, one claimed to have heard Max Geldman call President Roosevelt and Governor Stassen rats. The prosecutor could have only one intention in eliciting that reply to a loaded question—namely, to further prejudice the biased jury against the defendants.

Added proof that the FBI was coaching government witnesses

came out when Police Sergeant John J. Finn took the stand and
tried to justify the cops' conduct on July 14. During cross-
examination he was asked if he had discussed his testimony in
advance with anyone. "I just merely rehearsed," Finn answered,
"I mean, just went over the testimony with Noonan and J. H.
Rice [two FBI agents]."

While questioning prosecution witnesses, Anderson tried to
imply that the bullet that killed Emil Bergstrom came from a
picket's gun. He also insinuated that a cop who died after the
police riot, Patrolman John Gearty, lost his life because of an
alleged beating received from the strikers. Later in the trial,
however, Deputy Coroner Callerstrom testified that Gearty had
died from a heart disease of long standing.

All told, 158 witnesses were called by the government in the
third trial. Their rehearsed testimony was given in a courtroom
where a flag in a glassed frame hung on the wall. This led one
worker to remark: "They even have the American flag framed in
there."

In rebuttal the defense presented a considerable number of
witnesses. Their testimony showed that, acting without provocation, the cops had assaulted a peaceful picket line at the sewing
project. While cross-examining these witnesses, Anderson arrogantly sought to bulldoze them. In doing so he turned frequently
to the jury box to profess "righteous indignation" against the
defendants.

During the closing arguments, Assistant U.S. Attorney Giblin
painted a horrendous picture of the strike spreading to all parts of
the nation and "challenging" the government. He named Ed
Palmquist and Max Geldman as the "very fountainhead of the
Minneapolis WPA strike conspiracy." Giblin also stressed that
twenty-four of the twenty-five defendants were members of the
Federal Workers Section; that the FWS was the backbone of the
strike; and that the government understood the Workers Alliance
to have opposed picketing of the WPA projects.

Chief prosecutor Anderson wound things up by telling the bug-
eyed rural jury: "Minneapolis, so long as I am here, is not going
to become the Moscow of America. . . . Forty-seven states are
watching Minnesota and this jury."

All twenty-five of the defendants were found guilty of
"conspiracy" to violate the Woodrum law, and a number were
convicted on secondary counts involving incidents during the
strike. When the verdict was announced, none of the victimized

workers showed any emotion except restrained anger. They filed
silently from the courtroom and went to the Local 544 hall. There
a large body of supporters joined them in discussing plans for
continuation of the Federal Workers Section's fight on behalf of
the jobless.

While the third trial was in progress, Judge Joyce had
announced that the sentencing of all convicted WPA strikers
would be deferred indefinitely. His action was accompanied by
stories from "informed sources" that the White House was
shaken by mounting labor criticism concerning the handling of
the Minneapolis prosecutions.

AFL President William Green had recently sent a telegram to
the local defense committee, stating: "The indictment and
conviction of WPA strikers in Minneapolis has aroused resentment among all working class men and women."

A letter had been received from IBT President Tobin in which
he wrote: "Enclosed please find my personal check for $5 for
Labor's Dinner Meeting honoring WPA strike defendants. . . . Of
course my sympathies are with the men who are involved in the
case and whatever little help I have been able to render in my
humble capacity was gladly given in behalf of those who have
been persecuted for doing nothing but that which they believed
would be of aid to their fellowman."

Although Tobin could have done a lot more in his "humble
capacity" as head of the powerful IBT, he had at least solidarized
himself with the victimized WPA workers. Therefore, his message
was printed in the *Northwest Organizer,* so as to get the
maximum propaganda value from it.

A collective letter of protest was sent to Roosevelt by national
trade-union officials and prominent liberals. They asked him to
"cease such un-American practices" as the mass trial of WPA
strikers, adding that "the number of people indicted reflects a
kind of witch hunt." Citing Anderson's assertion that "Minneapolis . . . is not going to become the Moscow of America," they
contended that "raising this false issue was highly prejudicial to
the cause of Justice."

Trade unionists signing the protest included J.R. Butler, head
of the Southern Tenant Farmers Union; A. Philip Randolph,
leader of the Brotherhood of Sleeping Car Porters; George Counts,
president of the American Federation of Teachers; James Carey,
secretary of the CIO; and Joseph Padway, general counsel of the
AFL.

Liberals who added their signatures were Upton Sinclair, Arthur Garfield Hayes, David Clendenin, Roger Baldwin, John Haynes Holmes, Daniel Hoan, and Norman Thomas.

In Minneapolis the AFL unions voted to assess their members a dollar apiece to help provide defense funds. Organizations of militant farmers in the area also manifested concern about the government's attack on the WPA strikers. They feared that the "conspiracy" weapon might be used to take reprisals against them because of their opposition to Roosevelt's farm policy. Spearheaded by the Farmers' Holiday Association, a rural movement was launched to protest against the federal prosecutions and to actively support the defendants.

What happened next appeared to reflect Washington's response to the pressures from all those sources. O.J. Rogge, head of the Justice Department's criminal division, suddenly arrived in Minneapolis. It quickly became clear that he had come with orders to get out of the fight with the labor movement as gracefully as possible. Negotiations with the WPA defense committee followed. These negotiations concerned the disposition of indictments involving the 130 strikers who had not yet been brought to trial.

As a face-saver, Rogge resorted to the device of nolo contendere pleas (no defense). He first demanded that 40 of the remaining defendants make such pleas, but the defense committee flatly rejected that figure. An understanding was finally reached that 5 would plead no defense on minor charges other than "conspiracy." Those who did so were Owen Jacobsen, Roy Orgon, Glen Smith, Louis Lindsay, and Victor Chiodo, all members of the FWS. The indictments against the last 125 workers were then quashed.

Upon completion of the negotiations, Rogge appeared in Judge Joyce's court, where he stated: "The Department of Justice feels that the 32 most culpable persons have already been convicted. . . . The President felt the duty of the WPA workers had been made clear. . . . they have no right to conduct a strike."

The fact that only thirty-two workers had been involved in thirty-three convictions, as Rogge's statement indicated, reflected yet another aspect of the government's savagery. Leslie Wachter, a Federal Workers Section steward, had been tried and convicted on various counts in both the first and third trials.

After the head of the Justice Department's criminal division had appeared in court, Judge Joyce proceeded to sentence all the strikers who had been found guilty. He prefaced his action with a speech about "self-seeking leaders with ulterior motives" and referred to the strikers as "dupes." On that note he ordered that all but three of the men convicted in the trials be jailed for various terms, as follows:

A year and a day—Ed Palmquist, Max Geldman, and Leslie Wachter; seven months—Charles Grider; six months—William Riley, Victor Nicholas, and George Totino; four months—Milton McLean; ninety days—Eddie Alberts, Frank Stevens, Floyd Hurley, Myron Phillips, and Richard Connell; sixty days—Ralph Core; thirty days—Charles Connors.

Short sentences given to the other three—Ben Palmer, Oscar Schoenfeld, and Carl Pemble—were suspended and they were put on probation. Those who had pleaded nolo contendere—Roy Orgon, Louis Lindsay, Victor Chiodo, Glen Smith, and Owen Jacobsen—got probationary terms of twelve to eighteen months.

Only one of the women convicted, Minnie Kohn, was ordered jailed. Judge Joyce branded Kohn a "ringleader" and gave her a forty-five-day sentence. There were seventeen counts in the indictment against her. This alone showed that she was indeed a fighter.

As Max Geldman remembered Kohn: "Here again is an example of worker heroism during the class struggle. Minnie was no talker. I vaguely recall her attendance at meetings of the sewing-project workers. She was not even a steward, but once the struggle broke out she was a whole army of wrath. Minnie was amongst the first on the picket line, she and a number of others. Believe me they were a formidable troop. They planted themselves at the entrance of the building, forming a determined picket line.

"Since the majority of the workers at this project were female, Minnie and her squad developed a unique tactic to keep scabs from entering the building. As they were being escorted by the cops, the squad would rush in and virtually tear the clothes off the scabs. It was quite a sight. The strikebreakers naked amidst the jeers of the pickets.

"I really don't know much about Minnie's background. I can only tell you that she never faltered, took the trials in stride, served her time and came out as rebellious and defiant as when she went in."

The remaining thirteen women, who had been found guilty,

were given from one year to eighteen months on probation. They were: Bertha Gates, Pearl Richards, Marie Morgan, Harriet Munson, Ida Dunlap, Lois Viens, Sigrid Asunma, Myrtle Squarcello, Margaret Schoenfeld, Dorothy Green, Ann Wisdom, Stella Ross, and Nellie Waldron.

Obviously enough, the government feared that to actually imprison most of the women, as was being done with the men, would precipitate a new wave of protests from the labor movement. For similar reasons the Justice Department also seemed to have proposed that those incarcerated receive relatively light sentences. But Judge Joyce didn't appear too pleased with those tactics. In carrying them out, he referred to the strikers as "cruel" and "heartless," as "ruthless" and "cowardly." If any who had been put on probation violated the terms, he sternly warned, they would promptly be thrown in jail.

During the trials, the prosecution appeared to have deliberately padded the court record with extraneous matter so that an appeal to the higher courts would be almost prohibitive to the defense. Not only would the necessary printed transcripts of the trials be very costly, but there would also have to be an extensive outlay for appeal bonds. In addition, the national trade-union bureaucrats couldn't be relied upon to provide significant financial help. Funds to meet the heavy costs would have to be raised mainly within the Minneapolis movement, and there was no real chance of that. For those reasons the defense did not appeal the convictions, which meant that workers given jail terms had to begin serving their time at once.

Twelve were sent to the federal prison at Sandstone, Minnesota—Richard Connell, Myron Phillips, Eddie Alberts, Floyd Hurley, Frank Stevens, Milton Mclean, William Riley, George Totino, Charles Grider, Leslie Wachter, Ed Palmquist, and Max Geldman.

Three—Minnie Kohn, Charles Connors, and Ralph Core—were put in the Minneapolis workhouse. Victor Nicholas, at the time of the WPA strike, was on parole from a Minnesota penal institution in St. Cloud, where he had been serving a sentence having nothing to do with the strike. Due to the new conviction in federal court, however, he first had to serve the rest of his Minnesota jail term before he could begin putting in the time imposed by Judge Joyce.

As the sixteen strikers were being imprisoned, a demand was

raised by the WPA defense committee that they be granted a presidential pardon. Support was soon obtained from several prominent trade-union leaders, including Randolph, Counts, and Butler—all signers of the above-mentioned collective letter protesting the prosecutions—and Joseph Schlossberg, secretary of the Amalgamated Clothing Workers. With that added impetus, the campaign grew steadily. Demands for a pardon flooded into the White House from officials of national unions, both AFL and CIO; from central labor bodies in various cities; and from a goodly number of local unions.

Roosevelt refused to act, however, and the WPA workers he had railroaded to jail stayed there until their time was served.

Looking back on the experience after thirty-five years, Max Geldman remarked: "The 1939 WPA strike was the culmination of mass protest and anger at a system that robbed the unemployed of the dignity of workers engaged in productive labor. Not only were they alienated from such products as were turned out, like factory workers; they were completely alienated from the work process itself. Then came the mass layoff notices, which sent them back to the worst miseries of direct relief. There were spontaneous reactions. Workers threw down their shovels and manifested their anger everywhere.

"Was it a strike? No production was stopped, since 'made work' was involved. It was a political act, a demonstration of burning resentment against the government. It was a mass outburst such as makes revolutions possible, only it didn't involve workers engaged in actual capitalist production.

"Nationally, the jobless workers were weakly organized and their leadership was even weaker. Minneapolis became the center of the struggle. There the unemployed were well organized, as were the trade unions which backed them; and an experienced revolutionary leadership was present within the mass movement. But it was just in one city, and if it's not possible to build socialism in one country, it's much less possible to do so in one city. Roosevelt knew this as well as we did. With the cry, 'You can't strike against the government,' he came down on us with all the federal power, acting in collaboration with state and city repressive forces.

"I can't say we won the 1939 WPA strike, but we gave a good account of ourselves and left a bright chapter in the history of American class struggles."

17. The Economic Crisis Is "Solved"

Despite strong labor opposition, Roosevelt had stubbornly continued to phase out the federal relief program. In doing so he was simply carrying out the wishes of the ruling class, of which he was a loyal representative and a faithful servant. The capitalists were developing a need for cannon fodder and for cheap labor in the war industries. They wanted to drive the unemployed off public relief, to starve, to scratch for industrial jobs at cut-rate wages, or to go into the military forces.

In compliance with those aims the federal administration persisted in whittling away at the WPA rolls. During the protest strike it had gone ahead with the layoffs at an average national rate of 2,500 daily. The Minnesota figures reflected the general consequences. In that state, where there were some 66,000 WPA jobs in the fall of 1938, the rolls had been cut to around 31,000 by August 1939. This had happened, moreover, at a time when vast numbers were still unemployed. It was a situation in which, as the American Association of Social Workers pointed out, "The WPA cuts are not justified on the basis of disappearing need."

What is more, the bulk of the workers who were dropped under the eighteen-month clause in the Woodrum law were kept off for good. Within the first six months after the law was passed, about 750,000 had been laid off across the country under that clause. Although supposedly it was for thirty days, administrator Harrington admitted in a December 1939 statement that less than 150,000 of those involved had gotten back onto WPA. Local relief agencies everywhere were swamped with new applicants who had been cut from the federal program. As a result, workers trying to get enough help to at least feed their families had to wait in long lines at city welfare offices, where at best they got only meager handouts.

Not only did Roosevelt remain impervious to demands that his policy be altered so as to alleviate the human misery it was causing; his budget proposal for the coming fiscal year called for yet a further slash in WPA funds, paralleled by a new hike in military spending. As a corollary, he announced that 700,000 more workers nationally would soon be dropped from the federal relief rolls.

While all this was going on, the jobless were being subjected to other forms of harassment as well. In Minneapolis, reprisals were taken against the strikers upon their return to the WPA projects. A number were fired outright on charges of "intimidation," the action against them being predicated on reports from scabs and stool pigeons.

A blacklist of defendants in the WPA trials was set up locally by the main bosses' organization, the Associated Industries. These workers found pictures of themselves posted in the offices of concerns where they went to seek employment. They were turned down, even where other applicants were occasionally hired. One of the indicted workers had been lucky enough to find a job in private industry a few weeks after he was laid off from the WPA under the Woodrum law. When the grand jury action against him was made public, however, he was fired on the spot.

Capitalist pressure was put on the Minneapolis welfare board to cut the family budgets of those on relief. During the hassle that followed, the board managed to impose a reduction in the city supplement for workers on WPA.

Nationally, a drive opened up to refuse relief to single men who were eligible for military service. About the same time the WPA administration began a purge of "subversive elements" who "believe in the overthrow of the United States government." As a condition for continued employment, workers were required to sign a loyalty oath affirming that they "are not or will not become members of any Nazi Bund organization or Communist group" while on WPA. Efforts were made to bar from city relief those refusing to sign the oath.

Under these general circumstances, things had not gone well for the building-trades workers. When the protest action by the unskilled laborers ended and they went back to their WPA jobs, members of building-trades unions in some cities remained off the projects. While they held out against the wage cut, Roosevelt had been trying to break their strike.

In Minneapolis two AFL officials were included among those

indicted for "conspiracy" to violate the Woodrum law—Walter Frank, head of the lathers' union, and Myrtle Harris, a Central Labor Union officer. The charge against them was plainly intended to put pressure on the building-trades strikers locally. However, the two had been among the 125 whose indictments were quashed when the defense campaign forced the government to back off from further prosecutions, and that particular move fizzled.

A different form of legal attack was used in New York and other places. Several officials of building-trades unions were indicted by federal grand juries for "criminal conspiracy in restraint of trade" within private industry. They had been doing nothing more than following established trade-union practices in the construction field, which showed that the government actually had something else in mind. Its real aim was to demonstrate what could happen to these union officials if they didn't cease their interference with the carrying out of Roosevelt's policies in the WPA sphere. That intention was evidenced in the U.S. Attorney General's failure to make any real effort to secure convictions on the "restraint of trade" charges.

Faced with this several-sided governmental assault, the whole trade-union movement should have united in defense of the victims. All-out support should have been given to the indicted building-trades officials; to the Teamster organizers framed up in Sioux City, Iowa; and to the unskilled workers railroaded in the Minneapolis WPA trials. It was necessary, moreover, to raise the defense campaign to a political plane in the form of an open confrontation with Roosevelt.

There was a vital need to explain the link between the president's antilabor policies and his preparations for war. In that way the workers would have been helped to grasp the real score about the demagogue in the White House. They would have begun to see the need for a complete break with the Democratic Party and for the launching of an independent labor party, based on the trade unions. The whole class struggle could have been raised to a higher, more effective level as the workers were mobilized in mass opposition to both the domestic and foreign policies of the capitalist government.

Nothing of the kind was done, however, because the class-collaborationist mentality of the bureaucrats sitting on top of the trade unions made it impossible for them to give effective leadership. In the fight of the building-trades workers for union wages on WPA, official labor action was confined pretty much to a call for repeal of the Woodrum law. It proved to be a futile course. All that resulted was the granting of a few minor concessions, largely about secondary matters, on federal construction projects here and there. The attempt to establish a union scale on WPA was destined to peter out when the whole program was scuttled a bit later—"made work," scab wages, and all.

Due to the default in national trade-union leadership, the militants in Minneapolis found themselves caught in an increasingly difficult bind. Not only had the WPA layoffs been made to stick, but life on the projects was being made tougher than ever, as was shown by the firings for alleged "intimidation" and the demand that loyalty oaths be signed. Clearly, the Federal Workers Section could no longer block such antilabor moves, which showed the extent to which it had been weakened by the legal attack and the jailings. But the government hadn't succeeded in crushing the organization.

In a broad sense a sort of stand-off had developed. Although liquidation of the WPA could now be continued without serious interference, the FWS was still able to take meaningful action on various job grievances. It retained important trade-union support. Project supervisors were well aware of the power generated through the campaign in defense of the strikers who had been hauled into federal court. Resentment over the legal assault was also smoldering on the projects. This made the authorities fear that another eruption might develop if they cracked down too hard.

Thanks to those combined factors, the Federal Workers Section was soon able to launch a new organization drive. It caused a stir on the projects and produced a significant number of new members. Yet the gains could only be transitory, for the WPA labor force was dwindling rapidly.

By mid-1941 relatively few remained on the rolls of the "made work" projects, and those who did were about to lose their jobs in wholesale lots. So pronounced had the layoff trend become, in fact, that entire projects were being discontinued because the cuts left insufficient personnel to operate them. At the same time, with around nine million still out of work according to CIO estimates, the slashes in federal relief brought an increasingly heavy influx of needy families onto the public welfare rolls in most every town.

Except for a few finishing touches, the WPA had been abolished. But this action did not result from a correction of the basic economic dislocations that had brought about the massive unemployment from 1930 on. The causes of the job crisis were inherent in the system of production for private profit, which had not been changed. Roosevelt had in no way tinkered with the fundamental capitalist structure. At terrible cost to the working class, he was alleviating the economic problems by putting the country on a war footing. That was the ultimate capitalist "solution" for unemployment.

For the entire period during which that ruinous course was being imposed upon the nation, General Drivers Local 544 had not only fought against the president's brutal treatment of the jobless. It had also taken the lead in organizing opposition to his war policy within the Minnesota labor movement.

The stormy events of that campaign and their fateful consequences will be the theme of the fourth and final volume of these reminiscences about Teamster history.

Appendix
How the Teamsters Union Organized
Independent Truckers in the 1930s

[This article, first published in the April 12, 1974, issue of *The Militant* newspaper, was written in connection with the February 1974 strike of owner-operators in the over-the-road trucking industry. It expands significantly on the discussion of individual owner-operators in chapters 10 and 15 of this book and chapters 17, 19, and 22 of *Teamster Power*.]

During the depression of the 1930s individually owned trucks appeared in the transportation industry in ever-increasing numbers. A major factor in this development was an intensive sales campaign by the auto corporations. Their caper was to induce the unemployed to buy themselves a job by buying a truck. Workers who could scrape up the down payment were allowed to meet the balance of the purchase price on a long-term installment basis. Incentive for such purchases was given by the federal government, which used individually owned trucks on its "made work" projects for the unemployed of that period. State, county, and city engineering departments followed suit, especially in connection with road work.

Comparable trends developed within private industry. Firms having their own fleets of trucks often kept a surplus of rigs on hand by hiring independent owner-operators, who usually found themselves payless—despite the time put in—when they were not actually hauling something. Fluctuations in business volume were thus compensated for at the expense of the owner-operators and to the profit of the fleet owners. Broker setups appeared in the form of companies that relied entirely on individual truck owners to move goods. In such cases virtually the entire overhead cost of trucking operations was shoved on to the owner-operators, thereby impairing their capacity to earn a living. These and other

241

practices of a comparable nature held sway in coal and ice delivery, construction hauling, motor freight, and elsewhere in transportation.

Immediate profit-taking along these lines was not the only object the capitalists had in mind. Advantage was sought from ambitions that developed among independent owner-operators to expand their holdings and go into business for themselves. Illusions were fostered that such prospects were open to all individual owners, so as to trick them into identifying themselves with the problems of management. To the extent that the scheme worked, divisions were sown between owner-operators and the drivers of company fleets. Unionization of the industry was thereby impeded; the laws of the open-shop jungle could better prevail; and the trucking bosses were able to wax fatter in all respects.

These dangers to both categories of drivers were further accentuated by misleadership within the International Brotherhood of Teamsters. Little attention, if any, was paid to the problems of the owner-operators. Although sporadic efforts were made to organize fleet drivers, IBT policy was so ill-conceived and so poorly executed that not much headway could be made in that sphere either. As a result, the union remained weak, at best, and in several important respects it was quite impotent.

Such were the prevailing conditions throughout the trucking industry when Trotskyists in Minneapolis began to win leadership influence within the IBT during the second half of the 1930s. In shaping our overall class-struggle policy, close attention to the independent owner-operator question was included. We began by taking full account of the realities of the existing situation. Drivers owning their own trucks had become a factor of major dimensions within the industry. To consolidate the union power, they had to be brought into an alliance with the fleet drivers. Before that could be done, however, a course had to be developed that would serve the owner-operators' interests.

Careful examination of all the factors involved convinced us that those owning one truck, who did their own driving, should be approached by the union as fellow workers. Proceeding accordingly, we set out to organize as many of these individuals as possible. They were then extended the democratic right to shape the demands that were made upon their employers, the leasing companies. On that basis the union as a whole followed through by backing them in struggles to improve their take-home pay.

The validity of that policy was confirmed by its results. In the major struggles of that period against the trucking employers generally, the union's owner-operator members served loyally. They volunteered their trucks to transport pickets and shared in the picketing. A significant number of our casualties in battles with the cops were from among this category of workers. After the union had been consolidated, they continued to play a constructive role. Like other members of the organization, they looked upon those of their own kind who took an antilabor stance as finks and dealt with them accordingly.

Our course had checkmated the divisive schemes of the bosses. In Minneapolis the truck drivers and allied workers had emerged as a power, and the union was able to march forward in advancing the interests of all its members.

These experiences became an important asset when we launched an organizing drive in the over-the-road industry in 1938. There we found an even more complicated situation concerning independent owner-operators. Firms holding carrier rights issued by the government employed many of these independents, paying them flat rates by the mile, ton, or trip for rig and driver. It was truly a cut-throat setup. Diverse methods were used to heap inordinate trucking costs upon the owner-operators, thereby shaving down their earnings as drivers. At the same time, devious patterns were woven to confuse the true nature of the employer-worker relationship and turn the individuals involved in an antiunion direction.

Propaganda attacks were launched—especially by legal tricksters claiming to speak for the owner-operators—which were calculated to discredit the IBT campaign. One such blast came from David I. Lipman, who purported to head a "Truck Owners and Operators Association." Through an article in the December 1939 issue of the *Transport Driver,* a publication circulated among owner-operators, he sharply criticized Teamster Local 710 of Chicago. He charged the union with "lack of regard for the truckmen's interests" and claimed that the IBT had no right to represent his clients.

John T. O'Brien, then head of Local 710, asked me to prepare a statement for the local in reply to Lipman. I did so and sent the draft to him on January 3, 1940. It contained an extensive account of the owner-driver situation in over-the-road trucking.

Concerning the confused patterns of employer-employee relations in the industry, the statement said:

"The individual owner-operator is by the very nature of his position a composite in one degree or another of the two distinct factors in the over-the-road motor freight industry—the owners of trucks and the drivers. There is a more or less clearly defined category of individual owner-operators, and there are other categories called by that name but who are in reality something entirely different.

"There is the individual who owns one truck which he himself drives. Ordinarily he operates under lease in the exclusive service of one operating company. He represents the owner-operator type of driving service in its purest form and deserves the fullest measure of consideration for his special problems.

"It must also be recognized that even in this group there is a tendency to operate free-lance on a catch-as-catch-can basis. These individuals who operate in this manner are commonly referred to as gypsies, skimmers, wildcatters, etc., and are found hauling for one company today, another tomorrow, and the next day trying to drum up business as a one-man company. They are a serious problem to the industry.

"Even the most clearly defined type of owner-operator has a general tendency toward expansion, and the individual frequently becomes the owner of additional units of equipment. During this gradual process of accumulation he will first acquire one or two more pieces of equipment and will employ men to drive these while he continues as a driver of one of his units. As he continues to accumulate units he hires more and more men. This process transforms him into a combination owner-driver-employer.

"Finally he acquires enough equipment and hires enough men so that he must devote all or nearly all of his personal time to the problems of the management of his operations. He then is no longer in any sense a driver and is transformed into the status of an owner of trucks and an employer of men who does business with an operating company as a small fleet owner who hauls by subcontract under a lease system. Yet he continues to pose as an individual owner-operator and is erroneously posed as such by many others. We thus arrive at the ridiculous circumstance whereby, assuming such an individual to be the employer of ten men, which is not uncommon, the group is referred to as eleven individual owner-operators instead of being identified as an employer and ten employees, which is the true state of affairs.

"Occasionally a small fleet owner succeeds in acquiring the necessary operating certificates and permits and enough direct accounts to enable him to abandon his service under lease to an established operating company and to launch his own company. This action, which represents the realization in fact of the secret ambition of every 'gypsy' individual owner-operator, brings into the full light of day the true nature of the employer-employee relationship between the small fleet owner and the men who drive his trucks.

"It now becomes clear how many operating companies have cleverly devised a scheme whereby they obtain driving service at substandard wages. The drivers are held in a state of continuous confusion by the ever-changing employment and equipment ownership relations between the drivers and small fleet owner on the one hand and between the small fleet owner and the operating company on the other. The operating company evades all responsibility for employment relations with the drivers by hiring through the small fleet owner, who in turn far too frequently pays for driving service at varying substandard wage rates by a wide variety of methods."

With reference to the scope of Teamster jurisdiction in dealing with this situation, the answer to Lipman asserted:

"A man who owns the truck which he drives is merely an employee who is required to furnish his own tools as a condition of employment. He has a full legal right to be represented by a labor organization. The IBT will not relinquish this right, nor will it permit the issue to be confused by parading in alleged individual owner-operators who are in reality something entirely different. The true nature of these masqueraders has already been carefully defined above. . . .

"Those who are genuinely interested in the problems of the men who drive motor freight trucks across the highways will recognize that the IBT is approaching the problems of the individual owner-operators with the same serious consideration that it gives to the problems of the employed drivers [drivers employed on company-owned fleets]. The proper place for the individual owner-operator to get effective results is in the ranks of the IBT, shoulder to shoulder with the employed drivers."

An area committee, composed of representatives from key local unions, had been set up to lead the Teamsters' over-the-road campaign, to which Lipman and his kind were opposed. In dealing with the owner-operator question the committee had a clearly formulated perspective from the outset. The aim was to require leasing companies to pay individual owner-operators the cost of operating their equipment, plus its replacement value, plus the union scale as drivers.

It will be noted that the union was concerned only with the *cost* of operating the equipment, not with helping to secure any *profit* from the operation. If we had supported any notion of earning a profit on the vehicle itself, impetus would have been given to the petty-bourgeois aspirations inherent in the ownership of trucking equipment. Our aim was the opposite. We approached the equipment as expensive tools the individual owner-operators had been required to provide in order to get jobs as drivers. This served our objective, which was to make the leasing companies pay for the use of those tools, as though they were the owners. That would reduce their advantage down to having the owner-drivers buy the equipment initially, and there wouldn't be much percentage for the operating companies in such an arrangement. To the extent that we could succeed in that course, the trend toward an increase in the use of owner-operated rigs could be reversed; and a healthier situation could be established, with trucking firms again using their own fleets, operated by drivers paid on a regular wage basis.

In striving toward that goal we were aided by gains registered in securing higher wages and better conditions for fleet drivers. Those accomplishments were noted by the owner-operators, many of whom began to realize that they, too, would be better off as fleet drivers. As matters stood, however, they needed immediate help to secure the cost of operation of their equipment. In the rebuttal of Lipman's allegations, union policy on this matter was described as follows:

"Payment for equipment service has been computed in a wide variety of forms, consistently to the benefit of the operating company and to the detriment of the owner-operator.

"Whatever the declared rate may have been, an elaborate system of deductions made the real earnings something considerably less. Almost all of the hazards of the road, including cargo damage and equipment layovers, not to mention personal layover expense, were transferred by the operating company onto the shoulders of the owner-operator. Fake charges for 'spotting,' 'backup,' 'inspection,' etc., further reduced his income until the owner-operator received very little actual compensation in the form of earnings which could be taken home to meet the household expenses.

"The IBT has again in this case sought to attack the problem at the root. Equipment service must now be paid for the full mileage operated, and there can be no deductions by the operating company for any reason whatsoever. A statement of legitimate charges may be presented to the owner-operator. However, if they are not legitimate he protests in advance of payment and is no longer in the position of trying to get money refunded which was improperly withheld from his pay.

"The operating company is now required to provide insurance, certificates, permits, travel orders, out-of-state vehicle tax, bridge tolls, etc., and to pay any legal charges involved if these are not properly provided. The owner-operator has been freed from the gouging methods of those companies which made compulsory the purchase of gasoline, oil, tires, repairs, etc., through a company agency, with an unearned profit extracted by the company at the expense of a further reduction in the owner-operator's earnings."

Apart from the cost of equipment operation, the union required that individual owner-drivers enjoy the same wages and conditions as all other drivers. These earnings had to be paid separately from money received for rental of equipment. This made it harder for the leasing companies to cheat the individual owner-operators. A passage in the reply to Lipman outlined the union's approach:

"The International Brotherhood of Teamsters has sought through the new Area Over-the-Road Contract to correct this condition by placing employment responsibility where it rightfully belongs—on the shoulders of the operating company, which is now held responsible for the driver's wages, social security tax, compensation insurance, etc., regardless of whether he is employed by the operating company or through a small fleet owner.

"Not least in importance in the general problem is the driver who is given a paper title to the truck by the operating company, usually on a deferred payment plan, and is then paid as an individual owner-operator, not as a legitimate business relationship, but as a subterfuge to escape the payment of the union wage scale.

"Thus we find that while there are men who drive as actual individual owner-operators and who have a real employment problem, there are other categories incorrectly referred to as owner-operators who vary, in different shades, from the truck driver who is being cheated out of his just compensation by the subterfuge of a fake truck sale, to the individual who is in reality a small fleet owner and an employer. If we intend to be logical we must begin by recognizing that the first problem for the individual owner-operator is to identify the malpractices committed in his name by the operating companies and then join hands with the employed drivers for their mutual protection."

As can be seen from this sketch of the earlier situation, progress was being made in shaping a viable policy toward independent owner-operators in over-the-road trucking. But the process was suddenly cut short when the Trotskyists were witch-hunted out of the IBT and its leadership in 1941.

Since then the Teamster bureaucracy has reversed the trends we had set into motion. Democratic procedures used by the union's area committee in the pre-1941 period have been replaced by dictatorial methods in the present-day IBT conferences. More concern is shown for the wishes of the employers than is manifested toward the needs of the workers. The problems of the fleet drivers are neglected in many respects. At the same time, there has been an increasingly pronounced growth of independent owner-operators; and the union officialdom has little inclination and even less ability to cope with the situation.

As a result, the owner-operators are ceasing to look upon the IBT as the organization through which they can undertake to alleviate the difficulties now confronting them. Those who remain members of the union are tending to organize themselves into factions, which act independently of the Teamster bureaucrats and, to an increasing extent, in cooperation with nonunion groups of owner-operators. Formations of this kind are springing up in various parts of the country. Cut loose as they are from trade-union influence, factors that cause individual owner-operators to dream of becoming small fleet owners assume greater weight in the shaping of their policies. The negative aspects of that outlook impair the interests of all over-the-road drivers at a time when the union has become enfeebled because of bureaucratic misleadership.

Under those circumstances it becomes possible for the big trucking firms to mount a major attack on the IBT by maneuvering to intensify the hostility of owner-operators toward the organization. To the extent that they succeed in promoting such antiunion bias, every worker behind the wheel of a truck—owner-operators and fleet drivers alike—will be the ultimate victims. Only the bosses will be the gainers.

This danger can be averted through a shift in union policy toward application under modern conditions of the basic course that was being shaped prior to 1941. That would block the bosses from splitting the owner-drivers away from the organized labor movement. Instead, the catch-all category of independent owner-operators could be separated into its component parts. *Individual* owner-operators could be brought back into effective alliance with the drivers of company fleets. Small fleet owners, who masquerade under the designation "owner-operators," could be sorted out and placed in the employer category where they belong. Class lines within the industry would again become much clearer, and the workers would be in a better position to fight collectively in defense of their mutual interests.

There is an objective potential for such a turn in union policy that is manifested in diverse, confused form within the present opposition to the Teamster bureaucrats. What the situation now requires is the shaping of a course of action in support of the workers' just demands, aimed in the first instance at the bosses and their government. Within that framework, steps can be taken to oust the IBT bureaucrats from office, establish democratic procedures within the union, and make it a fitting instrument to serve the workers' cause.

Achievement of those ends requires an oppositional formation at all levels of the IBT based on a class-struggle program and capable of using class-struggle methods. Every militant worker and especially the socialists among them should be on the alert for realistic openings to help get such a movement started.

Index